MATERIALS FOR BUILDING
VOLUME 1

A

MATERIALS FOR BUILDING
VOLUME 1

Physical and Chemical Aspects of Matter
and Strength of Materials

LYALL ADDLESON, B.Arch., A.R.I.B.A.,
Dip.T.P., A.M.T.P.I.

Head of Design Section
Faculty of Environmental Science and Technology
Polytechnic of the South Bank, London

London
Iliffe Books

THE BUTTERWORTH GROUP

England
Butterworth & Co (Publishers) Ltd
London: 88 Kingsway, WC2B 6AB

Australia
Butterworth & Co (Australia) Ltd
Sydney: 586 Pacific Highway Chatswood, NSW 2067
Melbourne: 343 Little Collins Street, 3000
Brisbane: 240 Queen Street, 4000

Canada
Butterworth & Co (Canada) Ltd
Toronto: 14 Curity Avenue, 374

New Zealand
Butterworth & Co (New Zealand) Ltd
Wellington: 26–28 Waring Taylor Street, 1
Auckland: 35 High Street, 1

South Africa
Butterworth & Co (South Africa) (Pty) Ltd
Durban: 152–154 Gale Street

First published in 1972 by
Iliffe Books, an imprint of
the Butterworth Group

© Lyall Addleson 1972

ISBN 0 592 00235 7

Printed in England by Chapel River Press

contents

16.75

preface

Materials for Building uses a considerable amount of the material that originally appeared in the series of articles of the same name in *The Architect and Building News* between 1964-68. The decision to publish the articles in book form provided an opportunity to correct mistakes, add or delete, and as important, to bring everything up-to-date, including complete metrication. In the light of present practice, some may find the metric values 'too accurate'. Generally speaking the metric equivalents of imperial values rather than sensible metric values are given. In many cases experimental or test results have had to be converted, and here too much rounding off or over-simplification would have been inappropriate.

Materials used in buildings have to meet a number of different functional requirements while they are exposed continuously to a wide variety of destructive agencies. Factors associated with both of these include strength, water, heat, fire, sound and production. In building practice materials have to be selected to meet specific functional requirements and to ensure that harmful deterioration is delayed for as long as is practicable.

In order to obtain the best out of the materials available it is necessary to have an understanding not only of the properties of the materials themselves but also of the factors which influence their performance and durability. This series of books aims to provide a systematic coverage, on a comparative basis, of the relationship between materials for building as a whole and the factors against which materials are expected to perform. Consequently each of the factors in terms of its nature and characteristics are explained separately and then related to a specific range of materials. The properties of all materials relative to each factor are also included.

In this study an attempt has been made to gather together a considerable amount of diversified information from a number of sources and to relate it in a particular way. It is to be hoped that the form of presentation used particularly the graphics and the extensive use of photographic examples will facilitate an understanding of the problems involved and of their possible solution. Perhaps even stimulate further study.

This volume includes two parts. Part 1, 'Physical and chemical aspects of matter' aims to provide an appreciation of the structure and behaviour of materials by presenting, as a pattern of study, the relevant basic physics and chemistry. Particular emphasis is placed on the differences between physical and chemical changes in, and their effects on, materials. The principles of adhesion and capillarity are considered in detail, while porous and non-porous materials are discussed and compared. Part 2, 'Strength of materials' deals with the subject in the wider context and includes the resistance offered by materials to cracking and other failures caused by movements, local damage, shaping or fixing. The main structural requirements of materials are set out. Attention is also given to methods of loading with particular emphasis on the way in which loading may occur when materials are restrained from moving.

Many people and organisations have made this series possible and I am extremely grateful to all of them for their help and co-operation. Specific acknowledgment to publishers, authors, firms or organisations for permission to use their material is given where the material appears. I owe special thanks to George Mansell, formerly editor of *The Architect and Building News*, for his faith in me and for his unceasing encouragement. All the staff at *The Architect and Building News* were always helpful but Geoffrey Lee who attended to all arrangements for the articles deserves special mention. The photographic department at Dorset House never failed to develop and print my films on time and as required. Istvan Fenyvesi worked hard and conscientiously on the diagrams and charts and proved to be invaluable in the conversion to SI units.

I was fortunate enough to have had Miss Elizabeth Kirby to type the first part and Mrs. Sheila Todd the remainder so accurately and quickly.

I am always grateful to my students for their helpful criticisms and for their willingness to co-operate in teaching experiments. The things they have found out themselves and their penetrating questions have always encouraged me to explore further.

Last but not least, thanks to my wife for her patience and understanding while I was searching, writing or photographing, and for her secretarial and checking assistance.

London 1971   L.A.

GENERAL INTRODUCTION

The degree of protection, comfort and pleasure that a building of any kind provides throughout its 'working' life, depends in no small measure on the materials that are used to give physical form to the visions and aspirations of all those involved in its construction and care. The selection and use of materials that will be most appropriate for particular circumstances and requirements demands to a large extent an understanding of the possible potential of the materials available. Today the choice of suitable materials presents a difficult, although interesting, if not stimulating, challenge to the whole of the building industry and to those who commission buildings. Not only is there a wide range of materials from which to choose, but new materials and techniques are constantly being developed. Added to this is the ever-increasing speed of building. It is understandable, therefore, that the problems inherent in the design, construction and, eventually, the care of buildings have become increasingly complex.

In order to assist in overcoming the many problems now associated with building, a great deal of research-based information has been made available by various authorities. Much of this inevitably relates to materials. There are, however, many aspects of building practice, including those related to the selection and use of materials, where information which could be helpful is still not available, although attempts are being made, in various quarters, to fill the necessary gaps in knowledge. Lack of information on specific aspects of building, as in other spheres of life, can give rise to a certain amount of diffidence, if not anxiety, about the use of new materials and techniques. This is probably not a new phenomenon and, as important, has not prevented, if historical precedent is to be used as a guide, the successful development of innovations in building. The importance of this cannot be under-estimated. Furthermore, it does help to underline the fact that in the final analysis, *quality of building,* which includes the successful use of materials, cannot necessarily be achieved by slavishly following books, rules, diagrams or recommendations,

however valuable these may be as aids, particularly in preventing foolish mistakes or inferior work. It is equally important that some intuition and common sense is applied to the information available and keen and persistent observation of past performance of materials is also undertaken. In all this an understanding of the principles that underlie the use of materials and the factors likely to influence their properties are fundamental requirements and points of departure for study.

This particular study of materials for building does not aim specifically to set out or give rules and recommendations, although some are included where they may be useful, nor does it aim to cover, in detail, the properties and uses of every material. The primary aim is rather broader. An attempt is being made to cover, on an *essentially comparative* basis, not only the principles which govern, in general, the use of the whole range of materials, but also to outline the properties of materials and, as important the factors which affect these properties.

Although the relevant information included in this study is taken from that available from various sources (the Building Research Station, in particular) and already published, an attempt has been made to assemble, interpret and present this information in a particular way. In addition, and in order to try to help to cultivate an awareness of the importance of critical evaluation of the use of materials in existing buildings, whether old or new, as many examples as possible, particularly photographs, have been included. This method of presentation has, in general, been adopted in the hope that it might help to progress the studies of all those who wish to gain an understanding of the problems involved in the selection and use of materials. Among other things, it is hoped that this study will serve as a useful complement to the many references and works of others which have been relied on entirely. (These are referred to later in this introduction, under *Scope: 1. Objectives.*)

Although a brief outline has been

given above of some of the present problems in building and of the main objectives of this study, it has been considered advisable to expand on its *context and scope.* In practice it is necessary, if not imperative, to constantly take into account the *inter-relationship of many factors,* some of which may even be mutually incompatible. On the other hand, for the purposes of explanation it is usually more convenient to sub-divide the relevant information into more or less self-contained divisions. In this study the whole of the subject matter which it is intended to cover has been *divided into seven main parts,* each of which is in turn sub-divided into sections. Some of the parts and the sections are inter-related, with the inter-relationship noted in the text as necessary. One of the purposes of this introduction is then to provide some sort of link between the various parts. Among other aspects which need to be considered in general terms before studying any particular aspect are the effects of variations and the significance of the relationship between *durability and maintenance.* There is now a need for some notes on the use of the SI system of metric units. Consequently these are also included in this introduction. In order to cover the background to current developments and needs; the scope of this study; a brief description of the main parts into which the study has been divided; the significance of variations; the significance of durability and maintenance and the SI units, the following general headings are used: (1) Background; (2) Scope; (3) Main parts; (4) Variations; (5) Durability and maintenance; and (6) SI units.

background

1. The element of change

Change is an essential characteristic of life and, naturally enough, also of the buildings designed to meet the particular requirements of life at a particular time. Different requirements and attitudes at various times have encouraged and produced quite a variety of different forms and types of buildings and techniques used in build-

1

ing them. The success of any building at any time has, among other things, depended on the ability of the designers and builders of the time to make the best and, perhaps, the most imaginative use of the materials they were able to command. In some ways there is, therefore, nothing new about change as such. However, at this time we are already able to see the effects, and in many cases alas, the defects and chaos, that have resulted from changes in ways of living, working and taking recreation, and which have taken place at a rate far quicker than society can really cope with in the traditional terms to which it has mostly been accustomed. Little wonder that there is, then, particular concern by many people that this age should not repeat the mistakes made during the last century, when changes also took place at a phenomenal pace, although it is possible that this was not as rapid as recently and especially since the war.

One extremely important aspect of change is that it is part of an evolutionary process; another is that it usually involves a shift of emphasis, rather than a complete change in basic principles. However, the detailed application of principles to new situations can have significant effects and it is important that account is taken of these. Among changes which have taken place in recent years and which have had a direct impact on buildings, including in particular the materials used in their construction, is that of standards of performance. In general there has been a considerable increase in the visual, thermal and acoustic standards required for human comfort. Unlike historic example, these standards, for the most part based on scientific investigation, are being applied, and in many cases demanded, in a great many different building types and not merely kept for the 'special' or prestige building. Problems associated with comfort standards are, therefore, no longer restricted, but are now almost universally applicable. To a certain extent the problem would not be a very serious one if the higher standards now demanded could be provided at any cost. This is not the case and so desired standards have to be provided at reasonable cost or, better still, within a society's budget, which, taking the overall view, is nowadays fairly restricted. In the formative stages of any new development, cost implications are not always readily appreciated or allowed for. Incorporating higher standards of performance in buildings is no exception. Consequently the budgets of buildings which are expected to have higher standards of performance, as far as the visual, thermal or aural environments are concerned, have not always been increased sufficiently. This has meant that either some of the standards are achieved at the expense of others, or, that there is a general 'watering down' of all standards, or, that some other important requirements, like exclusion of rain or durability, are sacrificed.

'Change is an essential characteristic of life.' A reinforced plastics building developed for Bakelite Ltd.

'In general there has been a considerable increase in the visual, thermal and acoustic standards required for human comfort.' A large general office in Esso Petroleum Company's Victoria Street building. Architects: Denys Lasdun and Partners

Establishing a realistic budget for any given requirements of any building is no simple matter, takes time to get into 'the system', while the consequences of decisions taken at the design stage, some of which could have deleterious results, are not always fully realised. Thus, it has been necessary to adopt, as a principle at any rate, methods of re-assessing the properties and uses of building materials, and of finding ways and means of using their properties to the fullest possible advantage. In certain cases this has meant the production of completely different sorts of materials, where traditional materials have not met the particular standards of performance. The vast range of insulating materials, and particularly those of plastics, bears witness to this endeavour.

Buildings have always had as one of their functions that of protection, and materials were selected according to the kind of protection required. Traditionally, again, protection was mainly against external elements—rain, sun and wind—which had to be controlled in some degree to provide the comparatively low levels of standards of comfort then required. Now, almost of necessity, the present standards of the physical environment within buildings has led to man-made conditions, whether of lighting, heating or acoustics, which may require quite elaborate pieces of equipment throughout a building. Thus it is now essential for economic and other reasons that the agencies, such as heat, which produce these man-made conditions are not allowed to filter uncontrolled through the fabric of a building only to be wasted in the outside air or some other space. In this way materials have to perform in a variety of different ways on both sides of and within the fabric of any building—it is no longer merely a question of considering exposure to external elements. The latter are still extremely important, cannot be disregarded and, in fact, must be looked at in a new light, or take other factors, such as noise, more seriously into account. A general increase in the noise 'climate', both externally and internally, has made new demands on materials and the way in which they are used.

2. New building techniques

Running concurrently with these developments in environmental standards and materials is that of physical building itself. The scope of buildings has increased—many different types are needed. The scale of buildings has increased—bigger and, in many instances, higher ones are required to meet planning problems. And then added to all this, buildings are required at a far quicker rate than has been normal. Under such circumstances it is not difficult to understand how it is that misjudgements or misuses can have unfortunate results if not controlled at the early stages.

In order to try and meet the challenge presented to it for an ever-increasing number of buildings incorporating, among other things, high standards of comfort, the building industry as a whole in this country (and here must be included all the various skills which are necessary for a building project now) has commenced, and continues, to reassess its own methods and procedures. Already the results of these efforts are to be seen in the use of industrialised building methods, whether of a system or not. Much of the industry has now realised that traditional methods of building, and thus, of using materials in an essentially traditional way, are no longer suitable to meet the new requirements for a great many buildings. At the same time it is also realised by many that this type of building technique is not necessarily applicable or suitable for all kinds of buildings and programmes. For the reasons already stated, many look upon these new forms of building with their associated use of materials, both old and new, with a certain degree of scepticism and, in some cases unfortunately, derision.

Whatever view is to be taken of industrialised building or techniques, it is a fact that there always has been a trend to produce more and more of a building off the site, usually under controlled factory conditions. Industrialisation is in many ways a logical extension of this, and is, therefore, perhaps better seen, in the interests of better building, as part of the evolution of the building process. Prefabrication of one kind or another is not completely new, but its wider application brings with it new problems. This is admirably pointed out by R. B. White in his book *Prefabrication. A History of its Development in Great Britain* (National Building Studies, Special Report No. 36, HMSO, 1965), in which he analyses, critically, the development and significance of prefabrication in its widest sense.

The great 're-think' which has been going on has also revealed that much greater use must now be made of every scientific and technological aid. Experience has shown that there is an ever-growing need for information which will enable all those involved to operate on calculated risks rather than on blind chance. Scientists of all kinds are, therefore, finding that they can be of greater assistance in a sphere normally lacking in such skills. The presence of such skills in increasing numbers and from a wide range of disciplines is a welcome one. Among other things it also helps to emphasise the growing importance of having to study the nature of any problem from basic principles, and not merely relying on rule of thumb methods, or worse still, intuition for the solution of a great many problems. A new aid, the computer, has been added and is being used in a variety of ways in the solution of problems in both research and practice.

' . . . *the present standards of physical environment within buildings has led to man-made conditions, whether of lighting, heating or acoustics, which require quite elaborate pieces of equipment throughout a building.*'
Above, air inlet diffusers and below, air conditioning inlet ducts in the Esso Company's Victoria Street building

'*In certain cases this has meant the production of completely different sorts of materials . . . The vast range of insulating materials, and particularly those of plastics, bears witness to this endeavour.*' *Below, laying an expanded polystyrene insulation tray (Monsanto Chemicals Ltd.)*

'*A large part of the industry has now realized that traditional methods of building, and thus, of using materials in an essentially traditional way, are no longer suitable to meet the new requirements . . .*'

'*The scale of buildings has increased— bigger and, in many instances, higher ones are required to meet planning problems*'

3. Significant factors

Out of all these changes and developments two significant factors, both of which are closely inter-related, appear to be of importance, especially for those who are interested in and demand good building with all that that implies. One is concerned with novel techniques and the other with innovations in materials.

(a) *Novel techniques*

All developments which result in novel building techniques, whether industrialised or not, must be considered as an experiment. There is nothing new in this but, in the past, developments were able to take place gradually and, as important, with a limited number of materials. Difficulties could be ironed out in slow stages, and experience was passed on almost from one generation to another until, perhaps many, many years later, the particular system or technique was perfected. No doubt, a new development was already being born elsewhere.

Nowadays the position is quite different. Designers and builders alike do not, on the whole, have, nor can they be expected to have, enough *practical* precedent on which they can rely with absolute certainty. Scientific research has mainly been carried out under laboratory or controlled conditions, and this, together with some accelerated tests on materials and techniques, already shows that actual site usage, with its attendant difficulties of quality control, workmanship and exposure, may modify results previously obtained. Many people complain, as has always been the case no doubt, that not enough research is being done, among other things that is, into the problems affecting the use of materials, while others are disappointed and disillusioned that all published results cannot always be taken literally. Quite naturally the great urge to get on and do something often obscures the essential facts of the published results.

In all this it is possible that the implications involved in the perfection of any new technique are often overlooked, while the extent to which science and technology are expected to solve all the problems are often over-estimated. In principle, there is, in fact, very little difference in the procedure which has always been necessary, namely *trial and error*. Looked at in another way this means initial research, followed by development and application, and then evaluation of the results of the application. However, the process of further development, application and evaluation has to continue until perfection is obtained. In most cases redevelopment usually, but by no means always, involves slight modifications at each stage. Science, and the related laboratory tests which can be reasonably devised, assist by making it possible for the number of trials initially required to be reduced while they also assist in reducing the number of errors which will be made, during development and application. Thus the whole procedure can be speeded up, but not replaced. At the same time, it is also important to note that some intuition and, in some ways, inspired guesswork is still required.

More research is obviously needed and a great deal of investigation on the performance of materials in buildings already erected still has to be done. Despite the fact that this problem is aggravated by the great number of different techniques being employed, it is nevertheless, regrettable that there cannot be greater 'pooling' among all sections of the industry, whatever their skill, of the reasons for many failures. People, embarking on a problem for the first time, may, and often do, make the same mistake as has been made by others, because the mistake has not been able to 'see the light of day'. In other cases failures result merely from a lack of an understanding of the basic principles which affect the materials being used, or perhaps a complete disregard of those traditional practices that are still applicable. Here again one has to revert to traditional requirements, when such an understanding was not always necessary, as so much had already been proved by trial and error methods which allowed for fairly reliable rules-of-thumb to be applied to most problems.

(b) *Innovations in materials*
Innovations in materials have taken place at an alarming rate with the result that a vast range of materials is now available. Not only are there a great number of different types but also a number of different manufacturers producing them. With no standard, easy, and in some cases reliable, methods of assessing the properties of the general range of materials for a particular use, the whole question of choice is made extremely difficult, and, on the face of it, a highly complex one. The need for a central certifying authority which would deal solely with innovations in materials and techniques has long been realised. The report of the committee on Agrément* suggested that the delay of the spread of technical development in building at the present time could be attributed to three main causes. These are: (1) the difficulty that builders and designers find in keeping abreast of new products and techniques, and their reluctance to use or specify any that are not well established or have not been officially approved; (2) the general and understandable demand for clear compliance with Building Regulations; and (3) the disinclination of both public and private clients to adopt new and relatively untried developments.

Following the publication of the report on Agrément the Government set up the requisite central certifying authority, the Agrément Board, and

this commenced its work during 1966. In the main the central certifying authority confines its work to new products and techniques or to new uses of established ones. The authority aims to provide reliable and independent assessments for those manufacturers who apply for a certificate. Certificates are not intended to replace British Standards, but precursors of new or revised Standards. Consequently, until a new product is included in a British Standard, a certificate will initially be valid for a limited period, although provision is made for the extension of the period subject to certain requirements.

scope

1. Objectives

The general background has been presented in advance of a description and scope of the present study in order to give some indication of some current trends and difficulties now being encountered in building. These do not necessarily apply to each and every building as an assessment of this kind can never hope to do. Furthermore, there is no intention of implying that none of the new buildings have any measure of success. It really cannot be denied, however, that there have been failures and mistakes, and these must in the end assist in any endeavour to improve, if not perfect, any particular type of building technique. Recent experiences have shown that there is an urgent need for systematic appraisal of all aspects of building practice, including, of course, those related to materials. A recent report* by the Building Research Station has shown clearly the value of appraisals and the implications of carrying them out. This study does, in an extremely limited and general way, attempt to assess some aspects associated with the performance of materials, although it should be emphasised that greater emphasis is given to an analysis of the factors which influence durability.

At this time there are probably many who are not fully aware of the implications of present-day requirements, particularly as far as materials are concerned. At the same time they may not also be fully aware of the implications of those factors which influence the performance and durability of materials. On the other hand a great number will be entering the building industry for the first time completely unaware of the problems involved.

This particular study of the principles of the use and comparative properties of materials for building is, therefore, presented to those wishing to have an understanding of the problems and some guidance as to their possible solution.

In general, an understanding of the

uses and properties of materials is really required by nearly all the skills that make up the team necessary for a building project. The architect and his consultants have to know about the factors involved so that an intelligent selection of materials for a particular use or uses can be made; having made such a selection correct specification and detailing will then be necessary. With changes taking place in materials and techniques at an ever-increasing rate, it is becoming increasingly important that thorough communication between all sections is maintained, as has been shown in the recent report* published by BRS on the failure of an industrialised building. For those who will actually be taking part in the physical building operations it is vital that there is a clear understanding of the principles involved, so that operations may be carried out efficiently and with due regard paid to proper execution. Finally, even manufacturers must be aware of the problems so that they may produce materials which can meet particular requirements.

The degree of knowledge or understanding required by any one of the members of the whole building industry, or that required by any particular skill at any given stage in a building project, must, of necessity, vary between wide limits. On the other hand, there are the special requirements of students, who, among other things, need a pattern of study to follow. The latter has, in fact, been used as the basis of this study, and reflects, to some extent, the manner in which the study has been assembled and presented. No attempt has been made to emphasise any particular aspect to suit the requirements of any skill. It should be emphasised that the detailed requirements of the specialist or scientist are *not* included, although some aspects may be of interest to them. The aim is, then, to provide a general coverage of the subject matter, including where necessary some detailed considerations, in a systematic way, which should be of use to either the student or the practitioner.

As explained at the beginning of this introduction the intention is primarily to deal with materials as a whole, and so details of all the varieties of a particular kind of material are not covered. In this way it is considered possible to obtain an overall view of the problem, and, as important, be aware of the range of possibilities. The principles of use outlined, together with the properties given should provide some guidance as to the kind of material that may be required to satisfy a particular requirement. Once the kind of material has been selected, reference can then be made (from other parts of this study or other works as necessary) to details of any of its other characteristics. Throughout, particular attention has been given to those factors which influence both the properties and performances of materials. Where relevant some guid-

The Assessment of New Building Products, Report of the Committee on Agrément, HMSO, 1965

A qualitative study of some buildings in the London Area, National Building Studies, Special Report 33, HMSO, 1964.

*House of Commons Paper No. 36. HMSO.

ance is also given on the precautions which may be taken so as to achieve the greatest potential from materials under given conditions.

There are a great many useful publications, both old and new, which cover in various ways the uses and the properties of materials. Much of the information is scattered over a wide field, some of it is in a form which is too complicated for ready acceptance by many of the skills in the industry, while, in general, the written word tends to be the chief means of explanation. This study has as one of its main objectives the gathering in, so-to-speak, of quite a considerable amount of diversified information, interpreting it and relating it in a particular way which is explained later on. In so doing it is hoped to expose gaps in knowledge, and wherever possible to assess the significance of any 'missing links'. Furthermore, it is the intention to present the information in a format which should make an understanding of the subject a little easier. Thus, greater emphasis and reliance is placed on a variety of graphic means, including wherever possible many photographic examples.

It is important to note, at the outset, that this study could not have been undertaken without the aid of the many references available. The physical number makes individual recognition almost impossible. In consequence, gratitude is expressed by the author to all those who have already published information. In the text reference and acknowledgement is made, as applicable, to published works.

2. Method of approach

Some explanation of the approach and method employed in this study is necessary if its possible usefulness is to be appreciated. In general, an attempt has been made to adopt what is known as the scientific method, that is following through all the aspects which it is intended to cover in a systematic way. There is a considerable amount of science as such which explains many, though by no means all, of the 'mysteries' of the performance and properties of materials. Looked at in another way, a knowledge of science can go a long way to aid an understanding of the problems associated with the selection and use of materials. Consequently science cannot reasonably be entirely excluded from a study of the kind envisaged here. However, the interpretation, simplification and presentation of the science, as indeed any of the other information or facts given in this study, it should be emphasised, is as seen by one trained as an architect, with some practical experience and who is now actively engaged in teaching. In some senses, this study is considered to typify the range and degree of knowledge which should satisfy the requirements of general building practice and which should, at the

CLASS	TIMBER	MOISTURE MOVEMENT (% original length range 90% – 60% R.H.)									
		TANGENTIAL						RADIAL			
		value	3·0	2·0	1·0	0		1·0	2·0		value
I – small movement values	African Walnut	1·3									0·9
	Afrormosia	1·3									0·7
	Agba	1·8									0·8
	Balsa	2·0									0·6
	Cedar, South American	1·5									1·0
	Douglas fir	1·5									1·2
	Hemlock, western	1·9									0·9
	Iroko	1·0									0·5
	Mahogany, African (Khaya ivorensis)	1·5									0·9
	Mahogany, Central American	1·3									1·0
	Obeche	1·25									0·8
	Opepe	1·8									0·9
	Pine, yellow	1·7									0·9
	Rosewood, Indian	1·0									0·7
	Rhodesian, teak	1·6									1·0
	Spruce, European	1·5									0·7
	Teak	1·3									0·8
	Western red cedar	0·9–1·9									0·45–0·8
	Whitewood	1·5									0·7
II – medium movement values	Ash	1·8									1·3
	Elm, English	2·4									1·5
	Jarrah	2·6									1·8
	Keruing	2·5									1·5
	Mahogany, African (Khaya grandifoliola)	1·9									1·5
	Oak, English	2·5									1·5
	Parana pine	2·5									1·7
	Pine, Carribean pitch	2·6									1·4
	Pine, Scots	2·2									1·0
	Poplar, Black Italian	2·8									1·2
	Red wood	2·2									1·0
	Sapele	1·8									1·3
	Spruce, Serbian	2·3									1·3
	Sycamore	2·8									1·4
	Utile	1·8									1·6
	Walnut, European	2·0									1·6
III – large movement values	Ash, Japanese	3·5									1·5
	Beech	3·2									1·7
	Birch, Canadian Yellow	2·5									2·2
	Gurjun	3·3									2·0
	Oak, Turkey	3·3									1·3
	Olive, East African	2·9									1·7
	Tasmanian Oak	3·4									2·0
	Wattle, black	3·5									1·2

C.Introd./1 An example of a comparative chart. Moisture movement in timber (Reference: 'The movement of timbers; FPRL Leaflet No. 47 HMSO (revised 1961))

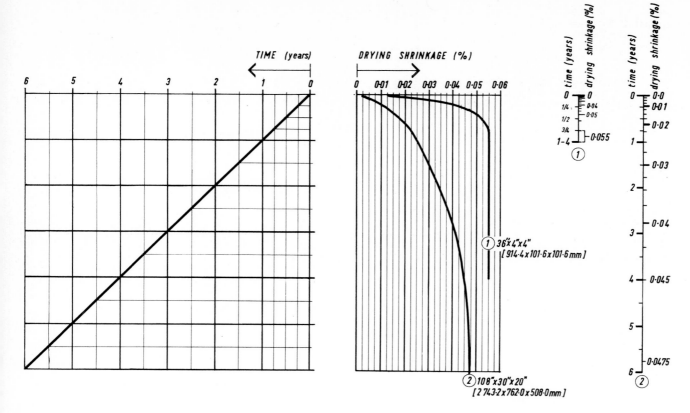

TIME (years)

DRYING SHRINKAGE (%)

① 36"x4"x4"
[914·4 x 101·6 x 101·6 mm]

② 108"x30"x20"
[2 743·2 x 762·0 x 508·0 mm]

C.Introd./2 An example of a comparative graph. The effect of size on drying shrinkage, 1 : 2 : 4 concrete specimens exposed to air at 17·8°C (64°F) and 65 per cent R.H. (Reference: 'The Chemistry of Cement and Concrete', by F. M. Lea (Edward Arnold Publishers Ltd) 1956, Fig 110, p. 353)

present time at any rate, be sufficient for the necessary understanding between the general practitioner and specialist, particularly the scientists whose assistance is obviously invaluable. As mentioned earlier, this study is not intended to cover the specific and detailed requirements of the specialist or scientist who should in any case be asked to investigate and report on problems which are outside the scope of the general practitioner.

The principles of the use of materials are explained, wherever possible, by diagrammatic drawings and sketches with the necessary supporting text. In many cases it has been necessary to exaggerate the scale somewhat. This is done merely to illustrate a principle and is in no way intended to simulate an actual material or form of construction. Generally speaking, precise methods of construction are not given as this is really part of another study. However, wherever possible, practical examples are included.

In considering the properties of materials mostly graphical methods are used in presenting the data. In so doing a number of different techniques are employed, depending on the nature of the information. In all cases the intention has been to use methods which make comparison possible by visual means.

However, values and other information are included where it is considered that such information may be required in any calculations. In some cases

selected properties have been used to illustrate a particular point, but on the whole it has been policy to include, so far as it is available, all the information relative to the whole range of materials in the various sections which are set out later. In this way the information should be of value, not only to students, but also to those in practice.

Some examples of the graphical methods are given here together with an explanation of their use:

(a) *Comparative charts (C.Introd./1)*
These charts are based on the histogram, or bar-chart, often used in statistical work. The precise numerical value of any particular property of a material is converted into a linear scale. In this way, a material with 'much' of one particular property will have against it a long line, or bar, while one with 'little', a short line, or bar. Where a particular material or group of materials has a range of values of a particular property, the least of the values is shown solid, while the difference between the least and the greatest is shaded.

One of the advantages of the comparative chart is that it only requires a brief examination to establish the relative merits of various materials, and then to select those possessing particular values, without getting involved with figures. The numerical values are, however, included for convenience.

In this study the comparative charts are used not only to compare a number of materials relative to one given property but also to two or more properties. In the example given here, the movement of different timbers in both tangential and radial directions are compared.

In order to preserve the method of assessment inherent in the comparative chart, it has been necessary, on occasion, to use the reciprocals of certain properties. Thus, for example, under thermal insulation, the $1/k$ (thermal resistivity) value is used and not the 'k' (thermal conductivity) value.

(b) *Comparative graphs (C.Introd./2)*
These are used to compare two different kinds of values which are related to each other in a definite way. In effect these are similar to the conventional two-ordinate graph, except here the two components have been set against each other, thus giving each component a visual value. In addition, it is possible to interpolate readings, but instead of reading up and across, or across and down as the case may be, it is only necessary to read from left to right or right to left.

(c) *Conversion charts (C.Introd./3)*
Based on the principle used in the nomogram, and often seen on thermometers with both Farenheit and Centigrade scales, these charts are also

useful for comparing two different properties or values. Many of the charts have been prepared from two-ordinate graphs, and as already mentioned the tediousness of reading in two different directions is avoided when using the chart. The accuracy of these charts cannot be any more than could be expected from a two-ordinate graph. In many instances in practice such accuracy is sufficient.

In preparing all the charts and graphs every reasonable care has been taken to include information from recognised authoritative sources. In all cases the source of the information is stated, as, among other things, it would be presumptuous to try to make any assessment of true authority.

Main parts

The whole subject matter to be covered in this study has been divided up into seven parts. In general, each part, in turn sub-divided into sections, represents a particular factor or element against which materials are expected to perform (the first part dealing with physical and chemical aspects of matter is the exception). In each part the actual factor, in terms of its nature and characteristics, is explained, and this is then related to the kind of material or materials which would be required. In addition, the properties of materials relative to the factor are included. The main parts, with an outline of their contents, are set out below, and this should amplify the general approach.

It is, however, inevitable that there will be some overlapping. This situation only helps to underline the important fact that a great many aspects are closely inter-related and that, in practice, it is always necessary to constantly take these inter-relationships into account. In order to avoid unnecessary duplication, any item which may repeat is dealt with in detail in one section and only referred to in any other to which it may also apply. Thus, for example, condensation could be included under water or thermal properties; it is, in fact, dealt with in detail under thermal properties, although repeatedly referred to under *3.00 Water and its effects*.

1.00 Physical and chemical aspects of matter

Some understanding of both physics and chemistry is necessary if any appreciation of the structure and behaviour of materials is to be gained. They are also vitally necessary to understand the elements which tend, or do in fact, affect any particular property of a material. As it is virtually impossible to condense that which exists in many standard works on the two subjects, this part sets out briefly the essential facts of these sciences as a pattern of study, while every attempt is made to relate the facts specifically to building materials.

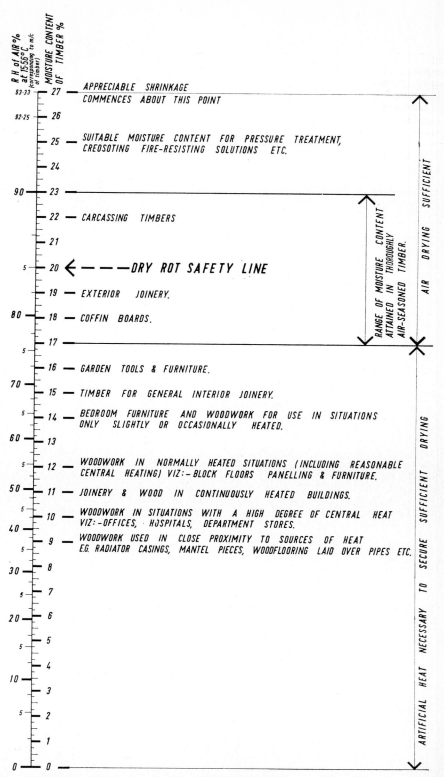

C.Introd./3 *An example of a conversion chart. Equilibrium moisture content of timber for various uses. Note: values for different species vary and the chart gives average values (Reference: 'The Moisture Content of Timber in Use, FPRL Leaflet No. 9, HMSO (revised, 1963))*

Particular emphasis is placed on illustrating the differences between physical and chemical changes in, and their effects on, materials, as these are the causes of so many failures in buildings (see pictures).

The principles behind adhesion, which plays such an important part in many building processes, are covered in detail, while consideration is also given to the importance and functioning of capillarity.

Some detailed consideration is given to the two main groups of materials used in buildings, namely porous and non-porous materials, and comparisons are made between the two.

2.00 Strength of materials

Taken by itself this is probably the most important property of nearly all materials. Strength is, however, not restricted to what may be termed basic structure alone, but is equally applicable to the resistance offered by materials to cracking or other failure, whether caused by movements, local damage, shaping or merely fixing.

Without trying to embark on an extensive structural analysis, this part does set out the main structural requirements of materials and explains the meaning of stress, strain, elasticity, creep and resistance to shock and fatigue.

Attention is given to methods of loading with particular emphasis on how loading may occur when materials are restrained from moving. This is done so that the causes of cracking in buildings may be understood. The various causes of movements are only indicated here and except for deflection which results from structural loading, are more fully discussed as appropriate under moisture, heat or sound.

3.00 Water and its effects

Water has always been one of buildings most vicious enemies. A considerable number of failures of materials are aided and abetted by the action of water, the results becoming more and more disastrous the more the water is polluted. Nowadays the sources of water in buildings have been greatly increased, and many problems due either to condensation or drying out are commonly occurring within the construction of a building.

A detailed consideration is given of the characteristics and behaviour of water and to the sources and causes of pollution of water in buildings. The capacity of materials to either absorb, repel or facilitate its passage is demonstrated, together with the manner in which the various materials may be used to exclude water. Under exclusion of water the performance of materials in walls and roofs are considered, while damp-proof courses and membranes, water vapour barriers, and sealants are also included. Particular attention is also given to the

problems now associated with 'entrapped water' in flat roofs. The mechanics and action of soluble salts, chemicals, the corrosion of metals and frost are fully described.

4.00 Heat and its effects

This part deals with the whole problem of heat and includes the nature and sources of heat, while the way in which it may be transferred is also considered in some detail. Terms normally used in thermal calculations have been included. In addition to outlining the thermal properties of materials in so far as insulation, thermal storage, condensation and pattern staining are concerned, the problems connected with movement due to expansion and contraction are explained. The effects of solar radiation on both insulation and movement are also included.

5.00 Fire and its effects

This subject could no doubt be included under thermal affects, but is usually separated as, again, it requires special consideration, and is in a sense a contingency. Although materials may or may not be able to provide fire-protection the actual form and construction as a whole plays an important part. The subject is, therefore, treated in a general way and gives an indication of the requirements of buildings and the resistance of various materials to fire.

6.00 Sound and its effects

Problems connected with sound in and about buildings are so directly concerned with complete structures that it is difficult to provide any clear-cut information on individual materials. In order to avoid the complexities associated with special sound or acoustic problems normally encountered in such buildings as theatres, concert halls and the like, consideration is given in an elementary form only. The nature and behaviour of sound are therefore discussed in outline only, so as to enable some distinction to be drawn between the three separate problems connected with insulation against transmission, absorption and impact. An indication, together with relevant values, is given of the kinds of materials normally used in meeting the requirements of these problems.

As sound is concerned with vibrations, the effects of the latter are included in this section.

7.00 Production and use generally

This section serves to sum up, mainly in illustrated form, the various production techniques, both on and off the building site, which are used and how these may be affected by materials or the special considerations which must take place under certain conditions.

Variations

It is important that attention is drawn to the significance of the element of variation that occurs in buildings as a whole. The effects of variations do influence considerably, both the selection and behaviour of materials. Because there are so many possible variations that can occur, it is also essential to explain what has been taken as the norm so to speak in this study, so that account can be taken of this contingency when using the information presented.

1. Factors of safety

Traditionally such variations as did occur, and particularly when these were minor, were not of such great importance as they are nowadays, mainly because traditional building incorporated quite high factors of safety. This no doubt happened naturally due to the fact that constructions were based on experience and rule-of-thumb and so some extra was added 'just to make sure'. Now, of course, the pendulum has indeed swung in the other direction, and so, far greater reliance is placed on scientific calculations, which afford methods of using materials to their fullest advantage. Thus, when compared with traditional building, present-day buildings based on calculation do have smaller factors of safety.

In the context of calculations it is important that cognisance is taken of the fact that the results of these can usually only be used as intelligent guides, unless all the factors used in the calculations are fixed and not subject to any variations. Under most practical building conditions this is most unlikely, and so it is, therefore, imperative that the *degree* of variation that may occur is accounted for and, in fact, is added in some measurable terms to the results of the calculations, or somehow incorporated into the calculations. An idea of the significance of all this can be given by considering *some* of the variations which may occur.

2. Physical environment

At the outset it is necessary to state, in general terms, the obvious! No two buildings of the same type are really alike; no two samples of materials of the same kind are really alike. Buildings create environments, both externally and internally, for human beings; in some degree they also create physical environments for themselves. The physical environments that exist in and around buildings have a direct influence on the behaviour of the materials used. Variations in the physical conditions are likely to and do, in fact, vary not only from county to county, city to city, town to town or village to village, but also as between town and country, town and seaside, and street and street (and, in

the extreme case, between various parts of the same site). Such variations as do occur may result from climate (national, regional or local), geological aspects or as the result of human endeavour (mining, roads, dams and the like). All these affect the conditions under which materials have to operate.

3. Quality and control

As for the materials themselves, quality and control at all stages are important. Three different aspects may be considered:

(a) The quality of the constituent components will influence the quality of the resultant material, while, as important, the degree of control which can be exercised in the selection of the components.

(b) The degree of control and the quality of workmanship which can be exercised and maintained during the manufacture of the material for use.

In both of the above it can be assumed that natural selection and manufacture (timber and stone, for example) are likely to produce greater variations in materials than in human selection and manufacture (concrete, metals, glass, plastics and timber products, for example). However, in the latter, great variations may still occur, especially when the ingredients are naturally found.

(c) The degree of control and the quality of workmanship which can be exercised and maintained during the application of the materials to be used in a building. Broadly speaking, and subject always to the human element involved, factory conditions are likely to produce less variations than normal building site conditions. In this respect it is interesting to note the obvious increase in the trend to establish as far as practicable factory conditions on building sites.

Another extremely important point which should not be overlooked is the effect of handling (on and off the site or factory), carriage and storage of materials before they are actually used in a building.

4. Assessments and limitations

All the likely variations that could occur do influence, to a very great extent, the manner in which information on materials should be presented and, following on from this, the manner in which this information may be usefully employed. One thing which cannot be done in this particular study is to make assessments of the severity of conditions which may apply in individual circumstances. For this a proper *analysis* of each particular site must be made. Another thing which cannot be done is to assess the likely quality or control that may apply to any given material or construction that is likely to be used in practice. Great accuracy in this would require the examination and testing of each sample before use. Generally speaking

in practical building items, the latter is impracticable and so, unless special circumstances apply, it is usual to rely, with some confidence, on the results of tests which give either reliable average values (can only be used when the likely variations between different samples of the same material is small) or a range of values. Under these conditions it is, therefore, only possible to tackle the problem within certain limits, which in this study are:

(a) Principles outlining the structure and properties of matter and materials assume ideal conditions, and are intended to show the best possible. Any changes or impurities which may occur should be taken to imply a variation. The precise degree of variation can only be ascertained from testing individual samples. (In practice, unless special conditions or circumstances apply, such tests may not be necessary.)

(b) The physical or chemical properties quoted are average properties for the particular materials, and generally assume what may be termed normal working conditions unless, of course, otherwise stated. In this context it is important to note that many tests have been made taking traditional conditions only, and particularly environmental conditions, into account.

(c) Principles setting out or illustrating the use of materials also assume ideal conditions with good quality workmanship and control and using materials of good average quality. Where applicable BSS is used as the criterion for this standard.

Finally, it is worthwhile noting that there are really no clear-cut or tailor-made answers to all the problems to be encountered in buildings, and particularly in the selection and use of materials for buildings. Each case must be considered on its own merits and above all the question of degree must be taken into account. Having made the necessary *analysis,* it is then of great value to have a clear understanding of the ideal which should be aimed for, so that some intelligent *synthesis* may result, taking all factors into account. At a time when the moon is within reach, perhaps all those concerned with building may be asked to raise their own sights a little higher.

Durability and maintenance

1. Significance

No study of the various and diverse agencies—a significant part of this study is devoted to these—which are likely to lead to deterioration or to cause decay of materials, would be complete without some consideration of the problems associated with durability and maintenance. Omission of the main aspects of these factors always has the danger of the study, carried out in isolation so to speak, resolving itself into a rather tiresome, if not forbidding, list which would appear to do nothing more than

A comparative example of the use of maintenance to increase durability is shown in the photographs. Both gates illustrated were made of the same timber, fixed and initially protected with paint at the same time. The one to 133 (left-hand side) has received regular maintenance, mainly painting, while the one to 135 (right-hand side) has received no maintenance at all and is shown (top) in an advanced state of decay. Five years later (bottom photograph) most of the timber has disappeared

Painting the Forth Railway Bridge— an operation which proceeds year in and year out—is a classic example, albeit not a building, of the use of maintenance 'to make up' for the short-comings of a material, in this case steel, so as to prolong its working life. (Courtesy; British Rail)

support the generalised statement that in time all materials decay and that deterioration of some kind or another commences almost immediately a material is used. In practical building terms, and taking into account the important part played by economic considerations, the essential aim must be to ensure that *the rate* of deterioration and decay is suitably controlled. Such control, in which good detailing and good workmanship are as important as the selection of materials themselves, must be closely related to particular circumstances and would, in the final analysis, virtually dictate the extent to which deterioration and decay may be 'allowed' over a given period of time. Thus assessment of durability and maintenance—the two are complementary to one another—is in many ways the point of departure for the *direct* and *realistic application* of the knowledge of those factors which may lead to deterioration or decay and, as important, the manner in which these inherent weaknesses may be overcome or controlled.

2. Aspects considered

At this stage, it is convenient to consider, in general terms, the main aspects of durability and maintenance, and at the same time to include some practical examples of the causes and effects of deterioration of materials. As regards the latter it is convenient to consider, for purposes of explanation, the effects of water. These have been summarised in Table 1 and other examples are given under '4. Factors influencing durability'. However, the aspects covered by way of explaining deterioration of materials and the principles discussed are equally applicable to all deteriorating agencies. It is perhaps also worthwhile noting that the principles involved are applicable to both 'traditional' and 'modern' methods of construction—the scale and emphasis which influence details are usually different.

Water probably contributes more to deterioration of materials than any other agency (one of the reasons for using the effects of water here). How-

ever, movements are also extremely significant but it is, nevertheless, important that all the agencies which may cause deterioration of materials are not overlooked. Accordingly these are summarised below. In each case the parts or sections in which they are dealt with are given in brackets.

(1) *Water and its effects.* (Part 3.00).
(2) *Changes in Temperature.* Result in expansion and contraction, leading to cracking. (*Section 2.00, and particularly Section 2.03, 'Cracking in buildings'; also Part 4.00.*)
(3) *Sunlight.* Influences changes in temperature but may also cause deterioration of some organic materials (e.g., paint, rubber, asphalt, and some types of plastics). (*Mainly in Part 4.00.*)
(4) *Wear and tear.* Mainly related to surfaces of materials and related to damage by abrasion. (*Section 2.04 under 'Abrasion'.*)
(5) *Impact.* May lead to cracking or local damage. (*Section 2.04 under 'Impact'.*)

Table 1.   Durability of materials relative to the effects of water

Deterioration		Substances involved in addition to water		Materials commonly affected
Cause	Effects	Type	Source	
1. changes in moisture content	(only physical effects included) (1) contraction during drying out (irreversible) or (2) expansion or contraction due to increases or decreases in moisture content (reversible), resulting in cracking, surface crazing, warping	none	—	porous materials but usually excluding expanded plastics
2. frost action	physical change occurring mainly in exposed and wet conditions and normally resulting in surface disintegration and cracking	none	—	porous materials, especially those used externally and below ground
3. atmospheric gases (naturally occurring and 'man-made')	corrosion erosion disintegration	acids alkalis salts	(1) natural constituents of air, e.g. oxygen, carbon dioxide and chlorides (at or near the sea) (2) industrial and other processes, e.g. sulphur dioxide from fuel burning	building stones; metals; some types of paint; some bricks; cement and lime based products; plastics (subject to type)
4. soil and ground-water action	corrosion erosion disintegration	soluble sulphates; acids	(1) clay soils, acid soils; ground-water (2) ashes and industrial wastes used as fill for 'made ground'	(1) cement and lime-based products as used in foundations, retaining walls, floor slabs in contact with the ground, but also other elements connected by capillary paths (2) metals used as service pipes, sewers, etc., in contact with the ground
5. water supply	corrosion choking	mainly acids but also alkalis and carbonates in hard waters	nature of water supply (pH values; hardness category)	metal pipes, appliances, boilers, etc., in plumbing and heating systems
6. efflorescence (evaporation/crystallisation of salts)	(1) appearance when white crystalline growth occurs on surface (usually harmless) (2) crumbling when crystallisation occurs within surface	soluble salts	(1) inherent in many materials (2) from other materials in close contact resulting from a chemical action (3) atmospheric reactions on certain materials involving a chemical change	porous materials but mainly bricks, sedimentary stones, concrete and some paints
7. sulphate attack (excluding soil and ground-water action)	expansion disintegration	soluble sulphates	bricks; stones; atmospheric action	cement- and lime-based products (mortars, renders, concrete)

continued

Table 1.—continued

Deterioration		Substances involved in addition to water		Materials commonly affected
Cause	Effects	Type	Source	
8. unsound materials	expansion disintegration	unburnt or partially burnt particles	(1) lime burning processes (2) industrial waste, e.g. coal, blast furnace slags	mortars, plasters, lightweight concrete blocks and other products
9. incompatible materials (in contact or in association with one another)	corrosion decay	various but all produced under damp conditions	(1) dissimilar metals	copper/zinc; aluminium/ copper or brass
			(2) copper and brass	vulcanised rubber
			(3) oak and other timbers	lead, iron, steel and aluminium
			(4) cement and lime	lead, zinc and some aluminium alloys, glass
			(5) bricks containing much soluble sulphate	cement renderings
			(6) building stones (some types)	with other types of stone and some bricks
			(7) magnesium oxychloride	most metals except lead
10. electrolytic action	corrosion of metals	electrolytic cell (not a substance) with presence of moisture essential. Extent of action dependent on amount of water-soluble matter present	(1) local differences in composition of the same metal (2) embedment of a metal in the soil (3) dissimilar metals in contact (4) stray or induced electric currents	all metals commonly used in buildings
11. fungal attack	decay	various fungus spores (dry rot—*merulius lacrymans* most important)	(1) inherent in material (2) transportation	timber particularly, but other organic materials (e.g. wallboards) may be affected
12. industrial processes	mainly decomposition; usually of a specific type depending on chemicals/ materials involved	various	(1) during processes (2) storage (3) spillage (4) fumes	most building materials— careful selection essential
13. cleaning and maintenance	physical and chemical changes	abrasives, acids and alkalis	cleansing agents	all building materials but particularly surfaces—careful selection of cleansing agents in relation to materials essential
14. domestic and industrial wastes	chemical changes	acids and alkalis	(1) sanitary installations (2) sewage disposal systems (3) industrial processes	materials used in all waste disposal systems. Concrete, mortars and metals may in particular be affected

References: (1) *Durability* BS Code of Practice, CP3—Chapter IX (1950)—main source of information.
(2) *The causes of dampness in buildings*, BRS Digest (1st series) No. 33.

(6) *Vibrations*. May lead to cracking, deformation or local damage. (*Section 2.02 under 'Time- and special loading-dependent properties'*.)

(7) *Fire*. One of the accidental causes of deterioration. (*Part 5.00.*)

Finally, for convenience, a bibliography on 'Maintenance technology' is included.

3. The problem

At any given time it is often lack of knowledge of a certain kind which is at the root of many of the problems to be encountered in considerations of durability and maintenance. However, in many ways the difficulties are increased by the wide variations in interpretation of the precise meaning of the two terms. The significance of this may be understood by an examination of 'official' definitions:

*Durability** is defined as *'The quality of maintaining a satisfactory appearance and satisfactory performance of required functions'.*

Maintenance† is defined as *'Work undertaken in order to keep or restore every facility, i.e., every part of a site, building and contents, to an acceptable standard'.*

Although these two definitions are, in fact, defining two different terms, they both contain terms basically similar and which allow a reasonable degree of interpretation. Thus, for instance, what is the precise meaning of either 'satisfactory' as used in durability or 'acceptable' as used in

* *Durability* BS Code of Practice, CP3—Chapter IX (1950).
† *Glossary of general terms used in maintenance organisation* BSS 3811 : 1964.

maintenance? Answers to these would, in the first instance, appear to depend on specific attitudes of mind, but as important on cost implications. In any given situation it is no doubt possible that some agreement could be reached by all parties concerned as to the precise meaning to be adopted. In part, this is one of the more difficult, but major, decisions to make. At the same time it is perhaps as well to note that the cost of physical building is exceedingly high when compared with the subsequent cost of maintenance of individual buildings and is, therefore, more unkely than not to lead to one attitude of mind at the design stage, that is when one type of decision has to be made, and quite another during the life of a building when another has to be made. Furthermore, decisions as to the necessity of actually undertaking any specific maintenance during the

Accessibility is closely associated with maintenance work and requires special consideration at the design stage, in all situations, irrespective of height. The photograph below illustrates the use of scaffolding for the maintenance of an old building, while that above illustrates one type of power operated travelling cradle to a new building. In the latter case the cradle would be used mainly for window cleaning, but would also be used in other maintenance work. It will be seen from the photograph that travelling cradles require special consideration in the design of the roof edge and parapet to accommodate the requisite equipment. In this particular example the mullions to the cladding have also been designed to accommodate the cradle. Storage space for equipment may also be necessary (Roof cradle on the new CWS building in Manchester photograph courtesy of Mills Scaffold Company Ltd.)

life of a building have normally to be made by only one party, that is the building owner, of the original building team.

For a number of different reasons the maintenance cost implications of decisions taken at the design stage have in the past generally been neglected. Now that the estimated national expenditure has reached somewhere in the region of £1,000 million per annum, absorbing roughly 40 per cent of the total labour force engaged in construction and with the stock of buildings rapidly increasing, attempts are being made for more systematic thinking into the whole problem. This was, in fact, urged at the Conference on 'The Maintenance of Buildings' sponsored by the Ministry of Public Building and Works (MPBW) and held at the RIBA on March 5, 1965.* Every effort needs to be made immediately to relate available information so that it will be of some assistance at the design stage. By implication, further research into certain aspects is needed. At the same time clear guidance of the kind and frequency of maintenance is also required.

The more recent investigations into the whole problem of maintenance have in many ways gone a long way to reinforce the close relationship that exists between durability and maintenance. They are, as has already been stated, complementary to one another. Thus, for instance, there would be no justifiable reason to reject the use of a particular material which for the present purposes could be regarded as having, in the given situation, a short life, provided (and this is important) it was *assured* of having regular and proper maintenance during the life of the building. Looked at in another way this could be taken as implying that maintenance can be utilised to 'make up' any inherent weaknesses in the material and thus increase its durability.

The fact that there are likely to be such wide variations, not only of interpretations as already described but also of conditions, only makes it possible to draw attention in general terms to those factors which need to be considered before any reasonable assessment of the required functions of materials can be made. In many cases it will be found that specific knowledge may be lacking; this then means that some intelligent revaluation of existing knowledge will have to be made. Difficulties such as these are more commonly encountered with either new materials or new techniques, when it should be noted that the required information cannot always be obtained from laboratory tests alone. In most cases tests plus experience, which would include field tests, are necessary. For this reason the basis of assessment

of any claims made should in fairness always be clearly stated.* The complexities associated with any building project, and perhaps more so those employing new materials or novel techniques, can in many cases be resolved, and in many ways made less exacting, only if all parties concerned, but particularly the building owner, are fully aware of the possible implications of decisions which are made at the design stage.

4. Factors influencing durability

Changes in properties of materials which affect durability are in the main dependent on four inter-related factors. These are: (a) Time; (b) Exposure; (c) Usage conditions; and (d) The amount of maintenance carried out. For convenience these are considered separately, but this should not undermine the fact that they are all closely inter-related.

(a) *Time*
The period of time during which a building or any of its elements or components is expected to remain operational, that is capable of performing required functions, and commonly known as 'The Designed Life', is of great fundamental importance. Traditionally it has been customary to classify buildings broadly into two classes, namely, 'temporary' or 'permanent'. There is, however, a growing tendency to be rather more specific and to attempt to quantify the period in terms of years. Thus buildings may, nowadays, be described as 'short-life' or 'long-life'. (The change in terms does indirectly help to reinforce the necessity to actually state a value.) These descriptions can more aptly also be used for materials or components.

At the outset it is necessary to determine the design life of the building as a whole. The length of the determined design life would act as *a guide* in the selection and use of materials in general. It should, however, be noted that short-life buildings particularly do not necessarily imply the selection and use of short-life materials. As in all cases the economic balance between initial and maintenance costs would be important. In this respect it is interesting to note that recent experience appears to indicate that in general many present-day short-life buildings, and taking into account the higher standards which are generally demanded, attract higher maintenance costs than would have been expected normally. It is also important to remember that present-day concepts do not restrict the actual size of a short-life building.

Irrespective of the life-category of a building as a whole, it is still important that consideration be given to the design life of elements or components. Generally speaking it is more usual to

separate the structural and non-structural elements into two groups for such considerations. For the structural elements, and these would also include any other closely related elements, such as damp-proof courses for example, which may be hidden in them, the chief concern would be to ensure that these do not require such maintenance that would include complete replacement. This does not and should not preclude the possibility or desirability in any given situation to 'design' for replacement. In the case of non-structural or service elements the selection and use of materials may be of either type. Where short-life types are to be used maintenance would have to include periodic replacement.

The whole question of *replacement* requires special mention. In all those cases where replacement is incorporated as part of the maintenance programme, then it is absolutely essential that the relevant elements or components are, in fact, easily replaceable. This has a marked effect on design! The ease of replacement considered sufficient must be related to the frequency at which this operation will be necessary. Associated very closely with ease of replacement is *accessibility*. This is also closely related to maintenance problems in general, and requires, among other things, serious consideration of adequate safety precautions for the men who will have to actually carry out the work. In tall buildings particularly, the use of scaffolding for maintenance purposes can be relatively expensive and inconvenient. At the same time cleaning, which may also be regarded as part of maintenance work, can also be inconvenient, if not hazardous, when carried out from inside buildings. It is, therefore, not unnatural to find that these buildings incorporate in their design some form of travelling cradle arrangements. However, the somewhat special conditions applicable to tall buildings should not detract from the fact that accessibility needs consideration in all situations irrespective of height. In this it is to be remembered that access is often also required to elements and components inside buildings.

(b) *Exposure*
In the context of durability, and perhaps even more so when considering the effects of water, it is grossly misleading to consider exposure as being solely related to those faces of materials which are fronting on to the aggressive agencies, whether these occur externally or internally. Such considerations are likely in some circumstances to lead to a misunderstanding of the significance of good detailing and good workmanship, which are as important as the selection of materials themselves. Many an inherently resistant material has been rendered weak because aggressive agencies have been allowed to 'strike' from the back.

Without in any way undermining

* In 1965, a MPBW Committee on Building Maintenance was appointed. The interim findings of this committee (*Building Maintenance—an Interim Report*, HMSO) published at the beginning of 1969, estimated that maintenance accounted for an annual expenditure of some £1,555m, and gave recommendations for dealing with what the report describes as 'the mongrel science'.

*This point is made in the 'Master List' (1.6 Durability) prepared by the CIB Working Commission (W31) as published in the *RIBA Journal*, December, 1964, pp. 526-528.

15

the importance of good detailing and good workmanship, an assessment of the severity of the *basic* exposure conditions, i.e. those against which the materials in general terms will be required to be resistant, is necessary. The most severe conditions can normally be expected to occur externally, but in some instances extremely severe conditions may occur internally. The severity of the basic exposure conditions of any particular element may be reduced by suitable protection, which in many instances may only require to be localised. At the same time the basic design, particularly the profile, of an element may be such as to increase the severity of the basic exposure condition. As an example consider Portland stone used as a facing to an external wall of a building, in which horizontal ledges have been formed. The latter are more heavily exposed and thus subject to greater deterioration than the vertical face. Such deterioration as will occur, and this could also include uncontrolled changes in appearance of the vertical face (see examples included under 'Flow' in *3.01*), could be mitigated if the ledge was covered by an impervious material which in addition should ensure that water is thrown sufficiently clear of the vertical face below.

The *juxtaposition* of various materials may also lead to an increase in the severity of the basic exposure conditions. It has sometimes been quite rightly suggested that the juxtaposition of incompatible materials is responsible for a high proportion of failures in materials. A common example to be found externally and easily recognisable is lime leached from materials containing the substance and subsequently deposited on adjacent materials. In some cases the lime may lead to serious forms of decay rather than merely causing disfigurement of the surface on which it has been deposited. Metals as a group may be more prone to corrosion when different types are in contact with one another under damp conditions. Acids and alkalis derived from other materials in contact with metals may also, under damp conditions, result in corrosion of the metal. It is virtually impossible, in practical building, to ensure that materials are used in absolute isolation. Thus the juxtaposition or contact of different materials is inevitable. In terms of durability attempts must then be made to ensure that the materials likely to deteriorate are suitably protected or otherwise isolated from the corrosive agents. Where such protection is effected by what have been termed 'sacrifice' coatings, such as paint, these would require periodic maintenance.

The examples which have been quoted, related specifically to the effects of water, are only a selection of many which could have been included. The significance of exposure and related properties of materials are considered in greater detail in *Part 3.00*. However, it is importance to

quote a further example in order to illustrate the significance of *good workmanship*. Damp-proof courses may very often be required to 'negotiate' acute bends. The success of a damp-proof course in preventing penetration of water is, among other things, dependent on the continuity of the impervious layer. Such continuity may be broken if the damp-proof course is carelessly bent so as to cause a fracture. (In this it is assumed that the material of which the damp-proof course is composed is capable, with care, of being bent without fracture.) In most situations any subsequent dampness due to the fracture would involve costly maintenance. On a broader front the limitation of some cracking is, to a large extent, dependent on quality control of workmanship.

(c) *Usage conditions*

Although usage is in many ways an aspect of exposure, it has been usual to consider separately the effect of special conditions which may be expected in various building types on the selection and use of materials. Thus, for example, industrial buildings are generally considered to impose greater limitations on the use of materials, while at the same time demanding materials which are 'more durable' than those required for, say, a domestic building. However, it is not always satisfactory to classify the severity of conditions imposed by usage in terms of building types alone. The actual activities which are to take place are far more important. Even in industrial buildings there may be areas subject to conditions which may be no more severe than those experienced in an office building, while in certain parts of an office building conditions may be as severe as in some industrial buildings. In any given situation it is, therefore, necessary to analyse carefully the activity to be anticipated in each area of a building in order to determine the limitations that usage will impose on the selection and use of materials.

In general terms usage affects surfaces of materials the problems of which are normally included under the heading of 'wear and tear'. In this the significance of wheeled traffic should not be overlooked. The problems of wear and tear are covered in some considerable detail under 'Abrasion' and 'Impact' in *Section 2.04*. In addition to these aspects, usage must include relevant consideration of the presence, in significant quantities that is, of water together with other corrosive agents such as acids, alkalis, salts, etc., and of those agencies which generally lead to physical changes such as loading, heat, etc.

Usage conditions may also affect maintenance, but in rather a different way from those already considered. This concerns disruption of use which is inevitable whenever maintenance work has to be carried out. The degree of disruption will obviously depend on the exact nature of work required to

be carried out at any given time. Even when such work is part of what can best be described as regular or planned preventative maintenance, this may be undesirable in some situations. The requirements of industrial buildings serve as an example of the extreme situation, where even minor disruptions may lead to serious losses in production. The cost of such losses would have to be included as part of the maintenance costs. In situations such as these the use of essentially 'maintenance free' materials and components may, despite their customary higher initial cost, be desirable. In other building types, and here schools provide a good example, it may be far easier to phase planned preventative maintenance so that it occurs during 'natural breaks' in the usage pattern.

(d) *Amount of maintenance carried out*

At this point, and having already outlined the other related factors of time, exposure and usage conditions, there is little that can be added of the significance of the amount of maintenance carried out on durability. Suffice it to repeat that the durability of either materials or of the elements or components of which they form part may be increased by regular maintenance. Furthermore, selection of materials must be accompanied by good detailing and good workmanship if the maximum durability and minimum maintenance is to be obtained in any given situation.

As a concluding note it is probably worthwhile including a well-intentioned and extremely significant statement from the introduction to *A qualitative study of some buildings in the London area* (NBS Special Report 33, 1964) p. 1:

'The weaknesses of well-tried materials are known and allowed for in good design; but even the best designer may have to use materials with known shortcomings because, for a particular purpose, there exists at the time no economically acceptable alternative.'

5. The future

Maintenance technology will command more interest in the future. The interim findings of the MPBW Committee on Building Maintenance (*Building Maintenance—an Interim Report,* HMSO, 1969) contain a wide-ranging series of recommendations specifically aimed to focus professional expertise on building maintenance. The report views as its greatest task 'the education of opinion to accept that building maintenance is entitled to professional status equal with building design or construction' and leaves the technicalities to be developed in a companion series of monographs to be published as material becomes available. The report does, nevertheless, recommend for further study aspects of cost, finance, research and training so as to help in providing the body of knowledge so conspicuously lacking in maintenance.

SI units

SI units are used throughout this study. However, it is important to note that the values quoted either in the text or in diagrams, charts, etc. are converted values, that is converted mainly from Imperial units. In some cases the converted values have for convenience been rounded off.

A number of publications and aids have already been published on the use of SI units. Some of these are included in the bibliography. The intention here is, therefore, to provide basic information on the use of SI units together with tables and scales for conversion of those units primarily used in this study.

1. Background

SI is the accepted abbreviation in all languages for Systéme International d' Unités (International System of units), the modern form of the *metric* system finally agreed in October, 1964, at an international conference— Eleventh General Conference of Weights and Measures (CGPM). This is a rationalised system of metric units coming into international use and to be adopted in the United Kingdom.

In 1965, the Government announced its support for British Industry's request that the Imperial system be replaced by the metric system of measurement. The change-over would take place over the next ten years with the British Standards Institution undertaking the central role of preparing co-ordinated programmes for each sector of industry. The programme for the change to metric for the construction industry was the first to be published (February, 1967). The bulk of the change-over for this industry should be completed by the end of 1972.

The change to metric is not seen simply as one of conversion from traditional British units, but rather as an opportunity of rationalising the sizes of components. In this connection emphasis is placed on the need for the co-ordination of sizes on a national scale which must be related to international dimensional standards.

2. The decimal system

Metric systems are characterised by the fact that they consist of two related systems, namely one for the units of measure and one for the decimals. The decimal system consists of multiples and sub-multiples as shown in Table 2. The names of the multiples and sub-multiples of the basic units of measure are related to the basic units used (unlike the British system where they are unrelated as in yard, foot, inch) and formed by means of prefixes which are the same irrespective of the basic units to which they are applied. For example:

1 kilometre (km) = 1 000 metres
1 kilogramme (kg) = 1 000 grammes
1 millimetre (mm) = 0·001 metre
1 milligramme (mg) = 0·001 gramme

The prefix name or symbol is written immediately adjacent to the unit qualified. For example:

meganewton (MN)
kilometre (km)
microsecond (μs)

Only one prefix is applied at one time to a given unit. Thus one thousandth of a milligramme is not referred to as 1 millimilligramme (1mmg) but as 1 microgramme (1μg), while a thousand kilogrammes are described as 1 megagramme (1Mg) and not 1 kilokilogramme.

The prefix always refers to the basic unit to which it is attached. This becomes important when multiples are raised to powers as the power applies to the whole multiple and not to the basic unit alone. For example:

$1km^3 = 1(km)^3 = 10^9m^3$ and not 1 000m³.

3. Basic and derived units

Unlike the technical metric system, which it replaces, SI represents a coherent and rational approach to the whole question of measurement. The SI is based on the six primary units given in Table 3. The SI also includes a number of derived or supplementary units given in Table 4 for use in various calculations such as structural forces, thermal values and other related properties.

As SI is a coherent system of units, it provides naturally for a coherent unit of force, namely the newton, and for the derivatives of that unit for quantities such as pressure, stress, work and power. This may cause some confusion initially as hitherto in both the British and technical metric system it has been common to use weight units as force units. In SI a clear distinction is made between *mass* (measured in kilogrammes) and *weight* which is a *force* (measured in newtons). As the newton is defined as that force which, when applied to a body having a mass of one kilo-

Table 2. Decimal multiples and sub-multiples of units

Multiplication factor		Prefix	Symbol
1 000 000 000 000	10^{12}	tera	T
1 000 000 000	10^9	giga	G
1 000 000	10^6	mega	M
1 000	10^3	kilo	k
100	10^2	hecto	h
10	10^1	deca	da
0·1	10^{-1}	deci	d
0·01	10^{-2}	centi	c
0·001	10^{-3}	milli	m
0·000 001	10^{-6}	micro	μ
0·000 000 001	10^{-9}	nano	n
0·000 000 000 001	10^{-12}	pico	p
0·000 000 000 000 001	10^{-15}	femto	f
0·000 000 000 000 000 001	10^{-18}	atto	a

Table 3. SI basic units

Quantity	Name of unit	Unit symbol
Length	metre	m
Mass	kilogramme	kg
Time	second	s
Electric current	ampere	A
Thermodynamic temperature	kelvin	K
Luminous intensity	candela	cd

Table 4. SI derived units

Physical quantity	SI unit	Unit symbol
Force (weight)	newton	$N = kg\ m/s^2$
Work, energy, quantity of heat	joule	$J = N\ m$
Power	watt	$W = J/s$
Electric charge	coulomb	$C = A\ s$
Electrical potential	volt	$V = W/A$
Electric capacitance	farad	$F = A\ s/V$
Electric resistance	ohm	$\Omega = V/A$
Frequency	hertz*	$Hz = 1/s$
Magnetic flux	weber	$Wb = V\ s$
Magnetic flux density	tesla	$T = Wb/m^2$
Inductance	henry	$H = V\ s/A$
Luminous flux	lumen	$lm = cd\ sr$
Illumination	lux	$lx = lm/m^2$

*The term 'cycle per second (c/s)' has been used in the UK for frequency.

C

17

Table 5. A selection of recommended SI units and conversion factors

Quantity	SI unit	Recommended unit	Recommended multiples or sub-multiples	Conversion of British units to equivalent values in SI units	
Space Length			km	1 mile	= 1·609 34km
	m (metre)	m	m	1 yard	= 0·914 4m (E)*
				1 foot	= 0·304 8m (E)*
			mm	1 inch	= 25·4mm (E)*
Area			km²	1 mile²	= 2·589 99km²
	m²	m²		1 yard²	= 0·836 127m²
				1 foot²	= 0·092 903m²
			mm²	1 inch²	= 645·16mm² (E)*
Volume	m³	m³		1 yard³	= 0·764 555m³
				1 foot³	= 0·028 317m³
			mm³	1 inch³	= 16 387·0mm³
			l (litre)	1 pint	= 0·568 litre
				1 gallon	= 4·546 litre
				(Note: litre may be written in full to avoid confusion with unity. 1 litre = 10⁻³m³ = 1dm³)	
Mass and density			Mg (t-tonne)	1 ton	= 1·016 05Mg (t)
Mass	kg (kilo-gramme)	kg		1 pound	= 0·453 592 37kg (E)*
				1 cwt	= 50·802 3kg
				1 ton	= 1 016·05kg
		g		1 ounce	= 28·349 5g
Mass per unit area	kg/m²	kg/m²		1 lb/ft²	= 4·882 43kg/m²
Density (specific mass)	kg/m³	kg/m³		1 lb/ft³	= 16·018 5kg/m³
Force (weight)			MN		
		kN		1 tonf	= 9·964 02kN
	N (newton)	N		1 lbf	= 4·448 22N
Pressure and stress Pressure			bar (10⁵N/m²)	1 atmosphere (std)	= 1·013bar
			hN/mm² (millibar)	1 in H₂O (4°C)	= 2·490 49mb
				1 in Hg (0°C)	= 33·863 9mb
	N/m²	N/m²		1 atmosphere (std)	= 1·013 × 10⁵N/m²
				1 in H₂O (4°C)	= 249·049N/m²
				1 in Hg (0°C)	= 3 386·39N/m²
Stress			GN/m² or kN/mm² MN/m² or N/mm²	1 tonf/in²	= 15·444 3MN/m²
			kN/m²		
	N/m²	N/m²		1 lbf/in²	= 6 894·76N/m²
Energy (work, heat)			GJ		
			MJ	1 therm	= 105·506MJ
				1 kWh	= 3·6MJ (E)*
			kJ	1 Btu	= 1·055 06kJ
	J (joule)	J			
			mJ		
Power			GW MW kW		
	W (watt)	W		1 hp (horsepower)	= 745·700W (J/s)
Heat Customary temperature Temperature interval	degree Celsius (°C) °C			(see conversion chart)	
Heat flow rate			kW		
	W (watt)	W	mW	1 Btu/h	= 0·293 071W (J/s)
Density of heat flow rate			MW/m² kW/m²		
	W/m²	W/m²		1 Btu/ft²h	= 3·154 59W/m² (J/m²s)

continued

Table 5.—continued

Quantity	SI unit	Recommended unit	multiples or sub-multiples	Conversion of British units to equivalent values in SI units	
Thermal conductivity	W/m °C	W/m °C		1 Btu in/ft²h °F	= 0·144 228W/m °C
Thermal resistivity	m °C/W	m °C/W		1 ft²h °F/Btu in	= 6·933 47m °C/W
Thermal resistance	m² °C/W	m² °C/W		1 ft²h °F/Btu	= 0·176 1m² °C/W
Coefficient of heat transfer (thermal conductance)	W/m² °C	W/m² °C		1 Btu/ft²h °F	= 5·678 26W/m² °C
Thermal diffusivity	m²/s	m²/s		1 ft²/h	= 2·581 × 10⁻⁵m²/s
Heat capacity	J/°C	J/°C		1 Btu/°F	= 1 899·0J/°C
Specific heat capacity	J/kg °C	Jk/g °C		1 Btu/lb °F	= 4 186·8J/kg °C
Specific energy (specific latent heat)	J/kg	J/kg	MJ/kg kJ/kg	1 Btu/lb	= 2 326·0J/kg
Moisture content Vapour permeability	kg m/N s	kg m/N s	µgm/N s	1 lb ft/h lbf ditto	= 8·62 × 10⁻⁶kg m/N s = 8 620·0µgm/N s
Permeance	kg/N s	kg/N s	µg/N s	1 lb/h lbf ditto	= 2·826 × 10⁻⁵kg/N s = 28 260·0µg/N s
Humidity ratio	kg/kg	kg/kg		1 lb/lb	= 1·0kg/kg
Moisture content	g/kg	g/kg		1 grain/lb	= 0·142 8g/kg
Vapour resistance		MN s/g		1 h lbf/lb	= 3·9 × 10⁻⁵MN s/g
Vapour resistivity		MN s/g		1 h lbf/lb ft	= 11·5 × 10⁻⁵MN s/g

*(E) = exact conversion factor.

gramme, gives an acceleration of one metre per second squared (N = kg m/s²) it incorporates gravitational pull. Consequently, as shown later in *Sections 1.07 and 2.02*, it is necessary to multiply mass by standard acceleration in structural calculations.

4. Conversion factors

Table 5 includes conversion factors for those British units commonly encountered within the scope of this study. The table also gives the recommended SI unit, multiples and submultiples. As regards the latter it is important to note that their choice in practice should be confined to powers of 10 which are multiples of ±3. This may help to explain why for example the centimetre (cm) is not a recommended unit: the recommended units are km, m, mm.

The degree of accuracy required when converting values from the British system to SI depends on the nature of the work in which the values are to be used. For a number of cases in building work an approximate value will suffice. The conversion charts given for heat and mechanics, in the Appendix, enable approximate values to be read off comparatively easily. The charts may also help as a visual aid for comparing the two systems.

Selected bibliography and references

1. British Standards Institution, PD5686 : 1969, *The Use of SI Units.*
2. National Physical Laboratory, *Changing to the Metric System* by Anderton, Pamela and Bigg, P. H., 2nd Ed., HMSO, 1967.
3. Institution of Heating and Ventilating Engineers, *Change to Metric*, 1968.
4. British Standard 3763 : 1964, *The International System (SI) Units*, British Standards Institution.
5. British Standards Institution, PD6030 : 1967, *Programme for the Change to the Metric System in the Construction Industry.*
6. British Standards Institution, PD6031 : 1967, *A Guide for the Use of the Metric System in the Construction Industry.*
7. *AJ Metric Handbook,* The Architects' Journal special issues, March 13, 20, 25, 1968. (Republished in book form.)
8. Ministry of Public Building and Works, *Going Metric in the Construction Industry.* (Series of bulletins: 1. *Why and when*, HMSO, 1967—others to follow.)

1.00 physical and chemical aspects of matter

introduction

THE successful use of materials for building, as in other spheres, depends almost entirely on the extent to which their limitations are known and 'respected' for any particular application. These limitations may be derived empirically, by trial and error, without the application of any or very little scientific knowledge. This approach, justifiable under some conditions, inevitably leads to the formulation of a series of inflexible rules for the specific application of specific materials. Interpretation of the requirements of new conditions is usually difficult or inhibited by doubt. The use of scientific knowledge still requires a certain degree of trial and error to determine successful methods of using materials. However, once the scientific basis for any particular use or application is known, it is easier to explain or understand the limitations imposed or the causes of failures. In some ways interpretation of the requirements of new or unfamiliar conditions is also facilitated. It is perhaps axiomatic that some understanding of the language of science, including its valuable form of shorthand, is necessary.

In general, the sciences which are most applicable, in so far as the performance of materials for building is concerned, are physics and chemistry. Looked at in another way, the limitations of materials depends on their structure and behaviour. Materials are composed of matter, that is the substances of which all physical things are made. By the application of principles or laws of either physics or chemistry (or both, depending on circumstances) it is possible to determine which substances can or will combine to form particular types of material. In this the properties of and relationships between various substances and the extent to which environmental conditions affect these properties and relationships have to be taken into account as well. The inter-relationship is, understandably, complex. However, the principles or laws do explain fully, or help to explain basically (the precise state of knowledge at any particular time may be relevant), the types of substances and the conditions under which they will combine, and,

within the context of materials, the conditions under which decomposition, deformation or destruction is likely to take place. In all cases, the effects of environmental conditions on the behaviour of substances, and, in turn, of the materials they form, are most significant. In this, the nature and behaviour of heat (other energies are also relevant) or water and the movement of materials are notable.

Physics and chemistry cover a wide field and it is difficult, if not impossible, to condense that which already exists in many standard works on the two subjects, not all of which are related specifically to materials for building. In addition, the degree of scientific knowledge which general practitioners and related students (this study is intended for them rather than the specialist) should have to enable them to use materials properly is not clearly defined. Sometimes for both explanation and understanding it may be more convenient to simplify certain scientific descriptions. On the other hand, it may be assumed that in the extremely complex cases, the specialist, particularly the scientist, whom the general practitioner should understand, will be called to advise or carry out the requisite research.

Bearing in mind that this study of materials for building is mainly intended for the general practitioner and is essentially concerned with properties and uses generally, this part is intended to serve as a general background for the ensuing parts and also aims to briefly set out, primarily as a pattern of study, the relevant aspects of the physics and chemistry of matter. (The references at the end of this introduction, some of which are related to building science, should assist further study.) In some cases, it has been convenient to include, in this part, detailed consideration of certain aspects, such as adhesion and porosity, for example. In other cases, certain aspects (heat and sound are obvious examples) are covered either exclusively or in greater detail in other parts. However, reference to any detail considerations given elsewhere in this study are noted in the text as relevant. In view of the impor-

tance of plastics, an outline of organic chemistry is included.

An outline of the coverage of this part including the general headings used is set out below.

1. Physical and chemical changes

The fundamental differences between physical and chemical changes, related specifically to building materials, are outlined. The factors which influence the extent of change are also included.

2. Matters of energy

The distinguishing features between and the basic inter-relationships of matter and energy are discussed.

3. The three states of matter

Solid, liquid and gas states are outlined and compared.

4. Internal structure of solids

The basic characteristics of the two different kinds of solids, namely crystalline and amorphous or non-crystalline solids are outlined. The formation of crystals is described; crystal types and their characteristics are outlined and the basic differences between materials composed of crystalline units on the one hand and materials having a complete crystalline structure on the other are noted.

5. Pure substances, mixtures and compounds

The characteristics and examples of pure substances, mixtures and compounds are given.

6. Solutions

For convenience common types of both *true* and *colloidal* solutions are included. Particular attention is paid to the significance of gels because of their importance in the moisture movement of timber and other hygroscopic building materials such as bricks, stone and concrete.

7. Basic physical properties of matter

Brief descriptions of physical properties such as area, volume, mass, weight, force (out of context but included for convenience), density and specific gravity are covered. Other physical properties such as molecular forces and those concerned with the energies of heat, light and sound are covered as convenient in other sections.

8. Basic structure of matter

The main points relevant to elements, atoms and molecules, that is the small particles of which matter is composed, are set out.

9. Chemical conventions

A brief outline is given of the 'shorthand' used to record the elements together with the number of atoms present, and to show the results of combinations of various substances.

10. Chemical reactions

This heading is used to set out the significance of chemical reactions such as combination, oxidation, and reduction, and the formation of particular substances such as alkalis, acids and salts. In addition a short description of *organic chemistry,* notable in the production of 'plastics', is included.

11. Molecular forces

An indication is given of the significance of the nature and behaviour of molecular forces in so far as it aids an understanding of other physical properties and phenomena, particularly those related to liquids such as evaporation, cohesion, adhesion, surface tension, meniscus, capillary action and viscosity. For convenience a detailed discussion of *adhesion* together with the precautions which should be taken to maintain good adhesion is included.

12. Porosity

The main purpose of this section is to draw a distinction between the two main classes of materials: porous and non-porous. The voids in the various porous materials are given particular attention.

BIBLIOGRAPHY
(1) GIBBONS, S. G., *Building Science, Book I*, Pitman, 1947, written for Junior building students.
(2) GEESON, ALFRED G., *Building Science* for students of Architecture and Building Volume 1, English University Press Limited, 1944, chaps. XIII–XVIII—structural mechanics, chaps. XIX–XXV—heat and electricity.
(3) ADAMS, E. C., *Science in Building* for Craft students and technicians, Hutchinsons Educational Limited, 1964.
(4) REID, D. A. G., *Building Science,* Volumes 1 and 2, Longmans Green & Company Limited, 1950 and 1954.
(5) STADDON, L. S., and McPHERSON, L., *A First Course in Science for Building Students*, University Tutorial Press Limited, 1944.
(6) WILSON, J. G., and NEWALL, A. B., *General and Inorganic Chemistry*, Cambridge University Press, 1966.
(7) CARTMELL, EDWARD, *Chemistry for Engineers*, an Introductory Course, Butterworths Scientific Publications, 1959.

1.01 physical and chemical changes

Allowance for expansion or contraction by means of joints

Allowance for expansion or contraction due to temperature changes

Inadequate allowance in brick boundary wall for expansion and contraction due to temperature changes

In very simple terms, the efficiency of any material depends on the *degree* of stability which can be maintained during its 'working' life. Under suitable conditions, which will vary for each material, all materials are capable of undergoing changes of one kind or another. Any change, however small, which occurs in a material will, or tends to, alter one or other of its properties. Whether or not the alteration of the particular property (or properties, as the case may be) is likely to be detrimental to the proper functioning of the material for its pupose, will depend on the type and on the extent of the change. In all cases *both* of these have to be taken into account.

The extent of the change will depend on, and be influenced by, the nature of the conditions, i.e. the *concentration of the cause* under which the change is to take place, *the rate of change* and *the length of time* during which the change can take place. However, at the outset it is more essential to distinguish the *basic difference* between the two distinctly different types of change which can take place, as both produce different results.

Physical changes

Physical changes in materials are those which last as long as the cause of change persists. In general, such changes are limited to a change in shape or appearance of the material concerned. This normally involves an alteration of the internal arrangement of the structure of the material which, and this is most important, has no actual effect on its basic composition.

Excepting for the moment the case of complete structural failure which could occur, the original shape of the material will be restored once the cause effecting the distortion has been removed.* Thus, a physical change is, within limits, easily reversible. One of the most important aspects of this type of change is that during the process

---

*An important exception to this general rule is plastic change of shape, when a material becomes permanently deformed as a result of the application of a force—see *Section 2.01* particularly *The basic mechanisms of elastic and inelastic action*, p. 93.

no new substance (or substances) are formed. In other words, the composition of the material remains unaltered.

Physical change is mainly caused by external conditions, such as change in temperature and/or pressure in or around the material, which cause forces to be 'created'. Examples of physical changes commonly encountered are:

(1) Expansion or contraction of metals and other materials on being heated or cooled.

(2) Expansion or contraction of many porous materials, like clay, stone, cement, and especially timber on absorbing or giving off moisture.

(3) Loading in a building, i.e. deflection of structural members.

(4) Expansion of adjoining materials as the result of a chemical action, or physical change.

(5) Water freezing, thawing or turning into vapour.

(6) Melting of lead, asphalt and thermoplastics.

Examples of physical changes

Wiping of a lead joint requires a change of state

Above, efflorescence. Below, efflorescence of stonework probably due to a combination of salt and atmospheric action and frost action

Asphalt has to change from solid to liquid for application and liquid back to solid for use and function

Application of hot bitumen used as an adhesive in roofing

Inadequate allowance in sand-lime brick for moisture shrinkage

Physical change resulting from expansion caused by a chemical change. (Top) Corrosion of iron standard in a portland stone upstand. (Bottom) Corrosion of steel reinforcement in a concrete column

Crazing of surface of porous material—cast stone—due to differential moisture shrinkage between the surface layers and the adjacent layer underneath

Extrusion of asphalt DPC due to temperature and load

Chemical changes

Chemical changes in materials, on the other hand, are those which are permanent, and result in completely new substances being formed. These are completely different from the original substances, with entirely new chemical properties. Apart from the exceptions, particularly in organic chemistry, chemical changes are not reversible. (In inorganic chemistry, calcium carbonate, a common compound in building practice, is a notable exception—see *Section 1.09 Chemical Equations*.) In general, there is usually a considerable amount of *heat* involved in a chemical change, while there is a change in volume and, in most cases, *expansion* takes place.

For some building operations to actually take place chemical changes are in fact essential; chemical changes which, however, take place after the completion of a building are, depending on the extent, usually deleterious. Examples of chemical changes commonly encountered in building practice are:

(1) Cement setting.
(2) Paint drying.
(3) Slaking of lime.
(4) Wood decaying or burning.
(5) Corrosion of metals.
(6) Sulphate attack.
(7) Decomposition of sedimentary stones.
(8) Carbonation of free lime in cement.
(9) Alkaline attack from wet cement.
(10) Crystallisation of salts.
(11) Setting of mastics and adhesives; site mixing of two-part applications.
(12) Fading and/or decomposition of paints, plastics, etc.

Control and inter-relationship

Because these two types of changes are so different, it follows that different precautions will be required if the changes are to be controlled in the proper way. The precise precautions which are necessary are discussed under the relevant causes of the changes. However, in order to understand the principles upon which these are based it is first necessary to have a basic understanding of the physical structure and chemical composition of materials.

In practice, the deterioration of materials is usually, in varying degrees, the result of *both physical and chemical changes*. Sometimes a physical change may encourage a chemical change, or a chemical change may facilitate a physical change.

It should be remembered that, although the deleterious results of changes are usually more evident in materials used externally, results of a similar kind can also occur internally in severe conditions.

Examples of chemical changes

Corrosion of a ferrous metal (Courtesy: R. P. Russell, student)

Solubility of a limestone causing staining of brickwork

Application of a two-part mastic which requires to be mixed prior to use for the requisite chemical change to take place; once applied further chemical changes takes place (Courtesy: Expandite Ltd.)

Decomposition of sedimentary stone due to chemical action

Paint drying, particularly oil paint, requires a chemical change to take place. Breakdown and loss of adhesion caused by impurities on the background during application or subsequent moisture permeating to surface of background

Right, corrosion of non-ferrous metal-aluminium. Corrosive products tend to form protection. Below, wood rotting. Example shows the results of dry rot

Above, the hardening of concrete relies on the chemical change taking place when cement sets. Below, sulphate attack (R. W. Goodman, student)

1.02 matter and energy

It is important to distinguish between matter and energy, especially in view of the fact that the latter, in its various forms, can affect the former in many different ways.

All matter is characterised by the fact that it has mass, occupies space, i.e. has volume and, furthermore, requires a force to set it in motion.

Energy, on the other hand, is defined as the capacity to do work. It therefore has no mass and does not occupy space. Heat, light and sound are all forms of energy commonly encountered in building problems, and are all capable of being transmitted. Thus forms of energy are capable of moving or creating pressure on particles of matter. In some cases the transmission of energy is aided by matter. There are also other forms of energy, such as mechanical, potential, kinetic and electrical energy. The principle of the Conservation of Energy states the following general law:

'Energy cannot be created or destroyed, but can only be converted from one form to another.'

This does not necessarily mean that all of a given quantity of one kind of energy can be converted into the equivalent amount of another particular type of energy.

All substances are, therefore, forms of matter and so are all the materials used for building. A most important aspect of matter is that it is composed of small particles or structural units, which may be atoms, molecules or ions, held together by 'binding' forces, the strength of which may vary. The precise amount of strength of these forces accounts for the fact that matter may exist in one of three states, namely, solid, liquid or gas. The precise state will be influenced by external conditions such as temperature and/or pressure, as these will affect the

Solid

Liquid

Gas

strength of the 'binding' forces. Some of the most common changes of state resulting from temperature changes of particular importance in buildings are those undergone by water which is:

> *solid* at *low* temperature,
> *liquid* at *normal* temperature, and
> *gas* at *high* temperature.

It is as well to note here that the possibility of these changes occurring are often forgotten when the effects of water on materials are being con-

sidered. Nowadays, sources of water have been substantially increased by, among other things, condensation (including that which forms within the thickness of the structure) which is simply a change from the gas (better known as vapour when in this form) to the liquid state, due either to temperature or pressure changes.

In general, the particular temperature or pressure state relationship in any material is significant because it may affect the manufacture, use and, as already noted, the performance of materials.

All materials used in building are forms of matter.
The photographs illustrate a selection of those used

Bricks and mortar

Timber in laminated construction

Timber and dense and lightweight concrete

Marble block

Granite

Wall cladding tiles in clay

Clay roof tiles and lead

29

Precast concrete cladding units with exposed aggregate (stone)

Concrete in the making for precast concrete cladding

Metal (bronze) and glass

Steel (Courtesy: Shell Photographic Unit)

From left to right, clay bricks, expanded polystyrene, lightweight concrete blocks, timber framing

Plastics weather boarding

Fibreboard acoustic ceiling tiles (Courtesy: Treetex Ltd.)

Moulded plastics bathroom unit (Courtesy: I.C.I. Ltd.)

Decorative plastics wall linings (Courtesy: I.C.I. Ltd.)

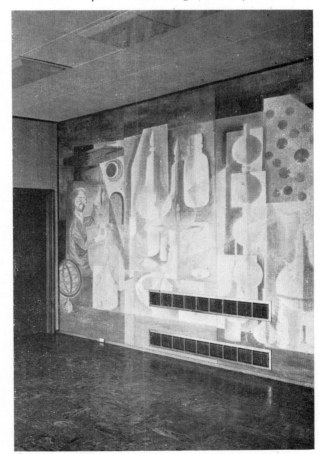

1.03 the three states of matter

Depending on its nature and prevailing environmental conditions, matter may exist in one of three states, namely, solid, liquid or gas. The fundamental differences between these are briefly:

(1) A solid has a definite volume and shape; (2) a liquid has a definite volume, but no definite shape, taking on the shape of its containing vessel; and (3) a gas has no definite volume or shape, but fills any vessel into which it is put, irrespective of shape or size.

In simple terms, the progression of a particular substance through the three states may be explained by the fact that when a gas condenses a liquid may be formed and this liquid may be frozen into a solid. The reverse may occur if the solid is melted to form a liquid and if this liquid is evaporated to form a gas. The change of state of water, as outlined in *Section 1.02* (p. 28), is important in everyday building practice.

The purpose of this section is to compare the three states of matter and to outline the significance of each state. An indication of the effects of the relationship between the nature of matter and environmental conditions is given in *Section 1.11* under *Forces between molecules* (page 60).

Solid

In the solid state, any given amount of matter has a definite volume and shape which, under normal conditions, is retained without the aid of any support from external agencies. This rigidity is maintained by the fact that the particles of which the solid consists are closely bound together into a compact mass and are relatively immobile.

The degree of rigidity possessed by a solid, that is its strength, is dependent on how closely bound the particles are or, in other words, the degree of strength of the bond between the particles. The volume and shape of a solid can be altered but only by the application of force, the extent of which will vary according to the bond between the particles and the particles of which the solid is composed. (Crystalline solids in particular require

the application of considerable force.) Thus solids will, subject to the strength of the bond, offer varying degrees of resistance to forces which tend to displace the particles and which would tend to alter the shape of the solid. Forces which will tend to alter the shape of a material may be created, either by simple superimposed loads on the material or by other agencies which may tend to either stretch, compress or otherwise deform the material. As regards the latter it may be noted here that considerable force may be exerted with the possibility of deformation (partial or complete) if a solid material is restrained from movement (see *Section 2.01* under *Deformation* and *Section 2.03* under *Cracking due to restraint of moisture and thermal movements*).

In addition to offering a resistance to being deformed, solids may also, again in varying degrees and within certain limits, return to their original shape once the force causing the deformation has been removed.

1. Useful classification

As a guide to the behaviour of solid materials when subjected to a force, it is useful to classify them into three broad types, namely *elastic, plastic* and *brittle*. Each of these is derived from the resistance which a solid material may offer to deformation.

(a) Elastic materials
A solid material is said to be *elastic* when, after it has deformed under load, and subject to a loading limit, it has the ability to 'spring' back to its original shape and size, once the load has been removed. In cases of excessive loading, even elastic solids will not return to their original shape and size. When this happens, they are said to have suffered permanent deformation, and to have a permanent set. In general, for a solid to have elastic qualities, it must have comparatively high resistance to deformation. Steel is one of the best examples of a solid of this type.

(b) Plastic materials
Solid materials which have little or no

elasticity and, therefore, deform even under *most* conditions of loading, are said to be *plastic*. Elastic materials, once they have passed the loading point when they will not recover their deformation, go through a state of *plastic flow*. Wet clay is an obvious example of a plastic solid, but lead can also be included.

(c) Brittle materials
Solid materials which do not become plastic under heavy loads but crack suddenly instead are said to be *brittle*. Cast-iron is an example of this type. Glass, not strictly a solid, is also extremely brittle. The brittleness of a solid may increase with use and exposure as, for example, asbestos-cement sheets.

In the above, no consideration has been given to the actual or physical size and shape of the solids concerned. These factors will affect the degree of resistance and, therefore, the extent of deformation which may occur subject to particular types of loading is more fully discussed in *2.00 Strength of materials,* particularly *Section 2.01* under *Behaviour of members subject to loading.*

2. Other distinctive properties

Finally, there are three other distinctive properties possessed in some degree by solids, namely malleability, ductility and hardness.

(a) Malleability
This is the ability of a solid to be beaten into sheets without rupturing, and is mainly confined to metals as a group. An example of a highly-malleable metal is lead.

(b) Ductility
The ability of a solid to be stretched or drawn into wire without rupturing. Again, this is mainly confined to the metals as a group. An example of a highly ductile metal is copper.

(c) Hardness
This may refer to the power of a solid to resist either abrasion or indentation. This term is normally restricted to surfaces.

Liquid

The fundamental difference between a liquid and a solid is that a liquid requires the support of an external agency to maintain its shape, usually referred to as a container. Liquids, like solids, do have a definite size, but take on the shape of the container into which they are placed. The reason for this lack, or absence, of rigidity is due to the fact that the particles of which a liquid is composed are, compared to solids, loosely bound together and are also more mobile. In other words, the forces holding these particles together are weak.

Because of its mobility, a liquid will readily change its shape when any force, however small, is exerted upon it. All liquids will not change shape at the same rate. The actual rate will be dependent on whether the liquid is viscous (slow rate of change) or mobile (fast rate of change), plus the extent of the force or pressure exerted (see *Section 1.11* under *Viscosity*, p. 77).

For most practical purposes, liquids are incompressible and transmit any pressure exerted upon them equally in all directions. The use of liquids in hydraulic machinery serves to illustrate this property fairly clearly.

Generally, liquids have 'flat top' surfaces, although surface tension forces will cause a curvature, known as a *meniscus* (see *Section 1.11* under *Surface tension* and *Meniscus,* p. 73).

Gas

All matter which is not in either the solid or liquid state is said to be in the gas state, and collectively referred to as gases. Again, this is important when considering water, as it may be in the gas state. In this connection it is worthwhile remembering that air always contains a certain amount of water vapour; in many cases the amount may be quite excessive.

Gases have no definite shape or volume, and are very easily compressible. This is due to the fact that the particles of the gas are extremely loosely associated with one another and extremely mobile. In fact, the particles (molecules) are not closely packed as they are in the other two states, but have a separate and independent existence. In general the attractive forces between the particles is almost negligible and the particles have rapid motion, colliding with one another and the walls of a vessel without loss of kinetic energy. As a result, they will flow in all directions and, above all, expand to fill completely any vessel.

Furthermore, one gas will readily diffuse, i.e. mix evenly, with another gas to form a uniform mixture, despite any differences in density which may exist between the particles of the gases.

Gases have the simplest constitution of any forms of matter. Whereas solids and liquids differ among themselves, the physical properties of all gases are remarkably similar.

33

D

1.04 internal structure of solids

A solid material may be defined as a rigid body which has a definite volume and shape, and, in order to distinguish it from a liquid or gas (particularly a liquid), does not flow on the application of a force. However, some substances, such as sealing wax, glass, pitch and thermoplastics, which look like solids and which might otherwise appear to have the properties of solids (comparative rigidity and capable of being shattered by a sudden blow), do flow if a *gentle* steady force is applied for a long period of time. Because of this ability to flow, amorphous solids resemble liquids possessing a very high degree of viscosity. Consequently a distinction has to be drawn between two types of solids namely *crystalline solids* (do not flow) and *amorphous or non-crystalline solids* (capable of flow), as their respective properties, and hence those of the materials which they form, are quite different. It may be noted that softness is not an indication of the type of solid that a substance may be. For example, a piece of sodium is softer than pitch, but sodium is a crystalline solid.

The main emphasis in this section is on the crystalline solids (occur more commonly), including their formation, types and occurrence in materials.

Crystalline solids

1. Arrangement of structural units

In a crystalline solid, the structural units, which may be atoms, ions, or more rarely molecules, are arranged in a definite and orderly manner, in what is known as a *space-lattice*. An example of the space-lattice produced by potassium chloride is illustrated in diagram D.1.04/1. A *space-lattice* may be defined *as the regular geometrical pattern in which the structural units of a crystal are arranged.*

There are various forms of lattice, but each different form is bounded by plane surfaces which meet at *definite* angles, producing external geometric forms which are correlated with the geometric internal structure and which are characteristic of the crystal of a given substance. Even if a crystal is

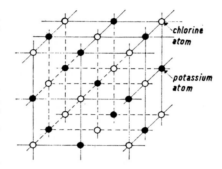

D.1.04/1 *Lattice produced by potassium chloride. Note: lines are used to indicate the arrangement of atoms. They do not exist in reality*

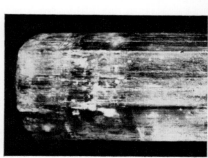

Various crystals showing characteristic geometric forms

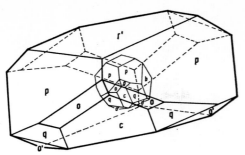

D.1.04/2 *Two crystals of ferrous ammonium sulphate, one drawn inside the other. Although possessing different shapes each has identical interfacial angles*

fractured, the new surfaces of each fragment are plane, and are inclined to one another at angles which are characteristic of the given substance. During crystallisation, local influences may result in the corresponding faces of different crystals, of the same substance that is, developing at different rates. Consequently the resulting crystals will have *different shapes,* but, although the relative areas of certain faces are different, the *angles* between the various faces remain the same. (See diagram D.1.04/2.) It may be noted that X-ray examination has also shown that, even in cases where there is no distinct geometric external form, the structural units are, nevertheless, still arranged in an orderly fashion.

According to the symmetry they display, crystals may be classified into 32 *classes.* These classes are grouped in seven *systems,* namely, the cubic, hexagonal, tetragonal, triagonal, orthorhombic, monoclinic, and triclinic. Although there are 230 possible modes in which a system of points can be arranged in space to give repetitive patterns, these 230 modes can be related to 14 space-lattices which correspond to the seven systems of crystal symmetry.

2. Properties

In addition to properties of crystals outline in (1) above and particularly the fact that a crystal is bounded by plane faces, with given interfacial angles being characteristic of a given substance, the basic properties of crystals may be summarised as:
(a) Crystalline solids have *definite* melting points.
(b) When struck, crystalline solids usually fracture along one or two particular planes, *cleavage planes,* which are related to the direction of the boundary surfaces.
(c) The application of considerable force is required to alter both volume and shape.
(d) Subject to the force applied and later released, the original volume and shape of a crystalline solid may be regained, that is crystalline solids possess *elasticity.*
(e) Crystalline solids contract under pressure and expand or contract with increases or decreases in temperature.
(f) Generally, crystals display different physical properties in each direction, that is they are *anistropic.*

Amorphous or non-crystalline solids

The basic differences between amorphous solids and crystalline solids may be summarised as follows:

1. Form
Amorphous solids are formless and have no cleavage planes.

2. Melting point
Amorphous solids have no definite melting points. On being heated, amorphous solids gradually loose their rigidity, that is, they soften, and their elasticity, that is they become more mobile, and pass continuously, without any sudden change in properties, into liquids.

3. Isotropy
Physical properties, such as thermal expansion, elasticity, and solubility have the same values in all directions in an amorphous solid and so it is said to be *isotropic.*

4. Super-cooled liquids
Because of their similarities with liquids, particularly the ability to flow, amorphous solids may be regarded as *super-cooled liquids,* in which the structural units have a greatly diminished freedom of movement.

Glass, particularly in its clear state, is now usually regarded as a super-cooled liquid, having small crystalline aggregations, distributed in a random and unconnected way in a non-crystalline matrix.

Formation of crystals

Crystals may be formed either when the temperature of a liquid is lowered, or, from a solution. The former is important in the metal industries, while the latter frequently occurs in porous materials and is of particular importance in problems associated with efflorescence. (See *3.05 Efflorescence.*) The mechanisms, so to speak, involved in the formation of crystals in either case are broadly the same. However, certain basic factors may alter the final shape and size of crystals. It is convenient to consider (1) the mechanisms generally involved in the formation of crystals, noting the causes of deviation from the ideal outlined in 'Crystalline solids' previously, and then the formation of crystals (2) when the temperature of a liquid is lowered and (3) from solution.

1. General considerations

(a) *Basic mechanisms*
The formation of a given crystal commences to take place as soon as the movement of the structural units involved has slowed down sufficiently for the forces of attraction between the units to be increased. During the 'slowing down' process, a nucleus (or nuclei, depending on circumstances) is formed around which the structural units dispose themselves at fixed points and not at random. Once occupying their 'fixed' positions, the structural units can still move, but, and this is important, their motion is restricted to a vibration or oscillation about their 'fixed' positions.

The nucleus does, in fact, form the 'starting point' for a tree-like growth, *dendrite* (from the Greek *dendron* = tree), which is three-dimensional, as shown in diagram D.1.04/3. The structural units do, however, continue to arrange themselves in a definite and orderly array, and so the growth of the crystal continues.

(b) *Variations in structure*
Depending on conditoins, the structural units of some substances may link together in two or more different kinds of structure, that is

D.1.04/3 *A dendrite to illustrate that crystal growth is orderly and three-dimensional. Growth of the 'arms' ceases as soon as any obstruction is encountered (Courtesy: Pascol, K. J., Properties of Engineering Materials, Blackie & Sons, 1961)*

different kinds of space-lattices. These substances are said to be *polymorphous.* If a substance exists in two different crystalline forms it is said to be *dimorphic,* and if in three, *trimorphic* and so on. Polymorphism is a special case of *allotropy,* a phenomenon peculiar to any given chemical substance, known as an *allotrope,* which can assume more than one form.

The significance of the allotropes of a given substance is that they often display remarkable and extensive differences of physical and chemical properties. *Calcium carbonate,* a substance which occurs in a number of building materials and uses, is dimorphic, with the two forms having identical structural units, namely calcium ions and carbonate ions, but arranged on different space-lattices. Calcium carbonate is also *monotropic* (type of allotropy). Under normal physical conditions one allotrope (calcite) is stable while the other (aragonite) is unstable and tends to change into the stable form.

Tin is also dimorphic—grey tin has a diamond lattice but white tin (stable above 13·2°C) has a face-centred lattice. Tin, however, differs from calcium carbonate in that it is enantiotropic. Each allotrope of a given substance in this type is stable over a given range of temperature (pressure has a negligible effect).

(c) Causes of distortion

The formation of a perfect crystal requires slow growth of the crystal so that the structural units may have time to arrange themselves properly, while the crystal must be free to grow in all directions. In the absence of these conditions, the crystal becomes distorted and there will be a divergence from the form of the perfect crystal. The flat fan-like or fern-like crystals which are formed when moisture freezes on a window pane are distorted crystals, because growth has only taken place in two dimensions. The beautiful leaf-like or lace-like crystals seen in snowflakes are another example. In their case, crystalline growth was more rapid in certain directions than in others, thus causing distortion. Although the external form of the crystal may have changed, the crystallographic system to which the crystal belongs *remains the same*. This is important.

2. Lowering the temperature of a liquid

In the liquid state the relative mobility of the particles of which the liquid is composed results in a disruptive and separating action. The forces of attraction between the particles are weak. However, as the temperature of the liquid is lowered, the forces of attraction between the particles are increased. Under favourable conditions the particles, which form the structural units of the crystal, join together, linking firmly together at definite points as previously described.

In the case of the solidification of liquids to form *metals*, it is usual for more than one nucleus to be formed from which dendritic growth proceeds. Thus adjoining dendrites will, when they meet, offer an obstruction to the further growth of the individual crystals. Obstructions (including dendrites) and external forces of many kinds may impede the growth of a crystal. Depending on circumstances, crystals may, therefore, grow to various sizes. However, the structural units still produce crystal structures characteristic of the particular metal.

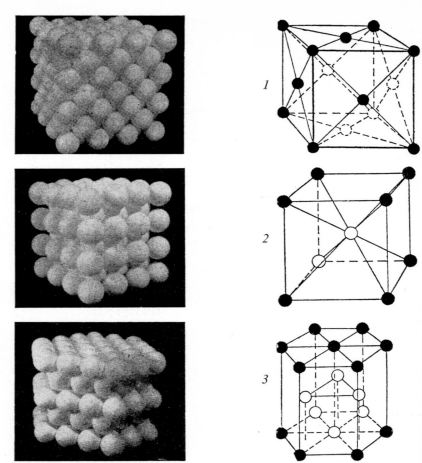

D.1.04/4 *Metallic crystals (1) Face-centred cubic unit cells, (2) Body-centred cubic unit cells, (3) Hexaganol unit cells. (Courtesy: Pascol, K. J., Properties of Engineering Materials, Blackie & Sons)*

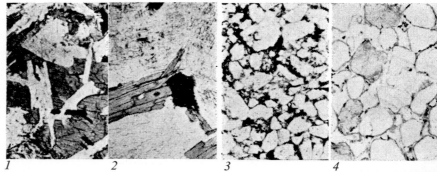

Structure of granite (1, 2) and structure of standstone (3, 4) (Courtesy: Geike, J. 'Structural and Field Geology', Oliver and Boyd)

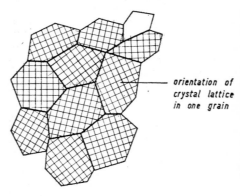

orientation of crystal lattice in one grain

D.1.04/5 *Diagrammatic illustration of metal grains and orientation of crystal lattice in one grain*

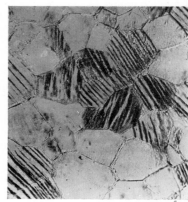

Magnified picture of aluminium clearly showing the metal grains

Other factors, such as impurities and the temperature gradient during cooling may also alter the structure of crystals. In metallurgy it is, therefore, important that all the factors which contribute to changes in crystal growth or to the structure of the crystals are carefully controlled. Distortion or deformation of the crystal structure results in changes in certain important physical properties of the finished metal.

3. From solution

In a solution the solid particles (the solute) are 'kept apart' by the particles of the liquid (solvent) in which they are dissolved. As the solution is concentrated by evaporation of the solvent, or as the temperature of the *concentrated* solution falls, the particles of the solute become more crowded together, or their kinetic energy diminishes to such an extent that the solid particles are able to join up into crystal units. The visible crystal is built up as more and more particles (the structural units) attach themselves in an orderly array.

Crystal types

As already mentioned, the structural units from which a crystal may be formed may be either atoms, molecules or ions. These various units give rise to the four crystal types set out below.

1. Atomic crystals

Atomic crystals, exemplified by diamond, carborundum and silica, are linked together by covalent bonds. The covalent bond is the sharing of a pair of electrons by two atoms (see *1.08 The Basic Structure of Matter,* under *Atoms,* p. 50). Being a rigid and intimate link between two atoms, it cannot be loosened or destroyed without chemical decomposition of the molecule. Due to the strong cohesive forces between the structural units, atomic crystals have high melting points. In another context they are extremely hard and durable.

2. Molecular crystals

The structural units of the crystals are molecules. Although the atoms in each molecule are firmly bound by covalent links, the molecules themselves are not linked to one another by any chemical bond. The molecules may, therefore, be described as neutral and held together by weak cohesive forces. Consequently molecular crystals have low melting points.

3. Ionic crystals

The structural units of an ionic crystal are held together by electrostatic forces. The crystal of sodium chloride is an example and is compacted together by electrical forces between the oppositely-charged ions of sodium and chlorine. The crystal disintegrates if these electrical forces are diminished by any means. The electrical attraction between the ions can be diminished by water. The ions fall apart, and so in an aqueous solution of sodium chloride the oppositely-charged ions of sodium and chloride move about with entire independence.

Ionic crystals have relatively high melting points.

4. Metallic crystals

In the case of metals, the structural units are positive ions with free electrons. The number of free electrons varies with temperature.

By and large, metals are close assemblages of face-centred cubic, body-centred cubic or hexagonal unit cells. (See diagram D.1.04/4.) The bonds between the atoms are specially undirected. Deformation by gliding can thus readily take place. This confers properties such as malleability and ductility.

Occurrence in materials

1. Naturally-occurring

For the present purpose naturally-occurring materials are deemed to include clay products.

Granites, which were formed from the molten state and under pressure, consist of a variety of crystals, such as quartz, felspar and mica, each of which has its own particular crystal structure. These different crystals have been fused together. However, the whole of the material cannot be said to be crystalline but, rather, that it is composed of crystalline units.

In the *sedimentary stones* (limestones and sandstones) many different kinds of crystals, commonly referred to as minerals, may be present. The crystals or minerals are usually embedded in a matrix which may itself be crystalline or amorphous. *Limestones* consist primarily of particles of calcium carbonate in a matrix of calcium carbonate. *Sandstones,* on the other hand, although consisting primarily of quartz particles (other minerals such as mica may be present), may have a matrix of silicon dioxide, iron oxide, calcite (calcium carbonate) or a mixture of these.

The composition of *clay products*— is also liable to wide variations in terms of crystal content. Among other things, clays themselves are likely to have different proportions of minerals while chemical changes of various kinds are likely during firing. During the firing process, vitrification results in part of the clay mixture melting and sticking the rest together.

From these general considerations it may be noted that, among other things, the degree of concentration of a mineral of any particular kind is likely to influence the overall properties of the whole material.

2. Metals

Whereas the naturally-occurring materials may be said to be composed of crystalline units, metals, on the other hand, are generally regarded as having a complete crystalline structure. The geometric boundaries of the crystals can rarely be seen with the naked eye. The crystals generally assume a polygonal shape (often referred to as grains—see diagram D.1.04/5) and so metals are said to be *granular.* Adjoining grains, it may be noted, are 'stuck together' by a different space-lattice structure at the interface of the grains.

The properties of any particular metal are influenced by the space-lattice peculiar to that metal, the size of the crystals or grains and the nature of the interfacial space-lattice. On the other hand, properties such as elasticity are affected by the orientation of the various crystals or grains to one another. (The orientation of the grains is determined by the orientation of the dendrite growth for a given grain.)

Finally, it is also important to note that the crystal structure of metals may be materially altered thereby also affecting some physical properties, by hot and cold working, that is by heat and pressure. (See *2.02. Mechanical Properties,* under *3. Relationship between stress and strain,* p. 97.)

1.05 pure substances, mixtures and compounds

One example of a pure substance is all parts of a sheet of glass (Courtesy: Pilkington Bros. Ltd.)

Pure substances

A pure substance is one which possesses the same properties throughout. Such substances are said to be *homogeneous.*

Examples of pure substances are all the parts of a sheet of glass or pure water.

All homogeneous materials may be divided into two kinds, namely, (1) *compounds,* characterised by the fact that their composition is fixed, and (2) *solutions* characterised by the fact that their composition is variable. The latter group should not, however, be confused with the strict definition of mixtures as outlined below.

Mixtures

A mixture consists of two or more substances whose individual properties remain unaltered. Thus the properties of the mixture vary from point to point, and is said to be *heterogeneous.* The substances making up the mixture can be present in any desired proportions, making the composition variable. *One* important characteristic of a mixture is that it is possible, by physical means, to separate each component from the mixture.

Granite is *one* example of a mixture found in building materials. The *main*

Iron, when combined with oxygen, forms an iron oxide—rust—which has different properties from the original iron

Chief differences between mixtures and compounds

	Mixture	Compound
1. Properties	Same as those of the constituents	Quite different from those of the elements present in the compound
2. Composition	Variable	Constant
3. Separation	Constituents may be separated by physical means, usually with ease	Constituents cannot be separated by physical means
4. Energy	Energy not liberated in the formation from the constituent elements	Energy (heat and/or light) usually liberated in the formation from the constituent elements

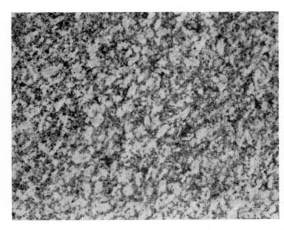

Granite is one example of a mixture found in building materials. The individual characteristics of the crystals result in the mottled effect

constituents of granite are three different minerals, quartz, felspar and mica. Unlike most other mixtures, the separate minerals can be separated by mechanical means with comparative ease. Heterogeneous bodies such as granite are, therefore, sometimes also known as mechanical mixtures. In the case of granite, as in some other mixtures, it is usually possible to distinguish the separate particles with the aid of a lens, particularly when the materials have previously been ground and polished.

The separate parts of a heterogeneous body are called 'phases'. Pure substances or bodies do, therefore, only have a single phase.

Compounds

A compound is formed as the result of chemical forces uniting two or more elements. The properties of the compound are, therefore, different from the properties of the combining elements. In fact, the compound is a *new* homogeneous substance and so the original components cannot be distinguished or separated out by physical means. During the chemical union energy (heat and/or light) is often liberated.

Iron, when combined with oxygen, as occurs in what is commonly known as rusting, forms an iron oxide which has completely different properties

from the original iron. The rusted portion and the original iron form a mixture, with obvious reductions in the overall properties of the latter.

Portland and other types of cement contain a number of compounds. These in turn react with the mixing water to form new compounds. The related chemistry is extremely complicated, but one important aspect is the fact that considerable heat is evolved during the reactions, particularly those during the initial setting and hardening processes. This heat must usually be carefully controlled.

Some examples of compounds will be found in *1.09 Chemical Conventions* under *Chemical equations.*

1.06 solutions

Solutions may be basically of two kinds, namely true solutions and colloidal solutions. A *true solution* is a molecularly *homogeneous* mixture of two or more substances, whereas a *colloidal solution,* or sol, is *heterogeneous* and is a system in which one of the components is *dispersed throughout* the other as small particles or droplets. Each type of solution is considered separately.

True solutions

A compound has a fixed composition. The composition of a solution may *vary* within very wide limits. This is an important difference. Solutions may be formed by the mixture of a variety of substances. There may, therefore, be solutions of gases in gases, in solids or in liquids; of liquids in liquids, in solids, or in gases; of solids in solids, in liquids, or in gases. Generally, the term *solvent* is applied to the component in the larger amount, and the term *solute* to the other components.

1. Solids in liquids

Solutions obtained by *mixing* a solid substance with a liquid (salt in water or sugar in water are obvious examples in everyday life) are the most familiar. They are a good starting point for the study of solutions. The *liquid* which holds the solid in solution *is the solvent:* the *dissolved solid* is the *solute.* As water is the most familiar solvent and of particular significance in the use of materials, the discussion which follows is confined to solutions of solids in water.

(a) *Saturation*
The extent to which a solid dissolves in water is limited; it depends on the nature of the solid and on the temperature. A *saturated solution* of the solid is obtained when no more dissolves, and *at a given temperature is a solution which is in equilibrium with undissolved solid.*
Super-saturated solutions, which are metastable, are those which contain more solute in a given weight of solvent than is required to form a saturated solution at the same temperature.

(b) *Solubility*
The *solubility of a solid* in water *at a given temperature* is defined as the *number of grams of the solid which dissolves in 100 grams of water to give a saturated solution at that temperature.*
Generally, the solubility of a solid in water increases with increase of temperature—calcium hydroxide, sodium sulphate and sodium carbonate monohydrate are among the few substances which dissolve more freely in cold than in hot water. Different solids, it should be noted, have different solubility curves.
Solids do not dissolve instantaneously when brought into contact with water; some form of mixing, the extent of which will depend on the nature of the solid and temperature, is required. However, the *rate* at which a given solid will dissolve in water at a given temperature does depend on the size of the particles of the solid; smaller particles dissolve at a faster rate.

(c) *Effects of evaporation and cooling*
Either the loss of water from a concentrated solution, through evaporation, or the cooling of a given concentrated solution will result in the soluate being deposited (see *Section 1.04,* under *Formation of crystals,* (p. 35).

(d) *Salts in solution*
Salts in solution account for a number of problems in buildings. One is the crystallisation of salts (usually as a result of evaporation) at or near the surface of porous materials; the phenomenon is known as *efflorescence* (*Section 3.05).* Another is *sulphate attack* (*Section 3.06)* in which, under certain conditions, sulphate salts (commonly encountered) react with some of the constituents of lime and Portland cement, particularly the latter, resulting in expansion and thus causing disintegration of materials such as mortars, renders and concrete of which they are constituents. Salts in solution also contribute to the problems associated with hardness of water (*Section 3.02)* and the corrosion of metals (*Section 3.07).*

2. Gases in liquids

Gases are only partially miscible in liquids. When water is the liquid, the amount of gas that will dissolve in a given amount of water is dependent on (a) the nature of the gas, (b) the temperature, and (c) the pressure of the gas in contact with the water.
Compared to other gases, such as oxygen and hydrogen, *sulphur dioxide,* an important constituent in polluted (smoky and industrial) atmospheres, and *carbon dioxide,* a natural constituent of the atmosphere (amount increases in polluted atmospheres), mix readily with water to form acids. These contribute to decay and deterioration of many materials, particularly some sedimentary stones and metals.
It may be noted that, unlike solids, the solubility of gases at constant pressure in liquids diminishes with increase in temperature.

3. Solids in solids

The solution of a solid in a solid usually takes place when the components are in a liquid state, as occurs in the alloying of metals. Common examples of alloys are: (a) *brass* (copper and zinc), (b) *bronze* (copper and tin), and (c) *steel* (iron and carbon). In all these cases the alloys have properties quite different from the constituent metals used to form them.

4. Gases and liquids

Whereas pairs of gases are mutually soluble (gases dissolve in each other resulting in solutions, often referred to as mixtures), not all pairs of liquids dissolve. They may be either (a) completely immiscible (oil and water), or (b) completely miscible (water and alcohol, or oil and alcohol) or (c) partially immiscible (water and ether).

Efflorescence: the crystallisation of salts takes place when the water in which the salts are soluble is allowed to evaporate

The mixture of carbon dioxide and/or sulphur dioxide with water form acids which help to decompose many materials, especially some sedimentary stones

Some examples of copper alloys—brass (copper and zinc) and bronze (copper and tin). Different proportions of zinc, tin and other elements with copper yield different kinds of brasses and bronzes

Sulphate action (attacks lime and especially Portland cement)

Steel—an alloy of iron and carbon

Colloidal solutions

An important characteristic of the dispersed or suspended solid particles in colloidal solutions is that they do not settle out under gravity, while they are not easily removed by filtration.

In colloidal dispersions, *disperse phase* and the *dispersion* are analogous to the solvent and solute in true solutions.

Some common colloidal dispersions are set out below.

1. Cloud and fog

Both of these are dispersions of liquids in gases.

2. Smoke

An example of a solid in a gas.

3. Emulsions

Emulsions are liquids in liquids as, for example, oil in water (milk) or water in oil (cod liver oil emulsion). When making emulsions which are normally used in buildings, such as paints, it is necessary for what is known as an emulsifying agent or stabiliser to be added in order to secure stability of the particles being suspended.

The detergent or cleansing action of soaps and other detergents is due to their ability to emulsify grease. Thus, solid particles or dirt are attached to the grease globules.

4. Gels

These are dispersions of liquids in solids and form a distinct colloidal system, setting in a semi-solid jelly-like condition. One of the most important properties of gels is that they are *hygroscopic,* that is, they take in water. Some, like gelatin, are capable of taking in volumes of water in excess of the volume of the gel itself. In the same way as water may be taken in, so may it also be given out. During these processes the gel either shrinks or swells depending on increases or decreases in moisture content. Gelatinous bodies are, however, divided into elastic, or non-rigid gels (like gelatin) and rigid gels (like silica gel). The former swell on the addition of water, finally pass into solution but reform as gels on drying. The rigid gels do not show this reversible behaviour and so, once formed, will not disperse again to a solution on the addition of water.

One particular characteristic of gels is that they do not really become chemically combined with water. The 'loose' chemical bond which is created between the gel and the water is a phenomenon known as *adsorption* (not to be confused with absorption), and sometimes referred to simply as *'sorption'*.

Sorption is a condition somewhere between a true chemical and physical

Cloud—an example of a liquid in a gas

Smoke—an example of a solid in a gas

The cleansing action of soaps and other detergents is due to their ability to emulsify grease

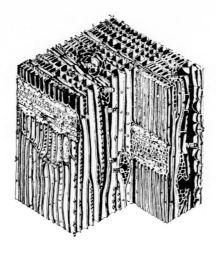
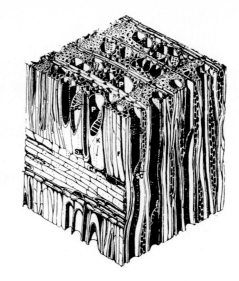

D.1.06/2 *Diagrammatic representation of the moisture movement of timber, in a tangential, radial and longitudinal direction*

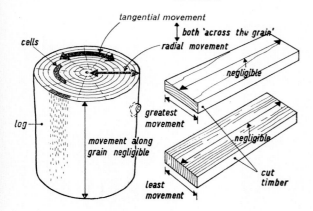

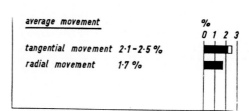

C.1.06/1 *Comparative chart of average moisture movement in timber*

bond. During the bonding process the molecules of the water become attached to the molecules of the solid, resulting in an increase in volume, but with no chemical action characteristics. Because of the expansion which takes place, great pressures can be created if the material is restrained.

Gels in materials

Many traditional materials, such as timber, brick, stone and concrete, are also hygroscopic and are liable, under suitable conditions, to increase or decrease their moisture contents, with corresponding increases or decreases in volume. These dimensional changes are known as *moisture movement* (see *3.03 Moisture content*). Some of the water taken in, or given out, is due to the fact that these materials tend to behave like rigid gels.

In addition, water known as *free water* may be held *chemically uncombined* in the interstices of the materials. This water, which 'finds' its way in and out of materials by capillary action, may, in a minor way, contribute to dimensional changes; the water certainly adds to moisture content. Whereas free water is, in a sense, the last to add to moisture content, it is, on evaporation, the first to leave the material. The moisture content of the gels themselves, which does, of course, contribute to the moisture content of the material, is primarily dependent on the relative humidity of their environment.

There is, however, a basic difference in behaviour between timber, essentially a fibrous material like cotton and wool, and the others (brick, stone and concrete).

In timber, the cells of which it is composed are arranged in chains in more or less concentric rings (see diagrams D.1.06/1 and 2). The cell walls, being the fibrous material, take in water by sorption and due to their formation expansion (or contraction) takes place to the greatest extent along the rings (i.e. tangentially); to a lesser extent in a radial direction while movement is negligible along the grain, as shown in diagram D.1.06/2 and chart C.1.06/1. Timber is thus anistropic.

In the case of brick, stone and concrete, there is a basic difference of structure, which gives greater mechanical rigidity and structural homogeneity. Thus in these materials, sometimes referred to as isotropic, dimensional changes due to shrinkage or swelling take place uniformly in all three directions.

5. Thixotropy

Rubber and some plastics having what are known as high polymers, do not dissolve in water. In solvents such as benzene they do swell and eventually

Illustrating thixotropic paint which is a jelly-like liquid. Once a shearing stress is applied the viscosity is lowered and the liquid 'flows'

form a viscous solution which becomes almost jelly-like. When the jelly-like liquid is poured, stirred or pushed through a tube, a shearing stress is applied, and the liquid 'flows' easily due to a lowering of the viscosity. Once the shearing stress has been removed, the liquid becomes rigid. This phenomenon is known as *Thixotropy* and is naturally used in the making of *Thixotropic paints*, sometimes also called non-splash.

1.07 basic physical properties of matter

A fundamental idea in physics, and one that is useful to remember, is that all physical quantities can be expressed in terms of three fundamental physical units; the units of mass (m), length (l), and time (t). The relation between the unit of a physical quantity and the fundamental units of mass, length and time is expressed by numbers which are called *dimensions*. For example, unit area has two dimensions in length ($l \times l$), expressed as l^2; unit volume has three dimensions in length ($l \times l \times l$), expressed as l^3; density is mass per unit volume and so its dimensions are m/l^3, or ml^{-3} as it might also be written. Dimensions of a physical quantity, it may be noted, define its nature and are, therefore, qualitative. The dimensions do not indicate the magnitude of the physical quantity. For example, the dimensions of all the materials given in the comparative chart, C.1.07/1, are all the same, namely, m/l^3 translated into kg/m^3, but their magnitudes vary—in fact, few are exactly the same.

Not all physical quantities define the nature of matter, or of the materials they form. Of those that do, area, volume, mass, weight, density and specific gravity are the basic ones, and are covered in this section. For convenience, however, force, though not a physical property of matter, is included. Other properties concerned with molecular forces, strength and those intimately connected with the energies (heat, light and sound) are discussed elsewhere.*

The dimensions of some of the more important quantities that occur in physics are included in Table 1.07/1 (see p. 48).

Area

An area, which may be any shape, is one of the simplest of physical quantities and is defined by multiplying two measurements of length, with the dimensions of l^2. The basic unit of

'The envelope of space occupied may be of any shape or form.' Right, brick. Above, steel sculpture (by Pevsner)

length in SI is the metre (m), but for practical purposes the millimetre (mm) is also used as in structural calculations, for small sections and specifications. Area is, therefore, expressed either as square metres (m²) or square millimetres (mm²).*

Volume

Volume is the *quantity of space* occupied by matter. The envelope of the space occupied may be of *any* shape or form. Volume is defined by multiplying three measurements of length with the dimension of l^3. Units expressing volume use the standard

linear measuring units, such as metres, millimetres as the base with 3 as the index to the base, and are expressed as *cubic units*. These are written either as cubic metres or millimetres (m³ or mm³). For the volume of liquids the litre (l) or millilitre (ml) are used (for practical purposes litre = dm³).*

Mass

Mass, one of the fundamental quantities in physics, is the amount of matter in a body and is proportional to the number of molecules in the body. Mass always remains constant (except in nuclear physics) and is not affected by the gravitational pull of the earth. Mass can be measured by

---

*Molecular forces are discussed in *2.00 Strength of materials,* but particularly sections 2.01 and 2.02; heat in *4.00 Heat and its effects;* and in *6.00 Sound and its effects.*

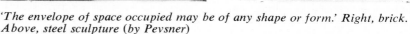

*In the British system the basic units of length are inches, feet and yards and for area they are square inches (in²), square feet (ft²) and square yards (yd²).

1in	=	25·4mm (exactly)
1ft	=	0·304 8m (exactly)
1yd	=	0·914 4m (exactly)
1in²	=	645·16mm² (exactly)
1ft²	=	0·092 903m²
1yd²	=	0·836 127m²
1m	=	1·093 61yd = 3·280 83ft = 39·369 96in
1mm	=	0·039 370in
1m²	=	1·195 99yd² = 10·763 91ft² = 1 550·0in²
1mm²	=	0·001 550in²

---

*The cubic units in the British system are commonly cubic inches, feet and yards (in³, ft³, yd³). For volume of liquids, gallons and pints are most common.

1in³	=	16 387·1mm³
1ft³	=	0·028 317m³
1yd³	=	0·764 555m³
1gal	=	4·546 litres
1pt	=	0·568 litre
1m³	=	1·307 95yd³ = 35·314 65ft³ = 61 023·7in
1mm³	=	0·000 061in³
1l	=	0·220gal = 1·760pts

comparing the weight of a body with the weight of a known mass on a pair of scales. It is measured in kilogrammes (kg).* It is important to note that in the SI system mass and weight are measured in *different* units—see 'Weight' below.

Weight

It is most important to distinguish the difference between mass and weight, particularly in the SI system, because unlike the British system, they are measured in different units and are not even numerically equal.

Weight is the attraction of the earth (gravitational pull) on a mass and is, therefore, a *force*:

Weight (w) = mass (m) × acceleration due to gravity (g)
Force (f) = mass (m) × acceleration (a)
∴ $w = f = mg$.

Weight is measured in newtons (N).† As the gravitational pull of the earth is not everywhere the same (varies by about 0·5 per cent), the weight of a given piece of matter is not constant, whereas its mass is. Weight decreases at high altitudes and increases at low altitudes.

However, for practical building work it is not necessary to take the *variation* of gravity into account. Instead the precise expression of weight (or force) on a gravitational basis is related to the international standard gravity value ('standard acceleration') 9·806 65m/s². Thus, as is common in structural work, the mass of materials, etc., expressed in kilogrammes (kg) must be multiplied by 9·806 65 to determine the weight or force involved. A conversion chart is given in C.1.07/2.

Force

Force is always concerned with motion or attempts at motion, and may be defined as 'anything that will cause a change in the state of rest or motion of a body'. Every body is subjected to a force caused by the vertical gravitational pull of the earth upon it. Broadly speaking the motion or attempts at motion may:
(1) move a body from rest;
(2) change the motion of a body already moving; or
(3) fail to produce motion or change of motion if opposed by another force.

*In the British system mass (often loosely referred to as 'a weight' meaning a weight-piece from a set of weights) is measured in pounds, hundredweights or tons.
1lb = 0·453 592 37kg (exactly)
1cwt = 50·802 3kg
1ton = 1016·05kg
1kg = 2·204 62lb

†In the British system the units used for mass (pounds, tons, etc.) are also loosely used for weight. For the latter, however, and in order to take gravitational pull into account the units should be expressed as pound-force (lbf), ton-force (tonf), etc. The conversion of lbf to values in kgf is identical with the conversion of values in pounds to values in kilogrammes (see footnote to *Mass* above) but 1kgf = 9·806 65N so that:
1lbf = 0·453 592 37kgf = 4·448 22N
1tonf = 1016·05kgf = 9·964 02kN
1N = 0·224 809lbf.

C.1.07/2 *Conversion chart for mass in kg to force (weight) in newtons*

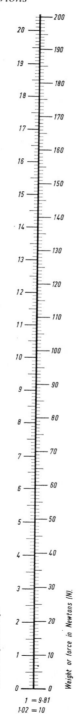

Mass in kilogrammes (kg).

Weight or force in Newtons (N).

1 = 9·81
1·02 = 10

MATERIAL		ref. value	DENSITY (ρ.) kgs/m³
asbestos cement sheeting		a	1121–1890
asphalte	light	"	1602–1922
	heavy + 20% grit	"	2323
BLOCKS hollow	clay	"	481–1009
	concrete	"	881–1009
solid	concrete	"	1121–2307
BOARDS asbestos – insulating		b	721–1202
blockboard		a	481
cork		b	112–465
expanded plastics		c	8–72
fibre –	hardboard	b	561–1041
	insulating	"	224–384
flax – resin bonded		"	673
jute – resin bonded		"	433
particle		"	481–801
plaster – gypsum		"	961
straw		"	256–352
wood pulp		"	88
woodwool slabs		"	400–801
BRICKWORK sand limes		"	1842–1922
common – lond. stk. flettons		"	1762–2003
diatomaceous		"	881–961
glazed		c	2083
pressed		"	2243
engineering		a&b	2195–2403
CONCRETE dense aggregate		b	1682–2483
no – fines		c	657–1922
lightweight aggregate			577–1762
aerated			320–1602
GLASS sheet window		b	2515
heat resisting		"	2243
loose wool blanket		"	144
GRANOLITHIC		"	2083
METALS aluminium		e	2563–2707
brass		a	8394–8507
bronze		"	8411–8891
cast – iron		"	7209
copper		"	8731–8939
lead		"	11326
stainless steel (av.)		i	8010
steel – mild		a	7690–7850
wrought iron		"	7690
zinc		"	7145
PLASTERING gypsum		b	1121–1282
perlite		"	401–609
vermiculate		"	481–961
sand:cement (sand:gypsum)		"	1570&1554
sand: cement: lime		"	1442
ROOFING FELT		b	961–1121
STONES		a&b	1762–2243
granite		"	2643
limestone		b	2083–2243
marble		"	2723
sandstone		"	2243
slate		"	2835
TILES (floor) terrazzo		b	2435
asphalt & asbestos		"	1922
burnt clay		"	1922
concrete		"	2163
cork		"	529
linoleum, inlaid		"	1121–1202
plastic		"	1041
" hard		"	1762
p.v.c. asbestos		"	2083
rubber		"	1522–1682
TIMBER seasoned softwood (av.)		a	481
hardwood (av.)		"	721
WATER ice		b	918–926
liquid		"	984–1000
snow – fresh		"	192
" – compacted		"	401
PLASTICS		f	1057–1794

C.1.07/1 *Comparative chart giving densities of common building materials. Figures have not been rounded off but are straight conversions from imperial units. References: (a) BS 648 : 1964. (b) I.H.V.E. guide, 1959. (c) BRS Digest 39 (2nd Series). (d) BRS Digest and Cement and Concrete Assn. (e) Civil Engineers Reference Book, Vol. 1. (f) Cousens and Yarsley, Plastics in the Service of Man, Penguin Books. (i) Specification 1964 (value 500lb/ft³)*

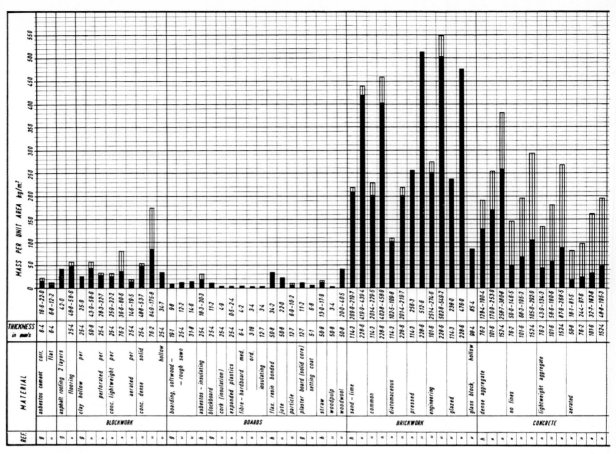

C.1.07/2 *Comparative chart giving densities of common building materials in kg/m² per stated thickness. References: (g) BS 648: 1964. (h) Calculated from standard results. (i) Specification: 1964*

Group	Material	Thickness (mm)	Mass per unit area (kg/m²)	Ref
BLOCKWORK	asbestos cement, conc.	6·4	16·6-22·0	g
	asbestos cement, flat	6·4	6·8-12·2	g
	asphalt roofing 2 layers		42·0	g
	flooring	254	49·0-58·6	i
	clay hollow, per	254	25·9	g
	perforated, per	50·8	43·9-58·6	g
	conc. lightweight, per	254	29·3-32·7	g
	aerated, per	254	259-322	g
	conc. dense, solid	76·2	366-80·6	g
	conc. dense, solid	254	14·6-19·5	
	conc. dense, solid	254	49·0-53·7	
	conc. dense, solid	76·2	84·9-175·8	
	conc. dense, hollow	254	34·7	
BOARDS	boarding, softwood —	19·1	9·8	h
	— rough sawn	254	12·2	h
	asbestos — insulating	31·0	14·6	h
	blockboard	254	19·3-20·3	g
	cork (insulation)	254	11·2	h
	expanded plastics	254	4·9	g
	fibre — hardboard, med.	6·4	0·5-2·4	h
	ord.	3·18	4·2	g
	insulating	12·7	3·4	
	flax, resin bonded	50·8	3·4	h
	jute	50·8	34·2	g
	particle	127	22·0	h
	plaster board (solid core)	127	6·9-10·2	g
	setting coat	5·1	11·2	h
	straw	50·8	6·8	h
	woodpulp	50·8	13·0-17·9	h
	woodwool	50·8	3·4	h
			20·0-40·5	
BRICKWORK	sand — lime	114·3	209·9-219·7	h
		229·6	419·9-439·4	h
	common	114·3	201·4-229·5	h
		229·6	402·8-458·9	h
	diatomaceous	114·3	102·5-109·8	h
		229·6	201·4-219·7	h
	pressed	114·3	256·3	h
		229·6	512·6	h
	engineering	101·6	257·4-274·6	h
		229·6	502·8-549·2	h
	glazed	114·3	238·0	h
		229·6	476·0	h
	glass block, hollow	90·4	85·4	h
CONCRETE	dense aggregate	76·2	129·4-190·4	h
		101·6	170·9-253·9	h
		152·4	259·7-300·8	h
	no fines	76·2	50·0-148·5	h
		101·6	68·3-195·3	h
		152·4	105·0-292·9	h
	lightweight aggregate	76·2	43·9-134·3	h
		101·6	58·6-180·6	h
		152·4	87·9-268·5	h
	aerated	50·8	18·1-81·5	h
		76·2	24·4-97·6	h
		101·6	32·7-162·8	h
		152·4	48·4-195·3	h

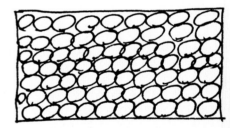

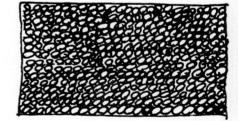

D.1.07/1 *Diagrams illustrating quantity of mass/density relationship. Top, light (less dense) and, bottom, heavy (dense)*

Expanded polystyrene showing raw material (beads) and moulded block. The beads are nett density and the block bulk density although both have the same weight

Units of weight are normally employed in measuring forces, the units being the same whatever the direction of the force may be (see 'Weight' above). For determination of the strength properties of materials force per unit area, namely *stress,* is used. (See *2.00 Strength of materials,* particularly Sections 2.01 and 2.02.)

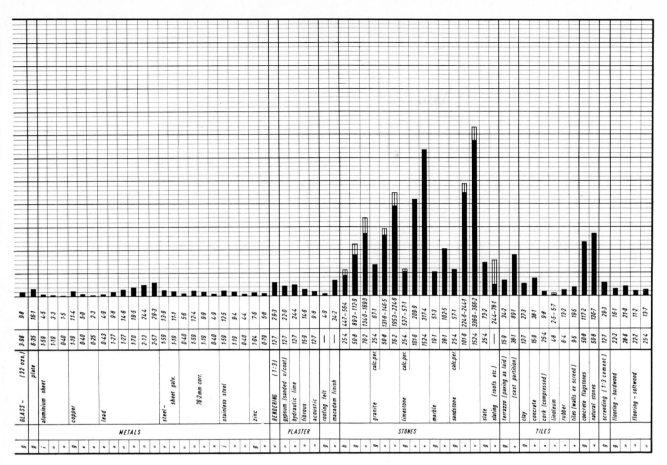

Right, C.1.07/3 *Specific gravity of common materials. References (f) Plastics in the Service of Man, Penguin Books, (j) Manual of Building Science, Douglas and Kent*

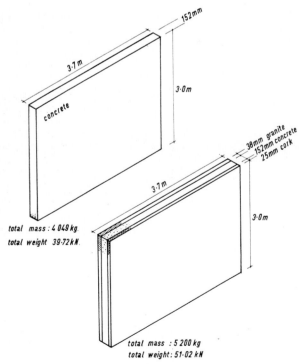

total mass : 4 049 kg.
total weight 39·72 kN.

152mm

3·7 m

3·0m

concrete

38mm granite
152mm concrete
25mm cork

3·7 m

3·0m

total mass : 5 200 kg
total weight: 51·02 kN

D.1.07/2 *Diagrams for weight calculations. Above, example (a), below, example (b)*

MATERIAL	ref	value	SPECIFIC GRAVITY 0 · 5 · 10
ASPHALTE	j	1·4	
BRICK		1·6-2·4	
BRICKWORK		1·8	
CEMENT		1·4	
CHALK		1·8-2·6	
CLAY		2·2	
CONCRETE		1·4-2·4	
CORK		·26	
GRAVEL		1·7	
LINSEED OIL		·94	
METALS - aluminium		2·7	
copper		8·9	
lead		11·3	
steel		7·8	
tin		7·3	
zinc		7·2	
STONE - granite		2·5	
limestone		2·0-2·7	
marble		2·7	
sandstone		2·2-2·4	
SAND - dry		1·6	
TIMBER - softwood		·48-·54	
hardwood		·74-·96	
TURPENTINE		·87	
WATER - liquid - fresh		1·00	
sea		1·025	
solid - ice		·92	
PLASTICS	f	1·06-1·38	

Quantity	Dimensions		SI System	
			Unit	Symbol
Area	(length)^2	l^2	square metre	m^2
Volume	(length)^3	l^3	cubic metre	m^3
Density	mass per unit volume	ml^{-3}	kilogramme per cubic metre	kg/m^3
Velocity	distance travelled in unit time	lt^{-1}	metre per second	m/s
Acceleration	change in velocity in unit time	lt^{-2}	metre per second squared	m/s^2
Force (and weight)	mass × acceleration	mlt^{-2}	newton	N
Work (and energy)	force × distance	ml^2t^{-2}	joule	J (N m)
Power	work done per unit time	ml^2t^{-3}	watt	W (J/s)
Moment of force	force × distance	ml^2t^{-2}	newton metre	N m
Stress (and pressure)	force per unit area	$ml^{-1}t^{-2}$	newton per square metre	N/m^2
Modulus of elasticity	stress divided by strain	$ml^{-1}t^{-2}$	newton per square metre	N/m^2
Surface tension	force per unit length	mt^{-2}		

Note: Quantities in italics are explained in this section.
References: (1) Stead, G. *Elementary physics*, J. & A. Churchill Ltd., p. 3, 1961.
(2) Anderton, P., and Bigg, P. H., *Changing to the metric system*, 2nd Edn., London, HMSO, 1967.

Density

Density is the mass in *unit volume* of material and is sometimes loosely referred to as 'relative weight'. Consequently the more matter (mass) that is contained in a given volume, the denser the substance, as illustrated diagrammatically in diagram D.1.07/1. Formula used is:

$$\text{density} = \frac{\text{mass}}{\text{volume}}$$

and is expressed in kg/m^3 for building work.* When dealing with materials a distinction has to be drawn between bulk and net density.

Bulk density includes in the volume measurement any air spaces or voids which may occur in a material. If is, therefore, the density of any material 'as found'. *Net density,* on the other hand, does not include in the volume measurement any air spaces or voids. It is, therefore, the density after any air spaces or voids have been removed.

As materials for building are mainly used as found, bulk density is normally used and simply referred to as density. Thus, unless otherwise stated, quoted densities are bulk densities.

Density is, in fact, one of the most important properties of any material as it compares 'lightness' and 'heaviness'. In addition to offering a very useful comparison of the relative 'weight' of materials, density is also used in connection with:

1. Structure

In the structural design of any element in a building which is required to support the weight of other elements (sometimes even the element's own weight) the weight of the latter must be calculated. To do this the densities of all the constituent materials of the element must be known together with the extent of the materials being used.
For example : (see diagram D.1.07/2)
(a) The total weight of a concrete

*For most building work density is expressed in the British system in lb/ft^3:
  1 lb/ft^3 = 16·018 5 kg/m^3
  1 kg/m^3 = 0·062 4280 lb/ft^3

wall, with a density of 2400 kg/m^3, 152 mm thick, and 3·7 m long and 3 0m high is:

Mass: 0·152 × 3·7 × 3·0 × 2400 = 4049·28 kg
(say 4049 kg).
Weight: 4049 × 9·81 = 39 719N = 39·72 kN.

(b) The same wall with 38 mm thick granite at a density of 2643 kg/m^3 on the outside, and with 25 mm thick cork at a density of 128 kg/m^3 on the inside would be:

Mass:
  Granite: 0·038 × 3·7 × 3·0 × 2643 = 1114·82
  Concrete: from (a) above: = 4049·28
  Cork: 0·025 × 3·7 × 3·0 × 128 = 35·52

  Total mass = 5199·62 kg
  (say 5200 kg).
Weight: 5200 × 9·81 = 51 015N = 51·02 kN.

2. Porosity of materials

Density does offer some guidance as to the quantity of voids in *porous* materials. In aerated concrete particularly, the density of the various grades available is entirely dependent on the volume of voids in any grade.

3. Testing for purity

Once the density of a particular material with a particular structure and composition has been established, guidance as to the purity of other samples of the same kind of material may be given by any variations in density of the sample as compared with the 'control'.

Practical densities

When dealing with the density of building materials it is normal in most instances to quote what is, in fact, an *average* density for a particular material. In normal building practice and in most cases it is usually either impracticable or unnecessary to actually weigh each unit of material before use. However, it is important that this point is borne in mind because there may be instances where it might be vital for the precise density of a particular material to be known. Furthermore, it may also be essential to select particular materials to comply

with a specific density.*

In some cases, such as with bricks, there would be little practical value in having the densities of the individual bricks as they are seldom used without mortar. Thus, densities are given for *brickwork* which include the combined densities of the brick and its surrounding mortar.

As many of the materials used in buildings are manufactured or employed in specific thicknesses, it is common to have densities of many materials translated into a density which is related to a particular thickness of material per unit area. This density or, better, mass of material per unit thickness and area, has many practical advantages. Firstly, the calculation of the mass of complete elements is greatly facilitated, as it is only necessary to calculate the area of the element of a particular thickness and to multiply this by the quoted value for that thickness. Secondly, provided the same units are used, a better comparison of the 'relative weights' of materials, as commonly used, can be obtained. This will be clear if a comparison between the comparative charts giving density in kg/m^3 (see C.1.07/1) and in kg/m^2 for quoted thickness is made (see C.1.07/2).

Specific gravity

Specific gravity is sometimes referred to as a 'relative density' and is a simple system for comparing various materials. The comparison is made by comparing the density of a material with the density of an unvarying material such as water.

Thus,

$$\text{specific gravity} = \frac{\text{density of material}}{\text{density of water}}$$

and is a *ratio*.
Specific gravity has greater use in the laboratory than in buildings.
The comparative chart C.1.07/3 gives the specific gravity of common materials.

*Practical densities have been developed mainly for structural purposes. Consequently care is needed when relating practical density values for other purposes, e.g. thermal and acoustic.

1.08 the basic structure of matter

Mention has already been made of the fact that matter is composed of small particles and that it can exist in either the solid, liquid or gas state, depending on the extent or power of the forces holding these particles together. The exact state is largely dependent on the nature of the physical environment in which the matter exists at any given time. However, all this does not give any indication of the exact nature or inner structure of the individual particles nor does it explain why some particles will combine with others to form particular substances. A complete understanding of the manner in which matter is built up to form the variety of substances in common use requires some knowledge of atomic theory. It is not intended to expound fully on present-day atomic theory but rather to set out briefly the main points relevant to elements, atoms and molecules.

Elements

Elements are the basic 'building units' upon which the formation of matter is based and they are substances which cannot be broken down or decomposed by any chemical means. All forms of matters can be built up by a combination of the elements. The manner in which the elements may be combined with one another or whether in fact one element will combine with another, is largely dependent on the nature of the actual atoms of which each element is itself composed.

There are 103 known elements. Each element has been given its own symbol, atomic weight and atomic number, as shown by the selection of elements included in the comparative chart, C.1.08/1. The occurrence of the elements on the earth's crust expressed as a percentage, is shown in chart C.1.08/2.

The atomic weight of an element is defined as *the weight of the atom of the element compared with the weight of an atom of hydrogen,* which is the lightest of all elements. (The fact that modern practice uses one-sixteenth of the atomic weight of oxygen hardly makes any difference in most cases.)

The atomic number (represented by

atomic no	ELEMENT	symbol	value	ATOMIC WEIGHT (approx)
13	aluminium	Al	27	
51	antimony	Sb	122	
56	barium	Ba	137	
20	calcium	Ca	40	
6	carbon	C	12	
17	chlorine	Cl	35·5	
24	chromium	Cr	52	
29	copper	Cu	63·5	
1	hydrogen	H	1	
26	iron	Fe	56	
82	lead	Pb	207	
12	magnesium	Mg	24	
25	manganese	Mn	55	
28	nickel	Ni	59	
7	nitrogen	N	14	
8	oxygen	O	16	
15	phosphorous	P	31	
19	potassium	K	39	
14	silicon	Si	28	
11	sodium	Na	23	
16	sulphur	S	32	
50	tin	Sn	119	
30	zinc	Zn	65	

C.1.08/1 *Comparative chart giving the atomic weights of elements*

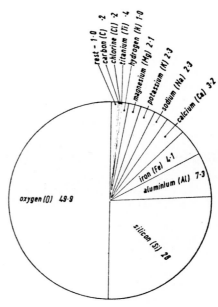

C.1.08/2 *Percentage occurrence of the elements in the earth's crust (Courtesy: Civil Engineers Reference Book)*

the symbol Z) given to each element, is used in two ways, namely, (1) *to describe* the position of the element in the periodic table and (2) *to express* (a) the number of protons in the nucleus of the atom of the element and (b) the number of electrons in the atom. The atomic number is the characteristic property of an atom which distinguishes the atoms of one element from those of another.

Atoms of elements cannot exist on their own as they possess unsatisfied *valencies* or combining powers, thus joining together to form molecules. Each element has its own valency; some have two or more valencies in which case each valency state appears as a separate series of compounds. Some simplified examples may explain this. (1) If an element with a valency of 1 (hydrogen is *one* example of many) combines with an element of valency 2 (oxygen is *one* example of many), it needs *two* atoms of the first to combine with *one* of the second; water consists of 2 atoms of hydrogen and 1 atom of oxygen, giving the formula H_2O. (2) Sulphur has valencies of 2, 4 or 6, and may combine with, for example, 2 atoms of oxygen ($S = 4: O_2 = 2 + 2 = 4$) to form sulphur dioxide (SO_2), or with 3 atoms of oxygen ($S = 6: O_3 = 2 + 2 + 2 = 6$) to form sulphur trioxide (SO_3). Iron, on the other hand, has valencies of 2 and 3 and combines with oxygen to form ferrous oxides, FeO ($Fe = 2$: $O = 2$), or ferric oxide, Fe_2O_3 ($Fe_2 = 3 + 3 = 6: O_3 = 2 + 2 + 2 = 6$).

It may be noted here, for convenience, that not only elements have valencies. There are certain groups of atoms which commonly occur together in many compounds, known as radicals (commonly referred to as *ions*), and in many respects behave *as if* they were single atoms. A typical group is the SO_4 group, or the sulphate radical (valency 2, hence the formulæ, H_2SO_4, sulphuric acid or $NaSO_4$, sodium sulphate, or $MgSO_4$, magnesium sulphate). Some other radicals which commonly occur in building problems are: sulphite, SO_3 (valency 2), carbonate, CO_3 (valency 2), bicarbonate, HCO_3 (valency 1) and hydroxide, OH (valency 1).

Valency does not indicate the nature of the linkages between the atom of a particular element and other atoms in a given molecule. There are two principal types of linkage, namely, covalent bond and the ionic bond. These are outlined under *Atoms*.

Atoms

Atoms are the smallest particles of matter and remain undivided in any chemical reaction. The atom can be regarded as the unit of matter which moves from one molecule to another during chemical change. Within limits, chemical theories can be explained by simply regarding the atom as a solid homogeneous sphere. However, in order to explain the peculiar relationships between the elements *and* to show

D.1.08/1 *Drawing to illustrate that an atom is a system and not simply a particle. (Courtesy: Science, Chemistry, Physics and Astronomy, Macdonald Illustrated Library, Rathbone Books Ltd.)*

 Proton

 *Neutron*

 Electron

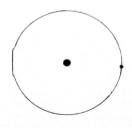

D.1.08/2 *Two representations of an atom of helium. The two negative electrons neutralize the core's positive charge. The neutron has no charge, it merely adds mass to an atom (Courtesy: Science, Chemistry, Physics and Astronomy, Macdonald Illustrated Library, Rathbone Books Ltd.)*

how atoms combine together, it is necessary to postulate a structure of the atom. To this end an outline of (1) the accepted structure of the atom and (2) bonding of the atoms are included under two separate headings.

1. Structure

An atom is now generally accepted to be *a system* rather than a particle (diagram D.1.08/1). The accepted structure may be summarised (see diagram D.1.08/2) as: (a) Atoms of all elements are made up of *three subatomic units,* the electron, the proton, and the neutron. (b) The atom consists of (i) the nucleus at the centre and (ii) a system of electrons in motion outside the nucleus.

The electron is negative electricity; a body with excess electrons is negatively charged; one deficient in electrons is positively charged. The electrons in an atom are arranged in shells about the nucleus as centre. The number of elecrons in a given shell of a given atom is limited.

The neutron is a component of the nucleus and has no electrical charge.

The proton is a component of the nucleus and carries a positive electrical charge equal in magnitude to the negative charge of the electron.

The nucleus consists of protons and neutrons (except the hydrogen atom which consists of one proton), and is referred to collectively as nucleons. The nucleus carries a positive charge, which is balanced by the system of electrons outside the nucleus.

2. Bonding

Broadly speaking the property of an atom which enables it to enter into chemical combination with other atoms is known by the term *valency*. When two atoms combine together to form a molecule, they do so by means of the electrons in their *external* shells. A shell is complete when it contains its maximum number of electrons (the maximum number in the outer shell is eight electrons). Normally, no completed, or temporarily completed, shell provides electrons for valency purposes. Thus the valency of an element and its chemical behaviour is determined by the configuration of its two outermost shells.

The peculiar stability of the electron configuration of the inert gases (the outer shell with eight electrons and the penultimate with 18 electrons resulting in such stability as to make the gases chemically inert) is the starting point for the *electronic theory of valency*.

Molecule of sugar

Molecules of water (left) and oxygen (right)

A model showing a small section of a long protein molecule. Light coloured hemispheres represent hydrogen molecules

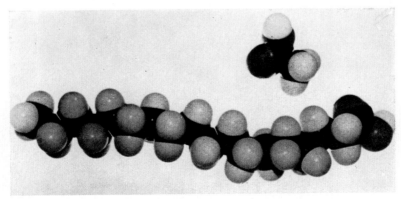

Molecules of stearic acid (bottom) and acetic acid (top). (All photographs on this page Courtesy: PSSC Physics, D. C. Heath & Co., Boston, U.S.A.)

This assumes that the atom of any element, other than an inert gas, tends by means of chemical combination, *to adjust* the number of electrons in its outermost shells so that it may attain the configuration of an inert gas. Changes in the number of electrons in the valency shells of an atom take place by the *sharing of electrons* between two atoms or by the *transfer of electrons* from one atom to another. These give rise to two principal types of linkage, namely the *covalent bond* and the *ionic bond*.

(a) *Covalent bond*

This bond is the sharing of a pair of electrons by two atoms. It may best be explained by examples of some of the molecules in which it occurs. These are illustrated diagrammatically in diagram D.1.08/3. The dotted circles around each atom represent the outer shell and enclose the valency electrons controlled by *each* nucleus. The number of electrons in each has the stable number of eight, except the molecule of hydrogen whose electronic structure resembles that of helium, an inert gas.

General properties of covalent compounds

(i) The covalent bond is directional, giving definite shape to the molecule of a covalent compound. Only by chemical decomposition can the atoms of the molecule fall apart or change their respective positions.

(ii) Covalent compounds are either gases, or else solids, or liquids which are easily vaporised because the external electrical field of a covalent molecule is either zero or comparatively small.

(iii) Covalent compounds are usually sparingly soluble in water. (Some covalent compounds that dissolve freely in water do so because they react with it chemically.)

(b) *Ionic bond*

This bond is formed by the *complete* transference of an electron from one atom to another. In general, the loss of an electron from one of the atoms and the gain in an electron in the other results in both atoms attaining the stable electron configuration of an

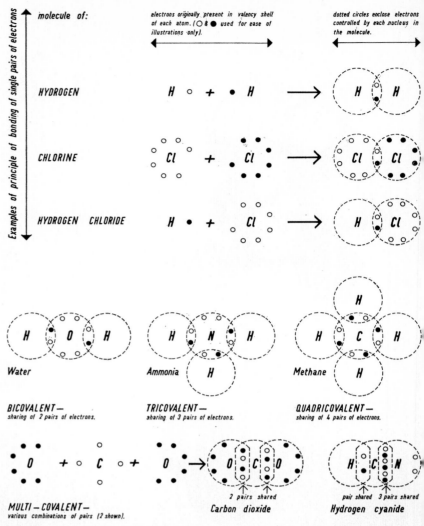

D.1.08/3 *To illustrate co-valent bonding—selected examples only*

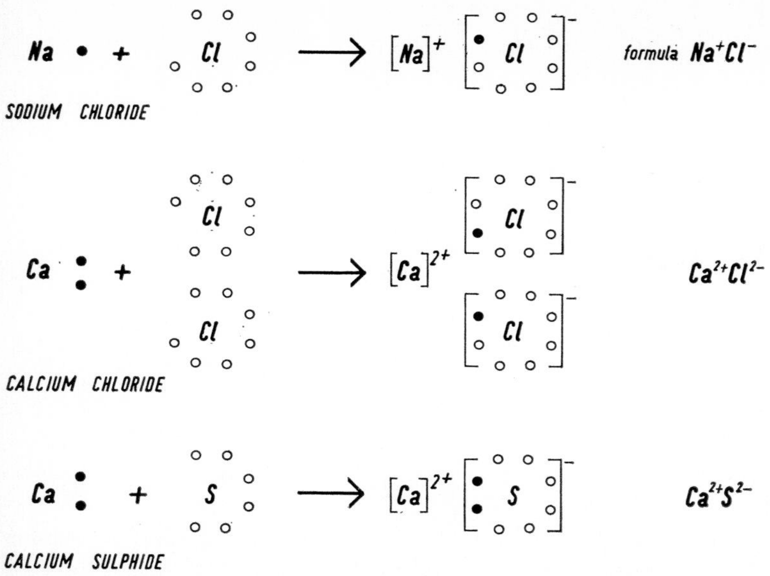

SODIUM CHLORIDE

formula Na^+Cl^-

CALCIUM CHLORIDE

$Ca^{2+}Cl^{2-}$

CALCIUM SULPHIDE

$Ca^{2+}S^{2-}$

D.1.08/4 *To illustrate ionic bonding—selected examples only*

inert gas. The modified atoms are known as *ions*; a positive ion is known as a *cation,* a negative ion as an *anion.* (See diagram D.1.08/4.) The link between the ions is entirely due to electrical forces between the charged ions. Two electrons may be transferred to or from a single atom, as in the cases of calcium chloride and calcium sulphide illustrated. The superscripts indicating the charges, as shown in the diagram, are omitted from the formula if there is no need to emphasise the ionic nature of a compound.

General properties of ionic compounds
(i) There is no intimate link between the ions, as the bond between the ions is the attraction between two opposite electrical charges.

(ii) Unlike the covalent bond, the ionic bond is non-directional. Crystals of ionic compounds consist, therefore, of ions arranged in close packed structures (see diagram D.1.04/1, p. 36).

(iii) The component ions fall away from one another, or disassociate, without the occurrence of chemical decomposition, when crystals of an ionic compound are dissolved in water. Imposing an electric field on the solution causes the cations and anions to move in opposite directions, and so the solution conducts an electric current. Because the ions in the melt are free to move independently, the fused compound also conducts an electric current.

(iv) Ionic compounds are solids which are not easily vaporised.

(v) Ionic compounds are usually (but by no means always) soluble in water.

Molecules

Molecules are the smallest particles of a substance capable of independent physical existence, and are built up of groups of atoms of the elements as these cannot exist on their own. The *molecular weight* of an element or compound is defined *as the weight of a molecule of the substance compared with the weight of an atom of hydrogen.* As in the case of atoms, two or more molecules may be linked together. The composite structure of molecules forms compounds.

1.09 chemical conventions

To facilitate the recording of the elements together with the number of atoms which may be present and also to be able to show the results of the combination of various substances, abbreviations and conventions in the form of chemical nomenclature, symbols, formulae and equations are used.

Chemical nomenclature

The names given to chemical compounds, that is those substances containing one or more elements, do have a relationship to the elements present, and so do give some indication of the proportion of some of these elements. In addition the termination of the word also indicates the type of element mainly involved. The more important of the names and their meaning are:

Oxides contain oxygen as in Ferric Oxide (Fe_2O_3); Calcium Oxide (CaO).

Sulphides contain sulphur as in Lead Sulphide (PbS); Calcium Sulphite (CaS); Hydrogen Sulphite (H_2S).

Carbides
Carbonates } contain carbon as in Silicon Carbide (SiC); Calcium Carbonate ($CaCO_3$).
Hydrocarbons

'. . . *um*' confined to metallic elements such as Aluminium, Calcium, etc.

'. . . *a*' used for certain oxides such as Silica, Alumina, etc.

'. . . *ide*' indicates the presence of only two elements as in Lead Monoxide (PbO); Sodium Chloride (NaCl).

'. . . *ate*' indicates the presence of three or four elements as in Calcium Carbonate ($CaCO_2$); Zinc Sulphate ($ZnSO_4.7H_2O$).

'. . . *ous*' indicates smaller proportion of non-metallic elements as in Ferrous Oxide (FeO); Sulphurous Acid (H_2SO_3); Stannous Oxide (SnO).

'. . . *ic*' indicates large proportion of non-metallic elements as in Ferric Oxide (Fe_2O_3); Sulphuric Acid (H_2SO_4); Stannic Oxide (SnO_2).

'*mono* . . . (one); *di* . . . (two), *tri* . . . (three), etc.'—prefixes used to indicate number of elements or molecules present in a compound as in

carbon *mon*oxide (CO); carbon *di*oxide (CO_2); *di*sulphur *di*chloride (S_2Cl_2); sulphur *tri*oxide (SO_3); *deca*hydrate ($10H_2O$).

Chemical symbols

Each element has its own symbol as shown in the comparative chart C.1.08/1 (p. 49). The number of atoms present in any molecule is signified by adding a small subscript as:

O_2—two atoms of oxygen;
O_3—three atoms of oxygen (O_3 is Ozone).

The number of molecules present in any compound is signified by prefixing the element with a number as:

$7H_2O$—seven molecules of water.

Chemical formulæ

A chemical formula expresses the exact combination of all the elements in a compound, together with the number of atoms and molecules present. There are three basic methods of indicating the manner in which the elements are associated:

(1) Closely associated: Calcium Carbonate $CaCO_3$ contains *one* atom of calcium, *one* atom of carbon and *three* atoms of oxygen.

(2) Some elements closely associated: Calcium Hydroxide (slaked lime) —$Ca(OH)_2$. The atoms of oxygen and hydrogen are closely associated to form Hydroxyl $(OH)_2$ and are bracketed.

(3) Some elements not chemically combined: Sodium Carbonate—$Na_2CO_3.10H_2O$. One atom of sodium carbonate in solution is not chemically combined with 10 molecules of water due to ionisation (see *Section 1.08*, under *Ionic bonding*, p. 52). When the water is driven off, Na_2CO_3 remains as a dry powder. In this case *the full-stop* separates the parts.

Chemical Equations

Chemical equations are *algebraic methods* of writing down chemical reactions or changes. The substances taking part in the reaction are shown on the left-hand side while the products of the reaction appear on the right-hand side.

This is a basic rule, but in addition each side of the equation must balance, while certain conventions are used to indicate direction of the reaction and, if required, information such as quantity, heat, electric charges, etc.

1. Balance

(a) Hydrogen and chlorine give Hydrogen Chloride, and could be written as:

$$H_2 + Cl_2 = HCl$$

but this does not balance, so it *must* be written as:

$$H_2 + Cl_2 = 2 HCl$$

This indicates that one molecule of hydrogen (containing two atoms) and one molecule of chlorine (also containing two atoms) form two molecules of Hydrogen Chloride.

(b) Similarly, one molecule of Calcium Carbonate yields (on heating) one molecule of Calcium Oxide and one molecule of Carbon Dioxide and is written as:

$$CaCO_3 = CaO + CO_2$$

(c) Two molecules of Sodium Chloride and one molecule of Sulphuric Acid react to yield two molecules of Hydrogen Chloride and one molecule of Sodium Sulphate:

$$2 NaCl + H_2SO_4 = 2 HCl + NaHSO_4$$

2. Quantitative relationship

The atomic weight of Ca is 40, of O, 16 and of C 12, so that

$$CaCO_3 = CaO + CO_2$$
$$(40 + 12 + 48) = (40 + 16) + (12 + 32)$$
$$100 = 56 + 44$$

The equation now also gives the quantitative relationship between the substances so that 100 parts by weight of Calcium Carbonate when heated will yield 56 parts by weight of Calcium Oxide and 44 parts by weight of Carbon Dioxide.

3. Direction

Chemical reactions can be either one-way or reversible reactions.

(a) *One-way*
The equals sign is usually replaced by an arrow:

$$2SO_2 + O_2 \longrightarrow 2SO_3$$
sulphur dioxide + oxygen $\longrightarrow$ sulphur trioxide

(b) Reversible

The single arrow is replaced by a double arrow:

$$CaCO_3 + H_2O + CO_2 \rightleftharpoons Ca(HCO_3)_2$$

calcium carbonate + water + carbon dioxide $\rightleftharpoons$ calcium bicarbonate

This reaction is reversed if external conditions are altered.

4. Heat

Energy is always liberated or absorbed when a chemical change takes place. Part of this energy is in the form of heat. Reactions which proceed with the *liberation* of heat are known as *exothermic* reactions and with the *absorption* of heat as *endothermic*.

The heat of reaction at constant pressure is denoted by $\triangle H$ and

$+\triangle H = absorption$ of heat by the system

$-\triangle H = liberation$ of heat by the system

The heat change which accompanies a chemical reaction is expressed by a thermal equation written *after* the ordinary chemical reaction.

$$C + 2S = CS_2: \quad \triangle H = +87.9\text{kJ}$$

(An example of an *endothermic* reaction.)

$$C + O_2 = CO_2: \quad \triangle H = -393.7\text{kJ}$$

(An example of an *exothermic* reaction.)

The heat of reaction plays an important part in building practice in the hydration of cement, which results in the liberation of heat. Depending mainly on the type of cement used, the rate and amount of heat evolution varies but nevertheless needs to be taken into account if, for example, the cracking of a cement-based product is to be reduced to a minimum. The evolution of heat may, on the other hand, be used to advantage during winter building.

5. Electrical charges

If required the nature and magnitude of electrical charges (see *Section 1.08*, under *Ionic bonding*, p. 52) may be denoted by using the relevant superscripts, as:

$$Na^+Cl^-, \ Ca^{2+} \ Cl^-, \ Ca^{2+} \ S^{2-}$$

The relationship of *hard* water and the lathering of soap (the soluble salt of Sodium Stearate, $C_{17}H_{35}COONa$) is included here for convenience. Certain metallic ions, notably those of calcium, magnesium and iron, react with Sodium Stearate to yield insoluble precipitates:

$$2C_{17}H_{35}COONa + Ca^{2+} = (C_{17}H_{35}COO)_2Ca + 2Na^+$$

Water containing these metallic ions in solution (see *Section 3.02*, under *Pollution*) will not form a lather with soap until sufficient has been added to precipitate all the metallic ions as insoluble stearate.

6. Rate of reaction

Equations of a different kind are necessary to calculate the rate of reaction. However, for the present purposes it is convenient to note the fact that the rate of a homogeneous chemical reaction is controlled by three factors: (a) the nature of the reagents, (b) the concentrations of the reagents, and (c) temperature. As regards the latter, in particular, the higher the temperature the greater the reaction rate.

7. General observation

When an assessment has to be made of the likelihood of any chemical change(s) taking place in materials (changes that may be deleterious is significant) it is important to understand what may best be termed the limitations of chemical equations. Whether or not an equation is 'fulfilled' as written depends, among other things, on the concentrations of the substances involved, their nature (precise chemical formula and physical nature of these in actual building materials is important) and environmental conditions. A simplified example may help to explain the significance of some of these factors.

Calcium Carbonate, an important constituent of limestone (commonly used in buildings), reacts with sulphuric acid (may frequently 'exist' in polluted atmospheres) to form calcium sulphate:

$$CaCO_3 + H_2SO_4 = CaSO_4 + H_2O + CO_2$$

The formation of Calcium Sulphate implies deterioration of the material. The extent of such deterioration would depend, for instance, on the nature of the Calcium Carbonate (the allotrope argonite reacting to a greater extent than calcite), its precise occurrence (particularly its distribution) in the material and the degree to which the acid (its concentration is also significant) can penetrate into the material and the length of time the acid is in contact with the carbonate. On the other hand, specific quantities of sulphuric acid would be needed, all other things being equal, to decompose all the Calcium Carbonate contained in the material. As observation shows, the requisite quantities for *complete* decomposition are not always available. As in all building work the *question of degree* is always important.

'Whether or not an equation is "fulfilled" as written depends, among other things, on the concentration of the substances involved, their nature and environmental conditions.' All the limestone (Calcium Carbonate) shown in the photograph could theoretically have reacted with Sulphuric Acid in the atmosphere to form Calcium Sulphate. However, the requisite quantities for decomposition of all the blocks were not available, and only one has decomposed

1.10 chemical reactions

Chemical equations represent the chemical reaction which takes place when one or more substances are chemically combined. The equations do not normally indicate whether any physical agency has been used to enable the reaction to take place. In addition some chemical reactions take place with particular elements to form particular substances, such as oxides, alkalis and salts, and which have particular characteristics. This section sets out briefly a description of these substances, while an indication is given of their occurrence and the part they play in building materials. Also included is a short description of a special branch of chemistry, that of organic chemistry, which in recent years has seen the rise in the manufacture and production of what are generally referred to as 'plastics' and which can truly be termed 'man-made' materials.

Combustion

Combustion is probably one of the most important chemical reactions that takes place and which affects life in general and buildings in particular. Oxygen is one of the essential elements required for combustion to take place. As a result some of the products of the reaction contain oxygen in them.

One very common example of this sort of reaction is that which takes place when coal is burnt. The coal may contain appreciable quantities of iron pyrites (FeS_2). During combustion oxygen combines with the sulphur to produce either SO_2 or SO_3, which are *acid gases* and which may react with other substances. The significance of the sulphur compounds in forming sulphates in clay bricks is outlined under 'salts' later. (See also *3.05 Efflorescence, 1. Salts originally present in materials, (a) Clay bricks.*)

Oxidation and reduction

The reactions in which oxygen (or an element chemically similar to oxygen, such as sulphur or chlorine) is added to an element or compound, or in which hydrogen is removed from a compound, is described by the term *oxidation*. The term *reduction* is used to describe the converse of oxidation. Both terms are used empirically and embrace reactions of widely divergent types and are not limited to the description of any particular type of change or molecular structure.

Some examples of oxidation include: (1) *Non-metallic elements and compounds*

$$\text{(a) } C + O_2 = CO_2$$
$$\text{(b) } 2H_2 + O_2 = 2H_2O$$
$$\text{(c) } 2SO_2 + O_2 = 2SO_3$$

(2) *Metals and metallic ions (cations)*

$$\text{(a) } 2Cu + O_2 = 2CuO$$
$$\text{(b) } 4Fe + 3O_2 = 2Fe_2O_3$$

(3) *Acid radicals (anions)*

$$\text{(a) } S^{2-} + 2O_2 = SO_4{}^{2-}$$
$$\text{(b) } 2SO_3{}^{2-} + O_2 = 2SO_4{}^{2-}$$

Acidic oxides, such as sulphur dioxide (SO_2), are oxides of non-metals and combine with water to form *acids. Basic oxides,* such as sodium oxide (Na_2O_2), are oxides of certain metals which combine with water to form *alkalis.*

Acids and alkalis

The elements can be divided into *metals* and *non-metals*. The metals include the *alkali metals* such as sodium and potassium and the *alkaline earth metals* such as magnesium and calcium; the non-metals include phosphorus, sulphur and carbon. Whereas metals often form oxides which react with water to form hydroxides or bases, the non-metals (usually gaseous) react with water to form acids.

1. Acids

A general definition of acids would be that they are compounds of acidic radicals with hydrogen. However, this simplified version must be qualified by the fact that true acids are those where the hydrogen can be replaced by a metal (usually sodium) either wholly or in part. Most, though not all, acids also contain oxygen; hydrochloric acid (HCl) is an important exception.

All acids turn blue litmus red and react with alkalis to form *salts*. Acids which are very active are said to be strong and those not so active weak. This should not be confused with a concentrated acid which contains a small proportion of water and a dilute acid which contains a large proportion of water. Either strong or weak acids may form either concentrated or dilute acids depending on the amount of water present.

A common example of the formation of an acid and one which plays a very large part in the deterioration of many materials, is that of either sulphurous or sulphuric acid. The cycle is as follows:

During the burning of coal either sulphur dioxide (SO_2) or sulphur trioxide (SO_3) may be formed as noted under *combustion*. Either of these two substances combine with water:

$$SO_2 + H_2O \rightarrow H_2SO_3 \text{ (sulphurous acid)}$$
$$SO_3 + H_2O \rightarrow H_2SO_4 \text{ (sulphuric acid)}$$

It should be noted here that when dealing with sulphate attack on cement or lime, and especially attack that may be caused through ground water, analysis of the water is made on the amount of sulphur dioxide or trioxide present, in order to assess what precautions are required to be taken. (See *3.02 Exposure* and *3.06 Chemical attack*.)

On the whole acids tend to attack building materials more directly than alkalis. Zinc (galvanised products notable) is one metal commonly used which is affected by an acid. Acetic and similar types of acids may cause problems in certain types of buildings where these may be present in large quantities.

Carbon dioxide in the atmosphere may combine with water to form a weak carbonic acid (H_2CO_3) which is capable of decomposing certain carbonates present in many materials.

2. Alkalis

An alkali may be defined as a soluble base or hydroxide; a base being a compound which reacts with an acid to yield a salt and water only. All alkalis turn red litmus blue and with the exception of ammonia (NH_3), contain oxygen, as shown in the following examples:

$$Na_2O + H_2O \longrightarrow 2Na(OH)_2$$
sodium oxide + water $\longrightarrow$ sodium hydroxide
(caustic soda)
$$CaO + H_2O \longrightarrow Ca(OH)_2$$
calcium oxide + water $\longrightarrow$ calcium hydroxide
(slaked lime)

Alkalis may be classed either as weak or strong—ammonia is a weak alkali, caustic soda a strong alkali, which tends to corrode and destroy tissue.

The traditional process of slaking lime on a building site for use with mortars and plasters is now being replaced by what is known as 'hydrated' lime. This is also Calcium Hydroxide with the water added by steaming; the resultant powder is dry and 'ready for use'. Cement is an important source of alkaline solutions. The alkalis involved may attack certain paints, for example, or leach bitumen from bituminous felt.

3. pH value

The symbol pH is used to denote the degree of acidity or alkalinity of a solution. Pure water at 23°C has a pH value of 7. A value *below* 7 indicates that the solution is acidic, while one *above* 7 that it is alkaline. Hydrochloric acid (a strong acid) has a pH value of 3, while caustic soda (a strong alkali) a pH value of 14.

The derivation of the pH value is from consideration of electrolytes. *An electrolyte,* which may be weak or strong, is defined as *a substance (other than a metal) which when fused or dissolved in water conducts an electric current.* Water is a very weak electrolyte and is slightly dissociated into hydrogen ions, H^+, and hydroxyl ions, OH^-:

$$H_2O \rightleftharpoons H^+ + OH^-$$

As the concentrations* of H^+ and OH^- in water must be equal

$$[H^+] = [OH^-] = 10^{-7} \text{ g.Eq/l}$$

and the ionisation constant of water is:

$$[H^+] \times [OH^-] = 10^{-7} \times 10^{-7} = 10^{-14}$$

In an acid solution there are *more* hydrogen ions than 10^{-7} and consequently *fewer* hydroxyl ions. If there are 10^{-4} of $[H^+]$ there must be:

$$\frac{10^{-14}}{10^{-4}} = 10^{-10} \text{ of } [OH^-]$$

as 10^{-14} is a constant applicable to all aqueous solutions, regardless of the presence of other ionic material.

The pH value is expressed as

$$pH = -\log_{10}H^+$$

In the case of pure water:

$$pH = -\log_{10} 10^{-7} \text{ (i.e. } \log_{10} 10^7) = 7$$

The *pH value* may be defined as *the logarithm to base 10 of the hydrogen ion concentration with the negative sign omitted.* Thus if a solution has a hydrogen ion concentration of 10^{-4}, its $pH = \log 10^4 = 4$, and so on.

Salts

Salts form a most important group of substances of particular interest in building materials. They result from a chemical reaction either by an acid and an alkali or an acid and a metal.

*Concentrations are expressed in g.Equivalents per litre (g.Eq/l).

Examples of Thermoplastics

A polystyrene lamp shade

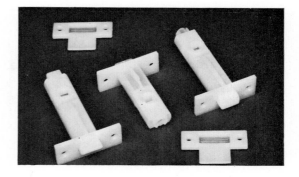

Nylon

*Polythene
(Courtesy: British
Visqueen Ltd)*

*Polymethyl methacrylic
(Courtesy: ICI Ltd.)*

PVC

(1) *Acid and Alkali:*

$$Ca(OH)_2 + H_2SO_4 \rightarrow CaSO_4 + H_2O$$

calcium hydroxide + sulphuric acid →
calcium sulphate + water.

(2) *Acid and Metal:*

$$Zn + H_2SO_4 \rightarrow ZnSO_4 + H_2$$

zinc + sulphuric acid → zinc sulphate + hydrogen.

A salt may be defined as a compound composed of ions (other than H^+, OH^- or O^{2-} ions), which, in the solid state are geometrically packed in the form of a crystal, while in aqueous solution the ions lead separate and independent existences.

The phenomenon of *efflorescence* is associated with the crystallisation of salts (*Section 3.05*), while salts in solution contribute to various forms of *chemical attack* (*Section 3.06*) including *corrosion of metals* (*Section 3.07*).

Salts, such as sodium chloride, are hygroscopic and may contribute to dampness, particularly of the surfaces on which they occur.

Sulphates of calcium, magnesium, sodium and potassium form an important group of salts particularly in problems of efflorescence and sulphate attack. The sources of these, and other salts are varied. The reason for the sulphate content of clay bricks, for example, is interesting. Although the actual mechanism involved has not been established conclusively, sulphur trioxide, sulphur dioxide, and oxygen may be involved as summarised below* (reactions with lime (CaO) are given).

$$CaO + SO_3 \longrightarrow CaSO_4 \text{ (calcium sulphate)}$$
$$CaO + SO_2 \longrightarrow CaSO_3 \text{ (calcium sulphite) which may be decomposed}$$
$$4CaSO_3 \longrightarrow 3CaSO_4 + CaS \text{ (calcium sulphide) which may be oxidised}$$
$$CaS + 2O_2 \longrightarrow CaSO_4$$

Organic chemistry

Organic chemistry is the specialised study of *carbon compounds*. This division is made because of the number and, perhaps more important, the complexity of compounds formed by this element. The structure of such compounds is of great importance and there is the obvious connection with many living substances. The cellulose substance of which timber is composed has the chemical formula $C_6H_{10}O_5$ when it is young but as it matures this formula changes to $C_{18}H_{24}O_{10}$ (lignin). Nowadays this branch of chemistry has progressed to produce a whole range of artificial materials which are generally of synthetic organic origin (i.e. man-made) and which are PLASTIC at some stage during their manufacture. They are collectively known as 'Plastics', and may be distinguished from other materials such as brick, concrete, etc., which are also plastic during some stage of their manufacture, but are not of a synthetic organic origin. Other materials such as *silicones* are also included in this branch of chemistry, and these may

*Reference: Butterworth, B., *Bricks and Modern Research*, Crosby Lockwood, pp. 47–48, 1948.

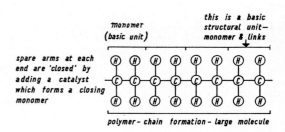

D.1.10/1 *Diagrammatic representation of the chemistry of plastics. (Based on Cousens and Yarsley, Plastics in the Service of Man, Penguin Books)*

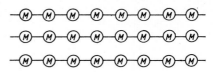

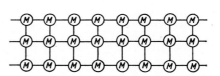

D.1.10/2 *Diagram showing the linking of monomers in plastics. Top, thermoplastics, right, thermosetting plastics*

Urea formaldehyde (Courtesy: Bakelite Ltd.)

Melamine formaldehyde (Courtesy: Bakelite Ltd.)

Phenol formaldehyde (Courtesy: Bakelite Ltd.)

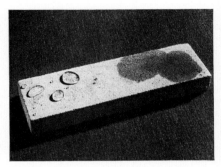

The waterproof half of the brick has been treated with silicon (Courtesy: Midlands Silicones Ltd.)

Examples of Thermosetting Plastics

range from free running oils to wax-like semi-solids and up to hard solids. Silicones are now widely used in the formulation of waterproofing compounds.

Due to the rather complex manner in which carbon may combine with other elements, it is not convenient, nor very explanatory, to record the results of chemical reactions by means of symbols only. Thus, it is more convenient to consider the combining power or valency of each of the elements in terms of arms which eventually form the links in the chain of molecules (D.1.10/1). In plastics it is normal to talk of chains of molecules. The unit in each chain is known as the *monomer* and this is repeated throughout the structure. The actual chain formation gives rise to a *polymer*, during a process known as polymerisation. By suitable 'manipulation' the chemist is able to cause a variety of combinations to take place and also to increase the length of the chain. Furthermore, he can also cause a substitution of atoms to take place. Thus, it is possible to produce a variety of monomers which can be subsequently polymerised to give chain products of widely different properties

Where spare valencies occur at the end of any chain, other substances known as *catalysts* are used to promote polymerisation so as to form a different unit and so complete the structure at the end of the chain. Normally the chains are so long that any difference at each end is negligible.

In the plastics industry it is, therefore, possible for a great variety of different types of plastics to be produced, and with each type having completely different properties. As a group, plastics may, however, be classified under two main headings, namely, *Thermoplastic* and *Thermosetting* (D.1.10/2).

1. Thermoplastic

Thermoplastic materials are those which can be softened and re-softened indefinitely by the application of heat and pressure. This process can only continue while the degree of heat is not sufficient to cause chemical decomposition of the material.

These materials are capable of flowing once they have been heated due to the particular method of linking of the monomers. Because the monomers are only linked in one direction, it is possible for the chains to move apart and while under pressure they are able to slide past one another to take up new positions. These plastics normally expand about five times as much as metals for a given rise of temperature, and this indicates that the thermoplastics do not have closely packed atoms in any crystalline form as in the case of metals. Despite the fact that there is no crystalline lattice the actual arrangement of the atoms in plastics is still very important.

Examples of thermoplastics are: nitro-cellulose, cellulose acetate, poly-methyl methacrylic, polystyrene, polyvinyl chloride (PVC), polythene, nylon.

2. Thermosetting

During the hardening process, thermosetting plastics undergo a chemical change, when they are subjected to the action of the required heat and pressure. Once the chemical reaction has taken place the shape of the material cannot be changed by subsequent application of heat and pressure. Under extreme conditions of heat chemical decomposition of the material occurs. However, in the initial stages of production thermosetting plastics are thermoplastic in character.

In thermosetting plastics the unit molecules have spare chemical attraction and so these are joined up in two directions. The chemical links are strong enough to maintain the chains at definite distances from one another. The strength is, in fact, sufficient to prevent sliding and so the material remains rigid at all temperatures short of decomposition, with no alteration in overall shape. The close packing of the molecules also makes it very difficult for solvents to enter between the chains and so cause dispersion. For most practical purposes thermosetting plastics are insoluble, although some solvents may cause swelling in certain circumstances.

Examples of thermosetting plastics are: phenol formaldehyde, urea formaldehyde, melamine formaldehyde, casein, silicon amino-silicon.

1.11 molecular forces

The precise chemical composition of any substance is dependent on the ability of atoms of the various elements to combine with one another to form molecules. (*Section 1.08*, p. 49.) Chemical symbols do not indicate the state in which the substance exists at any given time. The precise state will, among other things, be dependent on the *molecular forces* which exist between the molecules of the substance. The strength or weakness of these forces will be affected by the nature of the combining molecules *plus* the effect of the physical environment surrounding them. In addition to this the nature and behaviour of molecular forces also contributes to some understanding of other physical properties or phenomena of matter; many of them applicable to liquids.

In this section, the significance of molecular forces is outlined first, and then followed by consideration of phenomena applicable to liquids, namely evaporation, cohesion, adhesion, surface tension, meniscus, capillary action and viscosity. For convenience, adhesion is discussed in detail.

Forces between molecules

1. Effect of state

The molecules of any substance are always in a state of motion (diagram D.1.11/1). The degree of motion varies in each state of matter as follows:

In solids there is a small 'to and fro' movement in each molecule about a mean position. The strength of bond in this state is great enough to limit this movement and so the molecules are maintained very close together.

In liquids due to a reduction in the the strength of bond, the molecules are able to move more freely and in fact are also able to undertake short journeys from one part of the liquid to another.

In gases the strength of the bond is now so weak that molecules are

CONDITION   Allowable movement of one molecule.

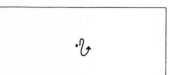

SOLID

A strong bond allows a little 'to and fro' movement.

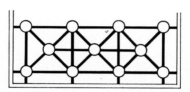
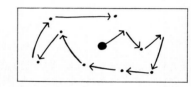

LIQUID

A weaker bond allows molecules to undertake short journeys.

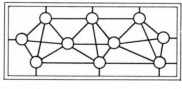
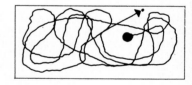

GAS

The weakest bond allows freedom of movement.

D.1.11/1 *Diagrams illustrating molecular forces*

INCREASE IN VELOCITY & MOVEMENT

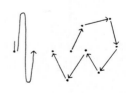
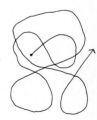

TEMPERATURE ———→ increase

SOLID | LIQUID | GAS

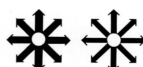

D.1.11/2 *Diagram showing the temperature-force relationship*

REDUCTION IN FORCE ———————→

able to move with comparative freedom from one position to another.

2. Effect of temperature

An increase in temperature causes an increase in the velocity of the molecules in all cases (diagram D.1.11/2). The increased velocity *reduces* the forces acting between the molecules, with the result that a solid will eventually have these forces reduced to such an extent that it changes into the liquid state. Further rises in temperature would then result in the gas state being reached. Within certain limits, all matter obeys these laws. Thus *different* temperatures are required to change the state of different substances; the precise temperature at which the change will take place will depend on the properties and particularly the nature of the forces between the molecules. Examples of two extreme ranges are ice which melts at just above 0°C and pure iron which melts at approximately 1550°C. (A range of melting points for some common materials is given in diagram D.1.11/3.) These general principles may not necessarily apply to the whole of any material, particularly those consisting of a number of different compounds. The effect of temperatures in these cases may be to change completely the chemical composition of the compounds or merely to change the state of some of the constituent compounds. In some cases the state of a material may not be changed, but different *degrees* of the same state may occur. In the solid state, such differences may result in the material becoming stressed if movement of one part of the material is restrained by another adjoining part. (See *Section 2.03*, particularly diagram D.2.03/5.) In addition to temperature pressure differences may also influence the forces between the molecules and hence the state of the substance.

3. Effect of mass and distance

The extent of the force which exists between the molecules is also influenced by *two* other factors. Firstly the *mass* of the molecules. Here the greater the mass the greater the attraction, and hence the force, between the molecules. Secondly the *distance* between the molecules. The greater the distance the less the forces of attraction between the molecules. Both these factors must always be taken into account. Thus it is true to say that there is a greater attraction between heavy molecules than lighter ones *at the same* distance. (Diagram D.1.11/4)

Evaporation

The process whereby the quantity of a liquid exposed to air is progressively reduced until it eventually disappears is known as *evaporation*. The rate at

D.1.11/4 Diagram illustrating mass-force and distance-force relationship

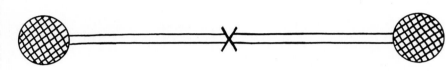

Distance

small

large

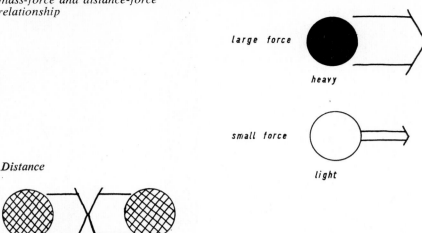

Mass

large force

heavy

small force

light

which a liquid will evaporate depends primarily on the nature of the liquid, its physical condition (temperature and surface area important) and the physical conditions of its environment (temperature, humidity and air movement important). The basic mechanisms associated with evaporation are the same whatever the liquid.

1. Fundamental properties of air

The following basic properties of air* are important to gain an understanding of the mechanism of evaporation, particularly as evaporation can only take place from the *surface of a liquid* which, for most practical purposes, 'fronts' onto air.

(a) *Vapour content*
The capacity of air to hold water increases with temperature, while the maximum amount of water vapour which air can hold at a given temperature is limited. When this limit is reached, the air is said to be *saturated*. The amount of water vapour in air may be expressed as *vapour pressure* and is nil at 0°C. The *relative humidity* of air is the amount of water vapour present compared with the amount required to saturate an equal volume of the *same* temperature.

(b) *Density*
The density of air is greater than water vapour so air tends to displace water vapour upwards.

*A more fully detailed discussion of the properties of air is given in Part 4.00, *Heat and its effects*.

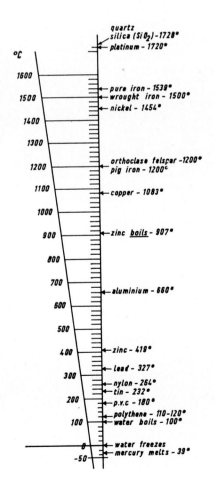

°C

quartz
silica (SiO₂) -1728°
platinum - 1720°

1600

pure iron - 1539°
wrought iron - 1500°
nickel - 1454°

1500

1400

1300

1200
orthoclase felspar -1200°
pig iron - 1200°

1100
copper - 1083°

1000

900
zinc boils - 907°

800

700
aluminium - 660°

600

500

400
zinc - 419°

300
lead - 327°
nylon - 264°
tin - 232°

200
p.v.c - 180°
polythene - 110-120°

100
water boils - 100°

0
water freezes
mercury melts - 39°

-50

D.1.11/3 Chart showing melting point for various materials

2. Basic mechanisms

The molecules at the free surface of a liquid are not restrained to the same extent as those in the interior and, because of their relative freedom, are able to leave the surface of the liquid and behave as a gas. The effect of the molecules leaving the surface of the liquid is to increase the vapour pressure of a 'layer' of air in contact with the surface of the liquid.

The vapour pressure of the 'contact layer' is then higher than that of the surrounding air. To establish a balance, the surrounding air removes vapour from the contact layer. This in turn allows further molecules to leave the liquid and so increase the vapour pressure of the contact layer. The balancing 'operation' continues until the surrounding air is saturated. Looked at in another way, evaporation cannot take place if the surface of a liquid fronts onto saturated air.

From this basic consideration the effects of various factors on the *rate of evaporation* may be noted:

(a) Effect of surface area

The larger the surface area the faster the rate of evaporation. It is important to note that evaporation cannot take place from the interior of a liquid. When considering the drying out of porous materials it should be remembered that this takes place by evaporation and that the evaporation can only take place when water reaches the exposed surface (or *just* below the surface in some cases) of the material (see *Sections 3·01* and *3.03.*)

(b) Effects of temperature

The rate of evaporation increases with temperature.

The movement of the molecules is increased as the temperature of a liquid is increased. The resultant reduction in the strength of the forces between the molecules enables them to leave the surface of the liquid more freely.

The temperature of the surrounding air has two effects. If this is higher than that of the liquid, then there is an exchange of heat (establishing a balance) between the air (looses heat) and the liquid (gains heat). This accounts for the relative coldness of damp rooms. On the other hand the higher the air temperature the greater its capacity to hold water.

(c) Effects of moisture content of the air

Evaporation proceeds more rapidly when the vapour content of the air is low than when it is high; evaporation ceases when the air is saturated.

(d) Effect of air movement

Water vapour rises and thus gives way to drier air. Induced air movement (e.g. by winds, fans, etc.) promotes evaporation by removing the air in contact with the liquid before it has reached saturation, *and* by bringing more unsaturated air into contact with the surface of the liquid.

Surface water on newly placed and levelled concrete. This water and the remainder still in the wet concrete has to evaporate eventually. The rate of evaporation must be carefully controlled (in this case some simple form of cover may be used) in order to reduce shrinkage cracking to a minimum

Volatile solvents used to aid spreading of paint must eventually evaporate

Operative protected from evaporation of highly volatile solvents

Photograph showing (from left to right) natural or true slump (good cohesion), shear slump (poorer cohesion) and collapsed slump (poorest cohesion)

3. Significance

The significance of evaporation in *some* aspects of building practice are noted for convenience. In general terms the ground may be regarded as a perpetual source of water. Many elements of buildings are either buried in the ground or in close contact with it. Water may rise in elements composed of porous materials to levels above the ground due to capillary action. Evaporation not only assists in maintaining a given level for a given construction, but also allows a continual 'flow' of water to take place. If the level is high enough evaporation towards the inside of a building will increase the dampness of that interior.

For these and other reasons, 'the supply of water' must be cut off by an impervious layer at some convenient level (see *Section 3.04, under Damp-proof courses*).

In many new buildings under construction the rate of evaporation is greatly increased, sometimes with deleterious results, by using heated moving air, thus taking advantage of two methods of increasing evaporation. These methods of reducing the quantity of water used in construction and held within the fabric of the building until it has evaporated, plus the greatly increased temperatures now prevalent in many new buildings, does tend to induce the loss of water particularly in the winter towards the inside, rather than the outside. In the early days of a new building humidity conditions are likely to be high, while rapid drying increases the risk of cracking or distortion of many materials—timber and wet constructions are significant.

In some building applications such as paint it is normal to encourage as much as possible the evaporation of the *solvent* used in the paint to aid spreading. These solvents are usually highly volatile liquids, that is those which tend to evaporate rapidly, and can be injurious to health if they are highly concentrated. For this reason it is important that there is *adequate* ventilation in those spaces where painting operations take place. Such ventilation also helps to increase evaporation. Where ventilation cannot be suitably effected, either because of the nature of the paint or other practical difficulties, it is then necessary to ensure that the operatives have an independent source of clean unvitiated air.

Cohesion

Cohesion is usually strictly confined to the forces of attraction within a material which exist between the molecules of the *same* substance in order to avoid confusion with the forces of attraction at interfacial surfaces that occur between different substances as in adhesion. (Adhesion may also occur between particles of the same substance but then only at interfacial surfaces.) Cohesion may also be equated with the chemical affinity between atoms. Although composed of different substances, materials such as mortar, plaster and concrete, can, more conveniently, be regarded as homogeneous, particularly when they are in a *wet* and *plastic* state. In this state cohesion in the material as a whole is important.

In the case of homogeneous materials, such as metals, heat does reduce the cohesive forces between the molecules, thus enabling these materials to change to the liquid or gas states. In the case of wet materials (mortars, plasters and concrete in the plastic state), the cohesive forces may be considerably reduced by the addition of excessive quantities of water. The water induces greater plasticity, i.e. ease of spreading the wet mixture. The cohesive forces in these materials, plus others such as paint, bitumen or asphalt, are important, as they must be of sufficient strength to enable application to take place and also to enable the materials to maintain their shape until hardening has taken place. Unfortunately there are as yet no simple methods which would be of practical value to assess accurately the cohesive forces required in a particular material. The slump test used in concrete practice does give some almost 'rule of thumb' guide. Much depends on experience. However, it is still of vital importance that in all cases where liquids are added to form a mixture their quantity should be commensurate with adequate cohesion and other requirements such as entering into a chemical reaction or providing plasticity.

Adhesion

In many ways it is difficult to make a clear distinction between cohesion and adhesion. If cohesion describes the forces of attraction between molecules or particles of the same substance within a material, then adhesion describes the forces of attraction between molecules or particles of different substances at interfacial surfaces. Adhesion may be defined as the property of matter by which close contact is established between two or more surfaces when they are brought intimately together. Force is required to separate the surfaces. Dust particles (one substance) settling and remaining on a ceiling (another substance) is a simple example of adhesion. However, so many building materials consist of different substances that it could be argued that it is adhesion that ensures they remain intact. But this applies to a material as a whole. For the purposes of this study adhesion is regarded, as is usual in building practice, as the forces of attraction at the interfacial surfaces of materials of different kinds.

However, it is important to note that, in terms of adhesion particularly, a distinction must be drawn between different states of the same material. For the purposes of adhesion the solid state must be regarded as one sub-

The use of a special adhesive for laying vinyl floor tiles

The photographs of plastering and brick laying illustrate the use of ordinary building materials rather than specifically manufactured adhesives

stance and the liquid or plastic state as another. An example may help to clarify this. Plaster is applied in a plastic state and usually in two coats, the second applied after the first has dried. Thus the first coat of plaster in the solid state is, in terms of adhesion, one material while the second coat of plaster is, during application, another material.

Adhesion has played an important part in many forms of traditional building techniques. Adhesion of bricks and mortar is an obvious example, but

63

adhesion is also necessary in plastering, glazing (putties), asphalting (vertical surfaces) and painting. In these cases, the adhesives are made of what may be called ordinary building materials. The use of special adhesives (glues) was, until recent years, to a large extent confined to joinery. With the development of synthetic resins and rubbers, it is now almost possible to stick 'anything to anything'. Among other things, the introduction of stronger and more durable adhesives has enabled great advances to be made in timber technology, particularly in structures; a variety of different floor and wall and other finishes (laminated plastics notable) can now be applied, while a whole range of new materials (chipboards and an increasing number of composite panels) has been made available. Adhesion also plays an extremely important part in the use of mastics (gap fillers—see *Section 3.04* under *Joint design*) which have been developed to meet the special problems now being encountered in many of the newer building techniques (curtain walling and large panel constructions are notable).

The principles upon which good adhesion rely are fundamentally the same whatever materials are used. In all cases the adhesive medium is applied in a liquid or plastic state to a solid material. The liquid or plastic medium usually, but not always (a number of mastics are the exception), becomes solid after application.

Satisfactory adhesion, and above all the maintenance of good adhesion, depends on ensuring that certain precautions are taken. The main purpose of this part is to outline the reasons for these precautions and to note all the factors which are likely to result in poor or complete loss of adhesion. For purposes of explanation, and to some extent for convenience, specific attention is given to the adhesion of ordinary building materials such as mortars, plasters and paint. The principles discussed are, however, equally applicable to the 'special adhesives', referred to earlier, although reference is made to these as convenient. Nevertheless it should be noted that the detailed application of many of the special adhesives may vary. It is in any case always important to follow the manufacturer's instructions for his particular material.

It is convenient to use the following general headings—(1) Basic mechanisms; (2) Effects of movement; (3) Practical precautions; and (4) Special adhesives.

1. Basic mechanisms

In most practical cases adhesion takes place between two substances by the combination of *two types* of adhesion, namely *mechanical* and *specific*. Mechanical adhesion is simply the interlocking of the two substances, while specific adhesion relies on forces of attraction between the *surfaces* of

Lath and plaster to a stud partition showing the manner in which the plaster eventually forms a mechanical key. Being a vertical surface the plaster tends to run down the laths but nevertheless a key is still formed

Expanded metal being used over timber (timber/plaster adhesion is extremely poor) to provide a key for plastering

Expanded metal being used over steel (no adhesion between steel and plaster) to provide a key for plastering

(Top) The use of bricks made with a special 'key' to add to the key usually provided by the porous nature of these materials but which may not always be sufficient. (Bottom) Scored undercoat of plaster to provide a key for finishing coat

The photograph shows water on a sheet of glass part of which has been greased. The water cannot wet the greased surface (left-hand side) and therefore forms globules but can wet the ungreased surface (right-hand side) and therefore is able to spread

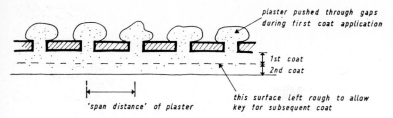

plaster pushed through gaps during first coat application

1st coat
2nd coat

'span distance' of plaster

this surface left rough to allow key for subsequent coat

D.1.11/5 *Diagram illustrating mechanical adhesion in lath and plaster*

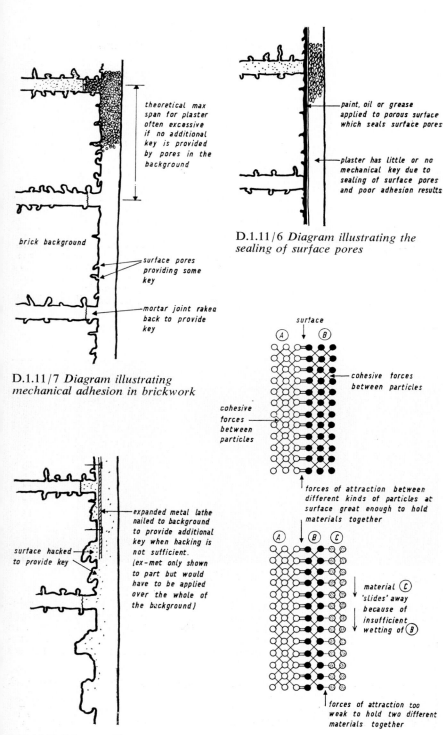

theoretical max span for plaster often excessive if no additional key is provided by pores in the background

brick background

surface pores providing some key

mortar joint raked back to provide key

D.1.11/7 *Diagram illustrating mechanical adhesion in brickwork*

paint, oil or grease applied to porous surface which seals surface pores

plaster has little or no mechanical key due to sealing of surface pores and poor adhesion results

D.1.11/6 *Diagram illustrating the sealing of surface pores*

expanded metal lathe nailed to background to provide additional key when hacking is not sufficient. (ex-met only shown to part but would have to be applied over the whole of the background)

surface hacked to provide key

D.1.11/8 *Diagram illustrating method of forming a mechanical key to porous surfaces which have been previously sealed (See D.1.11/6)*

surface

A   B

cohesive forces between particles

cohesive forces between particles

forces of attraction between different kinds of particles at surface great enough to hold materials together

A   B   C

material C 'slides' away because of insufficient wetting of B

forces of attraction too weak to hold two different materials together

D.1.11/9 *Diagram illustrating strong and weak adhesive forces between surfaces of various materials*

the substances. With the latter method, it is possible to unite two solids by ensuring that both surfaces are truly matched and highly polished. However this is not normally practical in building work.

(a) Mechanical adhesion
Mechanical adhesion could take place by physically interlocking two solids (the interlocking pieces of a jig-saw puzzle, for instance). However in practical terms it is more expedient to apply one of the materials in a liquid or plastic condition and to ensure that the solid (referred to as the background) on which the liquid is to be applied is suitably 'keyed'. The simplest example of this is traditional lath and plaster. (A diagrammatic representation of a ceiling is shown in diagram D.1.11/5.) Other methods are also shown, as for example raking back mortar joints (diagram D.1.11/7). In addition to these methods of providing a key, materials of a porous nature do in some degree possess a 'keyed' surface. Additional keying may sometimes be provided to porous materials during manufacture as shown in the photograph of specially made 'keyed' bricks. Where materials have smooth or unkeyed surfaces, as may occur with metals or when the surface pores of porous materials are sealed as by paint (D.1.11/6 and 8), some form of key has to be provided by mechanical or other means, such as buffing, filing, sand papering, etching or covering the surface with a 'keyed' material such as expanded metal lath or liquid bonding agents. The degree of 'keying' required in any particular case will, it should be emphasised, depend on the extent to which a particular adhesive material relies on mechanical adhesion. In the examples given plaster relies to a large extent on a mechanical key. The same is not necessarily true of paints and many of the special adhesives, although some form of key may still be advisable.

(b) Specific adhesion
In the same way as the molecules of the same substance are attracted to one another, so are the molecules of different substances (in different degrees) attracted to one another (diagram D.1.11/9). The degree of attraction will vary from substance to substance. At the one extreme, there can be a mutual attraction between the two different substances intense enough to *overcome* the cohesive force existing between the molecules of the individual substances, and thereby effecting a bond between the two different substances. On the other hand, the mutual attraction may not be intense enough to overcome the cohesive forces of the individual substances resulting in no adhesion taking place at all. Thus various intensities of adhesive forces may exist.

In the case of liquids, the surface of a solid is said to have been 'wetted' when there is sufficient mutual attraction between the solid and the liquid

65

F

to cause adhesion. It is important to remember that it is always the *two surfaces* and not the body of the materials which are relevant. Consider, for example, glass and two different liquids, water and oil. Water will wet clean glass and so will oil. However, if the glass is oily or greasy, then the water will not be able to wet the glass at all, because there is not very much 'wetting' of the water on the oil. If adhesion did occur, the oil would have to act as the adhesive. This accounts for the fact that, on clean glass, water will tend to spread over the entire surface, whereas it will form small globules, on glass that is greasy (diagram D.1.11/10). The importance of this lies in the fact that any liquid which is required to 'wet' the solid, must not have its 'wetting' properties interfered with by any substance which may exist on the solid at the time of application. Such substances are not confined to oil and grease alone but include dust, grit, dirt, salts, scum, laitenance, rust and mill-scale. These latter substances may help to produce *planes of weakness* in the adhesive bond (diagrams D.1.11/11 and 12). On drying, the solid material has only limited points of support, because of the impurities, and may therefore be more easily removed from its background by mechanical damage or even vibrations, because the limited adhesive forces are not sufficient to resist the forces created. In some cases the limited adhesive forces may not be sufficient to support the weight of the adhesive material in its solid state.

For easy application it is, therefore, easier to use the wetting properties of liquids, rather than to try and effect the even and true matching of the solids that would otherwise be required to effect specific adhesion. The actual degree of adhesion which can be obtained on any surface will in some cases be dependent on the surface area available. Roughening a smooth surface would be one way of increasing the surface area and this of course also helps to increase adhesion by mechanical means.

The importance of the *liquid content* in any substance should not be ignored. In instances where there is insufficient liquid, the wetting process cannot take place to the full, while other reductions on cohesive strength of the material being applied can also result. A typical example occurs with mortar or plaster. In either case, if the wet material is applied to a dry absorbent background much of the water will be absorbed by the background leaving little water for either wetting or to allow the wet material to set properly. The weakened material when set may then break or fall off. Similar conditions apply if paint is applied to a dry absorbent background. The paint will eventually peel off. In these cases the solution is to reduce suction. In the case of the mortar or plaster the surface of the background should be slightly wetted. Over wetting should be avoided, so as

D.1.11/11 (1) *Forces and* (2) *planes of weakness*

D.1.11/10 *Formation of globule due to lack of surface wetting*

D.1.11/12 *Diagrammatic representation of weak adhesive bond*

Loss of adhesion of paint applied on rusting steelwork

not to increase the water content of the wet material—excessive water content may increase shrinkage of the material when it dries out.* For the surfaces to be painted suitable sealers

should first be applied. The same principle will also apply to any absorbent surface which is to receive paper. In addition, it may be noted that the successful adhesion of many of the mastics

*The efficacy of wetting backgrounds for successful adhesion of plasters and renders is to a large extent dependent on the degree of absorption of the background. In general, traditional backgrounds such as clay brickwork for lime and cement-based plasters and renders are not highly absorbent. The absorption of many types of concrete (the lightweight varieties are notable) is, by comparison, extremely high, and wetting has been found to contribute little to adhesion. This has been found to be the case with *calcium sulphate*, i.e. gypsum plasters, in particular. The comment which follows is related specifically to this type of plaster. In some cases, air forced out of the background during absorption (i.e. the liquid from the plaster displaces the air in the interstices of the background material) has, because of the barrier created by the plaster, formed voids under the plaster, resulting in a hollow type of planes of weakness. Good adhesion can be obtained by using special plasters containing a water-retaining additive, or by treating the absorbent background with a bonding agent before plastering. (For guidance in general see *Choosing Specifications for Plastering*, BRS Digest (2nd Series), No. 49, HMSO, August, 1964.)

Loss of adhesion of paint applied to galvanised surfaces. Causes of planes of weakness are probably due to insufficient preparation of the surface

Loss of adhesion of paint applied to a concrete surface due to either moisture or laitenance causing planes of weakness

Detail of picture on the right illustrating the gap between the rendering and its background. The cause of the failure is probably due to a combination (often the case in loss of adhesion failures) of insufficient key and the development of planes of weakness

Due to loss of adhesion of the rendering originally applied to the concrete wall it has been necessary to hack off (a fairly simple operation in this case) all the rendering before applying new rendering. The photograph shows most of the rendering already hacked off

requires the priming of the faces of joints of absorbent materials such as concrete, before the application of the mastic into the joint.

In the case of liquids of an oily nature, such as those normally used in many kinds of paint and including bitumens, it is important that there should be no water on the surfaces which are to receive the paint. This is another instance of an intervening substance which will reduce 'wetting' properties of a particular liquid. In the case of painted plaster it is interesting to note that at all times the plaster has a greater affinity for water than it has for oil. Thus even after the oil paint has been applied and has properly adhered, it is possible for a loss of adhesion to occur should the plaster subsequently become damp.

2. Effect of movement

Forces set up as a result of movement, and especially when elements are restrained, are, in many cases, sufficient to break down the forces of adhesion. Movements of all kinds must therefore be controlled or limited as appropriate to circumstances. One common type of failure occurs with plasters or renders, particularly those with a cement base, applied to a background of wet construction and this is now used as an example to explain the effects of movement (diagram D.1.11/13).

Both the background and the adhesive are capable of moisture movement. Such movement persists until the materials have reached moisture equilibrium. Backgrounds which appear to be dry may still be damp enough for some moisture movement to occur. On the other hand the plaster or render after application must complete its drying shrinkage. During the drying process, either of the background or adhesive, it is possible for the shrinkage which occurs to be sufficient to 'shear through' the bond between the adhesive and the background. Excessive amounts of water do tend to increase drying shrinkage in addition to making the materials weaker. Some balance must therefore be created. Greater dependence on a mechanical bond will assist maintaining adhesion, but care must be taken not to depend entirely on this and in so doing disregard any precautions necessary to ensure satisfactory specific adhesion.

Any movements, whether moisture, thermal, etc., which may occur *after* application will, if they are large enough, also cause a loss of adhesion.

In this context it may be noted that some of the newer adhesives, including particularly mastics which rely on adhesion, are much more flexible than adhesives such as mortar, plaster and traditional gap-fillers, and can accordingly accommodate more movement. As in all cases the degree of movement must be closely related to the movement which can be tolerated by any given material.

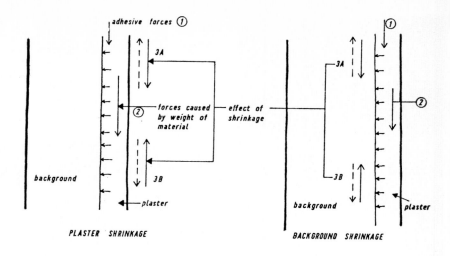

PLASTER SHRINKAGE

BACKGROUND SHRINKAGE

D.1.11/13 *Diagram showing effect of movement. When 1 is greater than 2+ (3A & 3B) then adhesion is maintained. When 1 is less than 2+ (3A & 3B) then adhesion is not maintained. Note: effect of expansion is the same in principle—direction of expansion forces opposite to shrinkage forces shown, i.e. dotted lines. A combination of both the above can take place at the same time*

Three typical examples of loss of adhesion of joints caused by excessive movement (moisture and thermal). Two examples (left) failure of mortar joints and example (right) of failure of a mastic joint

Loss of adhesion of pointing due to a special kind of movement—frost action. Similar types of failure may also be caused by chemical actions

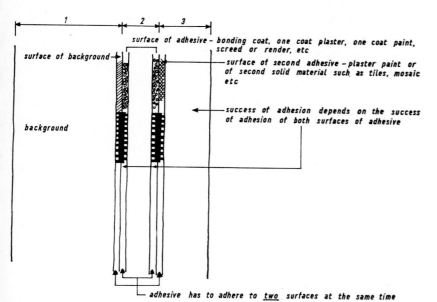

no foreign matter to come between 2 surfaces
no other forces greater than adhesive force to act between 2 surfaces

surface of background must adhere to <u>surface</u> of adhesive and vice-versa.

background

adhesive applied in a 'liquid' condition to solid background
as - mortar, plaster, render
- paint, asphalt tanking & upstands

surface of background ———————— surface of adhesive

surface of adhesive - bonding coat, one coat plaster, one coat paint, screed or render, etc

surface of background

surface of second adhesive - plaster paint or of second solid material such as tiles, mosaic etc

background

success of adhesion depends on the success of adhesion of both surfaces of adhesive

adhesive has to adhere to <u>two</u> surfaces at the same time

D.1.11/14 *Illustration of the importance of surfaces in adhesion. Above, two materials, two surfaces and, below, three materials and four surfaces*

Whereas most of the preceding discussion has been concerned with the application of adhesives in the form of surfacings, it should be noted that satisfactory adhesion may be required between abutting or overlapping units as occurs in joints—the use of gap-fillers is significant.

3. Practical precautions

Securing and maintaining good adhesion requires observance of a few rather simple precautions. When dealing with any form or type of adhesive it is of fundamental importance to remember two basic rules: (1) adhesion is essentially concerned with the bonding together of the surfaces of materials (see diagram D.1.11/14), while (2) no adhesive can effect a bond which is stronger than the surface to which it is applied.

As outlined earlier, adhesion is, in general, the result of the combined effects of both mechanical and specific adhesion. In many cases, the traditional adhesives such as mortars, plasters and renders are notable, it is difficult to lay down hard and fast rules as to the amount of adhesion that should be effected by either mechanical or specific means. Consequently as a general rule it is safer to ensure that provision is made for the *maximum amount* of each to take place. This rule may not necessarily apply to some of the special adhesives, particularly the newer ones, many of which have been specifically formulated to bond smooth surfaces together. The manufacturer's recommendations for the use of his products should, therefore, always be ascertained *and* followed.

The precautions which aim to secure *and* maintain good adhesion may be summarised as follows:

(a) Cleanliness
All surfaces to receive the adhesive should be clean and there should be no intervening or foreign substances between the adhesive and the background which will reduce the 'wetting' or other properties of the liquid content of the adhesive. Typical intervening substances are grease, oil, dirt, dust, grit, flaking paint, chemicals (particularly salts), scum, laitenance mill-scale, and rust.

(b) Dryness
Dryness, before and after application, is particularly necessary for those surfaces which are to receive adhesives with non-water bases. In the case of water-based adhesives a certain amount of dampness may be required to avoid excessive suction of the water content of the adhesive.

(c) Key
Some provision should be made to ensure sufficient key in the background material, unless recommendations for a given adhesive do not specifically stipulate the necessity of a key. Materials which do not normally possess 'keyed' surfaces, such as

69

metals, should have their surfaces roughened. Porous materials may require additional keying.

In recent years there has been a marked increase in the use of liquid bonding agents on dense concrete, not properly keyed during construction and which are to receive plaster or render. Bonding agents may be imperative on highly absorbent concrete surface (the lightweight concretes are notable) to secure good adhesion of calcium sulphate plasters in particular. Here it should be noted that the bonding agent has to ensure adequate adhesion between the concrete and plaster or render, that is, it is an *intermediate* adhesive. Bonding agents may be affected by moisture thus resulting in a loss of adhesion. The plaster or render and the background must therefore be maintained dry.

(d) Avoiding suction
Any absorbent materials to receive adhesive should be sufficiently sealed to prevent excessive absorption of the liquid content of the adhesive. This particular requirement may not necessarily apply to the specially manufactured adhesives.

(e) Chemical decomposition
Any agencies which are likely to lead to the chemical decomposition of either the adhesive or background after application must be avoided.

(f) Avoiding movement
Any excessive movement, including vibrations, either of the background, adhesive or of elements and units which may be joined by an adhesive, should be avoided in order to maintain permanence of bond.

4. Special adhesives

Within the context of this study, it has been convenient to use the terms 'special adhesives' to refer specifically to materials other than those made of what have been termed ordinary building materials such as mortar, plaster, render, asphalt (in limited applications) and paint which rely on good adhesion. In practice, of course, the term adhesives is used to cover the special formulations.

The enormous, if not formidable, range of adhesives which is now available has, to a large extent, been the result of developments in what are known as film forming materials. An important aspect of all specially formulated adhesives, and in particular those which have been developed since the war, is that they require *curing and setting*.

Chemical reactions do, therefore, play an important part when the adhesives are used. It is not the intention to discuss the chemical aspects of adhesives, but rather to outline, in general terms, the essential characteristics and applications of some of the more common types. The fact that chemical changes must take place in the

Some examples of chemical decomposition resulting in loss of adhesion. Top, mastic (loss of adhesion also due partly to movement). Left, mastic (two examples). Right, paint

'... the introduction of stronger and more durable adhesives has enabled great advances to be made in timber technology, particularly structure'. The photograph illustrates one of the timber roof structures now possible

Laminated plastics as wall or column cladding and plastics floor tiles can be bonded using adhesives based on natural or various forms of synthetic rubbers which are generally flexible

constituents of the adhesives should, it is hoped, at least draw attention to the importance of not only ensuring the correct selection of adhesive for a particular application, but also of carefully following the manufacturer's recommendations. It is also extremely important to remember to check that the adhesive and the materials it is intended to bind together are *compatible* with one another.

Through the use of synthetic resins, adhesives are now available which are strong enough to bond metal-to-metal for use in the aircraft industry. Consequently a practice appears to be growing up of distinguishing between structural and non-structural adhesives. The latter, in general characterised by their flexibility and ability to accommodate movements, include those adhesives which are suitable for light or intermittent, rather than continuous, loads. The essentially structural adhesives, characterised by their rigidity, are usually, but not always, reserved for bonding composite beams, as in laminated timber work, or in the manufacture of plywood, hardboard, chipboard and laminated plastics.

The main types of adhesives and their applications can be summarised as follows:

(a) Traditional glues
These include vegetable, animal, casein and blood-albumen glues for use mainly in internal joinery work. Most of these glues contain moisture and set by the evaporation of the moisture, aided by pressure and/or heat. Consequently, they can take up moisture again and are not waterproof. For joinery, or other timber products to be joined together for use externally, adhesives based on synthetic resins, which are resistant to moisture, should be used.

(b) Synthetic resins
The most widely used resins are phenol-formaldehyde, urea and melamine formaldehyde and epoxy. Being of the thermosetting type of plastics they are rigid. Apart from adhesives based on epoxies, synthetic resin adhesives are used for bonding timber products. Epoxy resins, on the other hand, are used for repairing metal and concrete structures.

(c) Polyesters
These are being applied to ceramics.

(d) Polyurethanes
For bonding timber and metal products.

(e) Rubbers
Adhesives based on natural and various forms of synthetic rubbers make up a fairly wide range of different formulations which are generally flexible. Among uses of the various types, the following can be included: bonding floor finishes such as vinyl; fixing plywood, hardboard, laminated plastics and other sheet materials as cladding; bonding insulation boards and acoustic boards and

tiles to prepared backgrounds; bonding expanded polystyrene and fixing ceramic tiles not only to rendered backgrounds but also to wood, metal and even tiles. Of particular interest is the range of 'contact adhesives'. These adhesives are applied to both surfaces to be bonded and left to dry (volatile solvents must evaporate). Once dried, the two surfaces of the materials to be bonded are brought together under ordinary hand pressure, whereupon a bond is immediately formed.

(f) Asphaltic compounds

These are modified with natural or synthetic resins and are used as roofing compounds, sealants and for bonding floor tiles.

(g) Butyl, polysulphide and others

These compounds are used in various types of sealants (mastics). A fuller account of these materials including their applications is included in *Section 3.04* under *Joint design*.

Surface tension (γ)

The free surface of a liquid behaves as if it were covered by a thin membrane of an elastic skin nature. This property is known as surface tension. Surface tension is measured in dynes/cm, i.e. force/length unit, as surface tension does not depend on extent but on the nature of the surface. The free surface energy is surface tension × area of surface. (See comparative chart C.1.11/1.) As with most properties, different liquids have different surface tensions. One of the most important characteristics of surface tension is the fact that within limits it is able to support a load. In practical terms and of interest in buildings the load is usually that of the body of the liquid beneath the surface (diagram D.1.11/15). This fact plus that of the 'wetting' properties of a liquid gives rise to capillarity, that is the ability of liquids, and particularly water to rise in narrow spaces.

The formation of this elastic skin over the surface of a liquid comes about in order to create a *balance* in the forces acting on the surface molecules. Molecules within the interior of a liquid are subjected to forces acting on all faces. However, those at the surface are only subjected to forces acting sideways and downwards. Consequently the forces acting on the surface molecules are unbalanced. The gas above the liquid does not normally exert sufficient force to maintain a balance of the surface molecules. Any given molecules at the surface are, of course, capable of moving inwards, but as soon as this happens other molecules will move in to take their place. Therefore, in order to maintain the balance the free surface of the liquid tends to become as small as possible (this tendency is due to an increase in the forces acting in a sideways direction) and in this way acts like an elastic skin. This skin does not materially affect the fact that surface

Felt being applied to a chip board infill panel with an asphaltic compound prior to the application of copper roofing

Use of a sealant (mastic) in external cladding

SUBSTANCE	VALUE	SURFACE TENSION (γ) - dyn/cm				
		0 100 200 300 400 500				
WATER	73					
PARAFFIN	25					
BENZENE	29					
TURPENTINE	27					
ALCOHOL	23					
MERCURY	465					

C.1.11/1 *Comparative chart of surface tension. The values are taken to the nearest figure and are for liquid/air surface tensions at 20°C. Surface tension decreases with increases in temperature. (Values taken from Civil Engineering Reference Book, Vol. 1, 1961, and Kaye & Laby, Physical and Chemical Constants)*

molecules can also escape as in evaporation.

If the body of the liquid were not subjected to any other force, including that of gravity, then it would tend to take on a spherical form due to the contraction produced by surface tension. In most cases other forces tend to flatten the sphere; the amount of flattening actually produced depending on the extent of the forces involved. The formation of globules of water on a greasy surface indicates that because there is no wetting by the water on the grease the surface tension contracts the body of the water. The size and shape of the globule will be dictated by the measure of the force created by the surface tension as compared with that of the weight of the water. In other words, the flattened surface of the sphere formed is due to the fact that the upward reaction which is provided by the surface tension is counteracted by the weight of the water itself (diagram D.1.11/16).

Surface tension is not necessarily confined to the boundaries of a liquid and a gas. It may also act on the boundaries between two immiscible liquids. In these cases it is possible to eliminate the effects of gravity and thus produce a perfect sphere. Some writers have suggested that surface tension although small in magnitude, may exist on the surface of solids, thus accounting for the difference in the characteristics of the surface layer and those of the interior of a material.

Meniscus

The curved surface which is produced when a liquid is placed in a container, especially one of glass, is known as the *meniscus*. In the case of the lighter liquids, such as water, the curve is concave, while heavy liquids, such as mercury, produce a convex surface (diagram D.1.11/17).

Concave surfaces are produced when the liquid is capable of wetting the surface of the container. In this case the liquid at the walls of the container

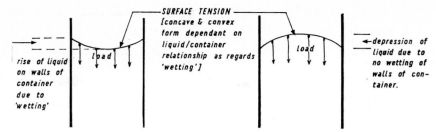

D.1.11/15 *Diagram showing surface tension supporting a load and meniscus*

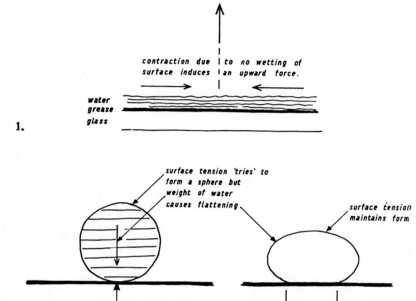

D.1.11/16 *Diagram showing power of surface tension*

The power of surface tension to form globules of water

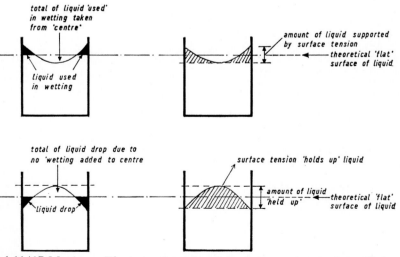

D.1.11/17 *Meniscus. The top pair of drawings show concave surfaces (light liquids) and the bottom pair convex surfaces (heavy liquids)*

73

tends to rise while the body of the liquid is held suspended by surface tension. When the liquid does not wet the surface the normal action of surface tension to produce a spherical form operates. Thus water will only form a truly concave surface in a glass container and when the glass is *clean*. Any greasing of the surface will reduce the wetting power of the water and thus reduce the amount of concavity. Should there be sufficient grease to prevent wetting at all, then the surface of the water will be convex as in the case of mercury.

Angle of contact

Mention has already been made, under 'Adhesion' (p. 63) that when a liquid spreads over the surface of a solid, the liquid is said to 'wet' the solid. This wetting takes place when the 'adhesive' forces at the interface of the liquid and the solid are greater than those of the 'cohesive' forces within the liquid. A spot of clean water dropped on to a *clean* glass surface spreads over the surface, whereas a drop of mercury will not spread but remain as a well-defined drop. A cross-section through the drop (diagram D.1.11/18) shows that the surface of the mercury meets the glass at an angle. The angle between the tangent drawn to the surface of the liquid at the place where it meets the supporting surface and the supporting surface *within the liquid* is called the *angle of contact*.

The angle of contact also occurs when liquids meet the sides of a container. As has already been illustrated in diagram D.1.11/17 liquids such as water curve upwards, whereas liquids such as mercury curve downwards. Diagram D.1.11/19 illustrates the angles of contact in the two extreme cases.

The significance of the angle of contact is that it is a measure of the wetting properties of a liquid. Looked at in another way, the angle of contact is a measure of the relative magnitudes of the adhesive and cohesive forces. If the angle of contact is *less* than 90 degrees the adhesive forces are the greater, and if it is *greater* than 90 degrees they are not. The angle of contact is of value in determining the extent to which capillarity will take place. (See 'Capillary action', p. 75.)

Finally it is important to note that the angle of contact for a given liquid is not constant. The angle of contact depends on the relationship between the liquid and the nature of the *surface* of the solid. Water spreads on clean glass (very low angles of contact) whereas it forms globules when the glass has a waxed or greased surface (high angle of contact). On the other hand, some substances when dissolved in water diminish the cohesive force so much that the solutions will spread over greasy surfaces. The diminution of the cohesive forces results in a reduction of surface tension.

74

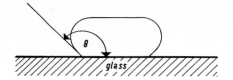

D.1.11/18 *Angle of contact for drop of liquid on a horizontal surface*

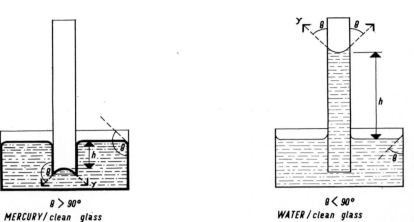

$\theta > 90°$
MERCURY/ *clean glass*

$\theta < 90°$
WATER/ *clean glass*

D.1.11/19 *Angles of contact for two different liquids (water and mercury) in contact with the sides of the container*

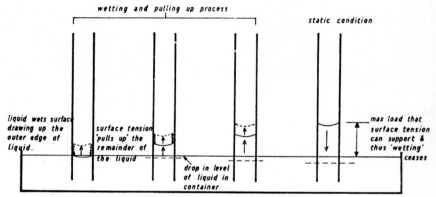

D.1.11/20 *Diagram illustrating the mechanics of capillary action*

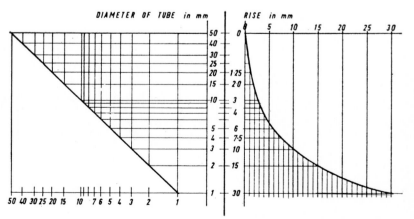

C.1.11/2 *Comparative graph showing the capillarity of water based on formula*
$$h = \frac{4 \times surface\ tension}{dia. \times density}$$ *where surface tension* $= 0.0743g/cm$ *and density* $= 1g/cm^2$ *(Civil Engineering Reference Books, Vol. 1). Notes: (1) Values have been rounded off. (2) The precise height or rise of water is dependent, inter alia, on the degree of cleanliness of the walls of the tube. Values should be regarded as the maximum possible under ideal conditions*

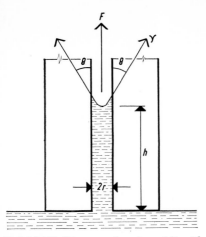

D.1.11/21 *Diagram for rise of liquid based on equilibrium of forces which includes the use of surface tension and angle of contact—see text*

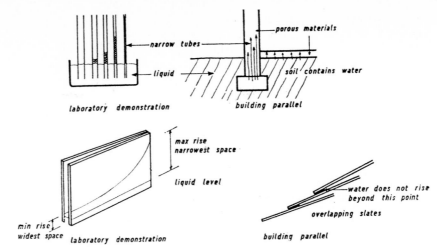

D.1.11/22 *Some illustrations of capillarity in the laboratory and in practice*

Capillary action

Capillarity is the name given to the capacity of a liquid to move upwards against the force of gravity. The name is derived from the fact that this upward movement was first observed in capillary tubes, that is, tubes with a narrow *circular* bore. However, the action is not confined to circular tubes, but will also take place in narrow enclosed spaces of non-circular shapes. The narrow spaces in which capillarity takes place are referred to more simply as *capillaries*.

In building practice capillaries may occur within materials (porous materials are notable) or may be formed in the joints of units of the same or different materials.

For the most part it is normal to consider the capillary action of water as this is the liquid most commonly encountered in buildings. However, it should be remembered that capillary action can take place with other liquids, although the occurrence of these will usually be restricted to some special cases only.

1. Basic mechanisms

It has sometimes been said that the rise of the liquid is due to the fact that surface tension pulls the liquid upwards. This is partly true, but it is better to consider the rise as a combination of the wetting and surface tension properties of the liquid. (D.1.11/20). When a liquid wets the surface of a container, that portion of the liquid in close proximity to the walls of the container will tend to rise and in a sense 'leave the rest of the liquid behind'. However, the molecules of the liquid cannot be separated that easily, so with the aid of the forces exerted by surface tension the whole body of the liquid is raised. The rise continues for as long as the liquid can wet the surface of the container and until the weight of the liquid beneath its own surface equals the weight carrying capacity provided by surface tension. For circular tubes

Sufficient plasticity is required in concrete in order that it may be placed (i.e. poured). This illustration shows concrete being used at ground level without reinforcement and being tamped into position

Like the photograph above this also shows concrete being used at ground level without reinforcement, but in this case being vibrated. Different methods of placing and vibrating are used in other situations and particularly in reinforced work

the following formula may be used to calculate the actual height of the column of liquid:

$$\text{height of column} = \frac{4 \times \text{surface tension}}{\text{density of liquid} \times \text{diameter of tube}}$$

From this formula it will be seen that for any given liquid the smaller the diameter of the tube the greater will be the rise in the tube (see C.1.11/2). On the other hand different liquids will rise to different heights in tubes of the same diameter, the rise being influenced by the surface tension and density of the particular liquid.

Another way of looking at the mechanisms of capillary action is to consider the equilibrium of forces involved (see diagram D.1.11/21). The rise of the liquid is due to the force with which the liquid is 'sucked up' in the capillary, while the extent of this rise (h) depends on the weight of the column of liquid (W) which opposes the sucking up force (F).

$$F = 2 \pi r \gamma \cos \theta \qquad (1)$$

where F is the force in dynes pulling the liquid up the capillary, r the radius of the capillary in cm, γ the surface tension of the liquid in dynes/cm at the temperature in question and θ the angle of contact in degrees.

$$W = r^2 hg \qquad (2)$$

where W is the weight in dynes of the column of liquid, h the height of the column of the liquid in cm and g the acceleration due to gravity (981 cm s^{-2}).

The force F is balanced by the weight W

$$W = F$$
$$\pi r\, hg = 2\pi r\gamma \cos$$

and

$$h = \frac{2\gamma \cos \theta}{rg}$$

It may be noted that the rise of a liquid only takes place when the angle of contact is *less* than 90 degrees.

To summarise then, the amount of rise of any given liquid in a narrow space will depend on:

(1) The extent to which the liquid wets the surface of the walls of the tube or space. Angles of contact are a guide; they must be *less than 90 degrees* for liquids.

(2) The force or weight carrying capacity of surface tension. The greater the force the greater the rise.

(3) The density of the liquid. Lighter liquids rise higher than the heavier ones, in tubes or spaces of the same bore.

(4) The diameter or width of the tube or space. The smaller the dimension the greater the rise for any given liquid.

2. Building significance

The simplest forms of capillaries encountered in building practice are those in the joints between abutting or overlapping units; the most complex are those resulting from the porosity of materials (see *1.12 Porosity*, p. 78). The capillaries in the porous materials influence both the absorption and drying out of water (see *3.03 Moisture content*). In

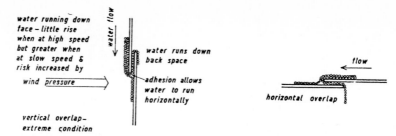

D.1.11/23 *Capillarity taking place without immersion*

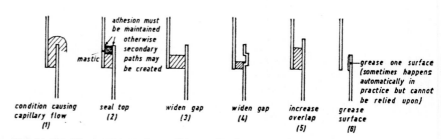

D.1.11/24 *Illustrations of possible methods of avoiding capillarity in overlapping joints (principle similarly applicable to butting)*

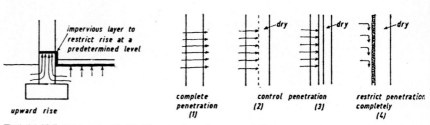

D.1.11/25 *Diagram (left) illustrating the principle of preventing upward rise of water. Four drawings on right illustrate the principle of preventing lateral penetration of water*

general terms all capillaries encountered in building practice are, when compared to the simple capillaries previously discussed, complex. Consequently, it is not always possible, or for that matter convenient, to evaluate the effects of capillaries encountered in building practice by means of formulæ. However, the results of investigations have enabled some fairly reliable rules to be established relative to given conditions and given materials. In recent years, it has also been shown that the angle of contact can provide a reasonable guide in some situations. Finally, it should be noted that capillary action is not confined to the rise of a liquid in truly vertical capillaries alone. Capillary action 'operates' even in horizontal capillaries and only ceases when a liquid flows in a downwards (as against an upwards or sideways) direction under gravity. However, the *rate* of liquid transfer is greatest when a capillary is horizontal.

It is normal to describe or illustrate capillary action by referring to narrow tubes immersed in a liquid and showing the rise in the tube above the level of the liquid in the larger container. However, it is possible for liquids to rise in capillaries provided the liquid is capable of reaching the orifice of the capillary. Under some conditions, therefore, it will be possible for sufficiently small quantities of liquid to travel as a small column up the complete height of a very narrow capillary. In building practice it is normal to have many different situations, as the illustrations in diagrams D.1.11/22 and 23 show, where water may reach the orifice of a narrow space. Of these, rainwater flowing down the surface of a wall tends to form a continuous, albeit moving, layer of water which is usually under pressure (wind blowing during rain—see *3.02 Exposure*). The effect of this is to increase the penetration of water, particularly in horizontal capillaries (porous materials and horizontal or bed joints are notable). On the other hand, as in the rise of ground water, the analogy of the tubes immersed in water applies almost completely.

It may be noted that evaporation from the exposed surfaces of the wall above ground level can provide an additional 'sucking up' force, which, subject to conditions, can be sufficient to 'pull' water well above the level to which it would rise if the sucking up force of the capillary action alone were operative. In effect the water will rise until the upward pull provided by evaporation is balanced by the weight of water in the capillaries.

In practical building terms every reasonable step should be taken to discourage capillary action at the interface of the junction of two or more units of materials. Some schematic examples of possible methods of avoiding capillaries are shown in diagram D.1.11/24—the widened gap in (4) is known as an *anti-capillary* groove.

In order to prevent the rise of water in porous materials either at or below ground level it is necessary for an impervious layer (d.p.c. or d.p.m. as relevant) to be inserted, as indicated in diagram D.1.11/25.

The basic methods by which water may be prevented from penetrating through a wall construction are either to provide a completely impervious skin (analogous to a raincoat) or to control the penetration of water into porous materials (see diagram D.1.11/25). As regards the porous materials, it is important to know how far water can be expected to penetrate into the material, how quickly this penetration will take place and how quickly the absorbed water will evaporate when the source of water has ceased. (A full discussion of all the factors influencing the use of both porous and impervious materials is given in *3.00 Water and its effects.*)

Viscosity

Viscosity is another property related to liquids. Under similar conditions water will flow much more easily than, say, oil, while oil more easily than treacle. Water is said to be *mobile* while the treacly variety is said to be *viscous*. However, water does have some viscosity, albeit very little. Thus liquids can be classified into those with very little viscosity grading to those with a very high viscosity. The latter in some cases almost resemble solids.

The amount of friction that exists within the interior of a liquid governs the amount of viscosity. In order to understand why there is any friction at all within the liquid, it is necessary to accept the principle that a liquid consists of various layers. During the flowing process, or to put it another way, for a liquid to flow, one layer of the liquid has to be able to slide past another. Frictional resistance between the various layers has to be overcome. Where this resistance is small, as in the case of water, the sliding takes place rapidly, resulting in the flow taking place easily. On the other hand, where the resistance is great, sliding cannot take place very rapidly and so flow takes place with more difficulty.

In general the denser the liquid the greater the forces of attraction between the molecules and hence the greater frictional resistance to be overcome. As temperature affects the forces of attraction between the molecules, viscosity can be reduced by increasing temperature, or increased by a reduction in temperature.

Viscosity does play an important part in some building operations and also in the manufacture of some materials. In *painting*, it would be difficult, if not impossible, to apply those ingredients which actually provide the protection and decoration, as these are highly viscous in their liquid state. For this reason a solvent or thinner which does not react chemically with the other ingredients is added to reduce viscosity for application. Once applied the solvent evaporates and leaves the essential ingredients behind. These in turn gradually become more and more viscous until the solid state is reached.

Asphalting is another operation which relies on accurate manipulation of the viscosity of the material and dexterity in application as the solid state is achieved in a comparatively short time.

The manufacture of *glass* also relies on the utilisation of the viscosity of the molten materials which gradually solidify.

In wet plastic mixes, such as mortars, plasters and concretes, water is used, among other things, to enable the dry materials to become, in some senses, viscous. Here the term *plasticity* is used rather than viscosity. Plasticity, that is ease of spreading a wet plastic mix, increases as the water content is increased and the greater the water content the greater the risk of shrinkage cracking, particularly in cement-based mixes. Consequently plasticity must be achieved by the use of specific materials (lime and special cements) or specially formulated additives rather than an increase of water. (For mortar mixes see *Section 3.04* under *Joint design.*)

1.12 porosity

Nowadays there are obviously many different ways in which materials could be classified. In fact, there are already quite a number which are related to a particular performance which materials are capable of, such as thermal insulation, sound insulation, absorption of water and so on. These classifications, useful as they may be, are in many ways restrictive, and do not necessarily cover the whole range of materials. Therefore, the traditional method of classifying building materials according to their basic structural arrangement, that is according to the quantity of air spaces they contain, is still useful. Furthermore, the *porous materials,* that is those which contain many voids or air spaces within their structure, and the *non-porous materials,* that is those with few voids or air spaces, in addition to their basic structural difference, do, in general terms, also show marked differences in their physical properties and behaviour. Of these, *one* of the most important is the difference in their performance in relation to water. Thus, on the whole, but with some exceptions, porous materials either absorb or allow the penetration of water, while non-porous materials, subject to no defects occurring, are generally impervious to water, although they may display some surface absorption.

Another distinguishing feature which to a large extent accounts for the difference in structure between the two groups is the methods of 'manufacture' in each case. The non-porous materials are all formed from the molten state and many of them have a crystalline structure as a result. Porous materials, on the other hand, have been formed either from materials containing vast quantities of water in their original form or water added or air trapped during manufacture.

As water absorption or penetration may in some instances be one criterion for the choice of a particular material it is worthwhile noting at this point that some impervious materials may at times allow water penetration. This sometimes occurs with granite, which to all intents and purposes can be regarded as an impervious material. Being a material of natural 'manufac-ture' it sometimes happens that very fine fissures occur through the body of the material. Under this condition water may, by capillary action, then penetrate through the material. For this reason some caution is required before deciding on the use of granite, or any other material liable to similar defects, in certain situations. In addition, careful selection to ensure the correct quality of the material concerned is also necessary.

It is convenient to discuss the formation and general characteristics of porous materials in detail, and then, with this as a basis, to compare briefly the characteristics of non-porous materials. Consequently of the four general headings used, three are related to porous materials. The headings are: (1) Pores; (2) Formation of pores; (3) Significance of pore arrangement; and (4) Non-porous materials.

Pores

In the earlier sections mention was made that atoms should not really be regarded as particles but rather as systems. The same also applies to the molecules of which any substance is made. Because of this there are likely to be spaces within the molecules, i.e. within the tangible particles. However, when considering building materials spaces *between* the particles of which the material is composed are referred to as 'pores'. These pores are air spaces or voids between the grains or tangible particles of which the material is composed. (Diagram D.1.12/1.)

Formation of pores

By definition all porous materials such as timber, brick, some stones, concrete, mortars, plasters, insulating and other boards, expanded polystyrene, etc., contain voids or air spaces. However, the actual structure and to some extent the physical behaviour of a material is dictated by the *arrangement* of the pores. Materials vary greatly in their arrangement of pores. Thus, in the case of timber the pores are highly regular in shape and more or less

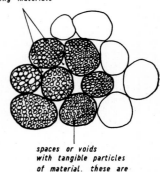

air spaces or voids <u>between</u> the tangible particles of material are regarded as <u>pores</u> in building materials

spaces or voids with tangible particles of material. these are <u>not</u> regarded as pores in building materials

D.1.12/1 *Diagrammatic representation of 'pores' in building materials*

evenly arranged in what is often termed a cellular structure. Brick and concrete on the other hand have pores which are irregular in both shape, size and number.

One important characteristic of the pores in most, though by no means all, materials is that they tend to form irregular capillaries. In materials like brick, sedimentary stones and concrete, for example, the pores form an extremely complex three-dimensional network—the three-dimensional aspect is important. In 1921, the American physical chemist Washburn* classified the pores in bricks into six types. Five of these, namely (1) channel, (2) loop, (3) blind alley, (4) pocket, and (5) sealed pores, are shown diagrammatically in diagram D.1.12/2. The sixth type, micro-pores, included all pores that are so small that water could not enter. Consequently the existence of these micro-pores has been doubted.

The formation of the pores in the various traditional materials has come about for different reasons but in nearly all cases it can be associated with the driving off of water, as

*Reference: Butterworth, B., *Bricks and Modern Research*, Crosby, Lockwood & Son Ltd., pp. 67–68, 1948.

Some examples of porous materials

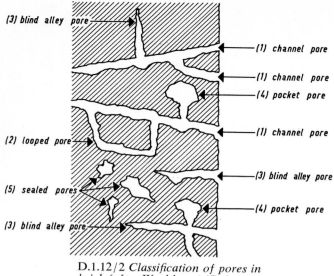

D.1.12/2 *Classification of pores in brick (after Washburn) (Reference: Butterworth, B., Bricks and Modern Research, Fig. 10, p. 68, Crosby, Lockwood & Son Ltd., 1948)*

Timber

Clay bricks and blocks

Sedimentary stones

described in the examples of timber, brick, sedimentary stones and concrete included below. An indication is also given of the methods by which pores are formed in the insulating materials.

1. Timber

During the growth of the tree the cells contain tremendous quantities of water (the water content of a growing tree is 50-200 per cent of dry weight). After felling and particularly during seasoning, a large proportion of this water is evaporated, resulting in the contraction of the cells. However, this contraction does not result in the fusing of the cell walls, so that there are still voids, minute as they may be, within the material. In some ways these voids are highly efficient capillary tubes. The shape and size of the capillaries are primarily dependent on the type of timber, as shown in the three photo-micrographs of transverse sections (p. 81). Although the capillaries do run through the height of the tree, they are by no means continuous and may also be broken by cells running in a radial direction. (See diagram D.1.06/1 (p. 43) included under 'Gels' in *Section 1.06*.)

2. Clay bricks

The raw material, that is clay, used in the manufacture of bricks, has to be mixed with water in order to obtain a mix of sufficient plasticity for moulding. The quantity of water varies with the type of clay. During the drying out which may include part of the burning or firing process the water is driven off. The voids left after the water has been driven off will, in varying degrees, be filled during vitrification, when part of the clay melts and sticks the rest together. The clay can be said, in some senses, to have closed up. The type of clay and its ability to close up, so to speak, after the water has been driven off will influence the size, shape and number of voids left in the material. In this context engineering bricks have very few if any voids, yet they are made of clay and water is used in their production. The amount of porosity varies enormously with different types of bricks, while there is usually quite a variation in the porosity of bricks of the same type.

3. Other bricks

Calcium silicate and concrete bricks may, in terms of the formation of pores, be considered in a similar way to concrete (see under *Concrete* below).

4. Sedimentary stones

These may be either lime- or sandstones which have been laid under or with the aid of water. In the case of limestones the essential grains consist of carboniferous matter including sea life, shells and the like, while sand or silica is the essential grain in sandstones as its name implies. Whatever the type, the grains were deposited in layers one on top of another with the water aiding the cementing together of the grains. In this various cementing agents were involved in the different stones. Voids previously occupied by the water were therefore left in the material once the water had evaporated; the size and number of voids depending to a large extent on the amount of water involved or trapped within the material before evaporation could take place.

5. Concrete

The quantity of water used in the making of concrete is only *one* of a variety of reasons for the presence of voids within the material. The size and shape of the particles used together with the degree to which these have been compacted before setting and hardening takes place are all contributing factors. However, when the water has evaporated it does tend to leave voids which, when all other things are equal, are minute particularly in well-made dense concrete.

Lightweight concretes, on the other hand, are specifically made with thermal insulation in mind, and consequently means are used to incorporate as many voids as possible. The voids may be incorporated by basically one of two methods. *Either* an aggregate which itself contains a high percentage of voids (exfoliated vermiculite, pumice, clinker, foamed slag, pulverised fuel ash, etc.) may be used *or* special processes may be used which encourage the formation of comparatively small but copiously distributed voids throughout the material. The

Lightweight concrete blocks

Fibreboards

Expanded polyurethane and expanded polystyrene. Right, woodwool slab (example shows special edge reinforcement sometimes used)

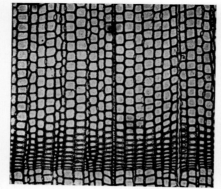

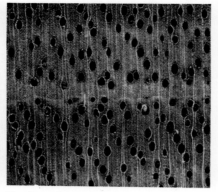

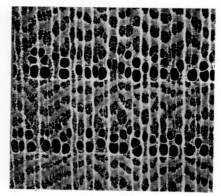

Softwood (Scots pine) ×75 magnification. Transverse sections which illustrate solids and voids in hardwoods and softwoods

Hardwood (Tasmanian oak) ×10 magnification

Hardwood (wych elm) ×10 magnification

1

2

Micro photographs (×20) showing the difference in internal arrangements of sedimentary stones (porous) and marble (generally non-porous). 1. Limestone. 2. Granite. 3. Sandstone. 4. Marble (Microphotographs prepared by the Geological Survey Museum and are published with the permission of the Controller HMSO (Crown Copyright))

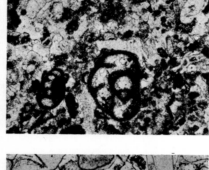

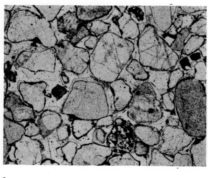

3

4

Illustration of the porosity of a Thermalite block (the block on the left showing the pores was used as sculptor's material)

An example of aerated concrete (Siporex) (Courtesy: Constern Concrete Ltd)

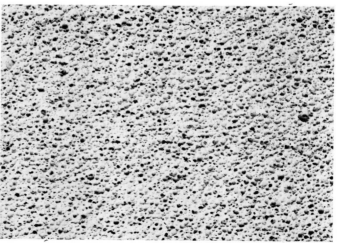

G

latter type of concrete is usually known as aerated concrete.

6. Mortars, plasters and renders

Mortars, plasters and renders are other porous materials in which water has been used and subsequently evaporated. The formation of the voids occurs for reasons similar to those already outlined for concrete, except that there are important differences in the way the mortars, etc., are placed and compacted. This usually results in materials with a higher percentage of voids than normally found in well-made dense concretes.

7. Insulating materials

Among the so to speak more recent and now more widely used porous insulating materials many have air entrained during manufacture.

Fibreboards consist of naturally occurring materials, such as timber, which have been reconstituted and then adhered together with the aid of heat and/or pressure. The amount of air or void in the material can then be controlled.

Glass wool is also manufactured in such a way that air is trapped between the fibres.

Expanded plastics. Of more recent origin are a whole range of *expanded plastics* (expanded polystyrene, polyurethane, PVC, rubber, ebonite, and phenolic, polyurethane and urea formaldehyde foams) each of which has a cellular structure. The many thousands of cells are each filled with air—the lightness of most of the materials (densities range between about 16 and 80kg/m³) is due mainly to the large proportion of air included (this may be up to 98 per cent). Air is entrained in all these materials as a result of the chemical reactions which take place in the relevant constituents during the setting and curing rather than as a result of the expulsion of water.

An important characteristic of the air cells in nearly all these materials is the fact that the cells are self-contained and not interconnected as in the case of most other porous

Photographs illustrating in very simple terms the preparation of concrete. Top, the dry materials. Middle, adding water. Bottom, the plastic mix. (Courtesy: Cement and Concrete Association)

Close-up of fibreglass Crown fibres. The fibres have been pulled apart slightly to show effect. (Courtesy: Fibreglass Ltd). Right, close-up of fibre insulating board showing the fibrous construction magnified six times. (Courtesy: Fibre Building Board Development Organisation)

materials. Consequently the materials do not normally possess much ability to absorb water, although some may be affected adversely by water. Some, such as urea formaldehyde foam which can be pumped into cavities, are of a greasy nature when set and consequently result in angles of contact (as far as water is concerned particularly) greater than 90 degrees. Fissures in materials such as these may not, therefore, allow capillary action.

Significance of pore arrangement

The *porosity* of any material is the ratio of the volume of voids in the material, and is usually expressed as a percentage as shown in the formula:

$$\text{Porosity} = \frac{\text{Volume of voids}}{\text{Total volume of material}} \times 100$$

Detailed knowledge of porosity as such does not usually have very much practical use. This is one of the reasons why there is not very much information available for all materials. Many of the actual properties of the porous materials are more dependent of the actual arrangement, size and shape of the pores.

The pores in porous materials may vary in shape and size, while they may or may not be linked by channels of pores. The channels may naturally enough be either fine or coarse. The properties set out below should serve as a *general guide* to illustrate the significance of the pores in a material. When considering various materials account must always be taken of the fact that the particular properties of the actual grains of which the material is composed will determine, however slightly, the general nature of the material itself.

1. Density

This is one property in particular that is dependent only on the nature of the grains and the air voids as such. Actual arrangement plays no part at all. Thus density decreases as the volume of voids increases.

2. Strength

Strength of porous materials is normally related to compressive or crushing strength only, as these materials are normally extremely weak in tension. One major exception is timber, which, on a mass for mass basis, is comparatively efficient in tension. This is mostly due to the particular cellular structure of timber. However, in general, strength increases as porosity decreases.

D.1.12/3 *Diagram showing pore structure absorption. Basic influencing factors (no account taken of 'sorption' by material itself, wind pressure, etc.)*

potential for water absorption.	surface pores	formation of pores into channels	interconnexion of channels
small	small area exposed	coarse	limited
large	large area exposed	fine	less limited

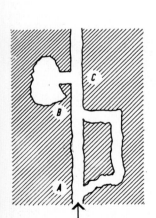

Water entering under the influence of capillarity, divides into two streams at 'A', one up the main channel and the other the loopway. Air is pushed out in front of each advancing stream. When main channel is full to point 'B', water is only half way round the loop, thus a small bubble of air is cut off. Water passing 'C' (entrance to pocket pore) is unlikely to allow all the air to escape.

D.1.12/4 *A simplified illustration of trapping of air in the pores of a brick when water soaks into it (Reference: Butterworth, B., Bricks and Modern Research, Fig. 11, p. 70, Crosby, Lockwood & Son Ltd., 1948)*

D.1.12/5 *Influence of pore arrangement on permeability*

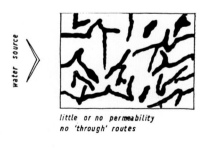

little or no permeability no 'through' routes

permeability 'through' routes

Some examples of non-porous materials

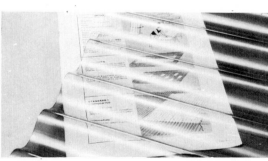

Polythene d.p.c. (Courtesy: Visqueen Ltd)

Marble and slates

Asphalt

PVC sheeting

Granites, slate and marbles

3. Absorption

Absorption, which takes place primarily by means of capillarity although diffusion of water vapour is also significant, is a very important property of porous materials. The actual amount affects the dryness of a material and also the defects which may arise from the action of water, with or without other agents.

Here a number of different factors may influence the amount of water that may be absorbed (diagram D.1.12/3). Firstly, the number of pores actually facing onto a source of water —the greater the number the greater the absorbing area of material. Secondly, the size and interconnection of pores—the smaller the pores and the greater the interconnexion by means of fine channels, the greater the amount of absorption. Finally, the absorbent nature of the 'grains' of the material itself by sorption. For most practical purposes it is usually sufficient to know the rate of absorption of the various materials, especially as the rate of evaporation is usually equivalent to the rate of absorption.

It is convenient to note here the fact that *saturation* of a porous material does not necessarily imply, in practical terms that is, that all the voids are filled with water. Among other things, it is impossible for water to gain access to sealed pores (see diagram D.1.12/2). On the other hand, the arrangement of the pores may result in certain quantities of air to be trapped in pores otherwise filled with water. The reason for this is explained in simple terms in diagram D.1.12/4. In practice it may well happen that after 'initial' saturation, the air trapped in the pores may find a way out, thus enabling further quantities of water to replace it. This for most practical purposes is insignificant. However, it is important to note that when materials are being tested for saturation in the laboratory, various methods, such as boiling for protracted periods, are employed in order to remove the air (except for sealed pores). The values so obtained are, therefore, likely to exceed those which should occur in most practical cases, extreme conditions apart.

4. Permeability

Permeability also affects dryness and the extent is dependent on the same factors as absorption, except here the number of 'throughways' in a material caused by interconnecting fine channels is especially important (diagram D.1.12/5). Again the rate at which water will permeate a material is important. Permeability only occurs as a result of 'through' routes in materials and so it is not essential that any given material should first become saturated.

5. Moisture content

The water absorbed by a material will cause the material to undergo a movement due to the expansion which takes place; on evaporation shrinkage causes a movement in the other direction. The actual amount of movement will to a large extent be dependent on the amount of water absorbed plus the actual nature and behaviour of the material when water is being taken in. (See *Section 1.06* under 'Gels', p. 42). Highly absorbent materials are therefore likely to have greater movements.

6. Thermal insulation

As *still dry* air is a most efficient insulator, it follows that the thermal insulation provided by a material will increase as porosity increases. For the greater part this is true, but here the nature of the grains of material will be important plus any 'through routes' for heat along the grains. As will be shown later insulation plays an important part in condensation problems. At the risk of over-generalising at this stage, it is true to say that porous materials, as a group, help to counteract the formation of surface condensation.

7. Sound insulation and absorption

Problems connected with sound are more involved with complete structures than with individual materials. Thus, subject to exact structural implications, the denser the material the better it is likely to act as an insulator against *sound transmission*. The precise arrangement of pores does not play a very important part.

For *sound absorption* on the other-hand, and especially high frequency sound, the lighter the material the greater the absorption. In this case pore arrangement is important as greater absorption is obtained when in addition to interior voids there are many connecting surface pores. Some materials do, in fact, have this requirement greatly enhanced by mechanical means with the creation of holes and grooves. For utmost efficiency the latter should never be covered by 'impervious' materials such as paint.

Finally, treatment of *impact sound* requires the use of resilient materials, which normally contain many air cells. The structure of the cells do have to ensure that the material is capable of 'springing back' after vibration. Special springs, sometimes used, would not have any porosity at all.

8. Surface texture

Subject to manufacturing techniques porous materials have inherent characteristics for the provision of surface texture, as compared to non-porous materials where surface texture has to be 'contrived'.

Non-porous materials

Non-porous materials as already stated are those which have been formed from the molten state, whether naturally, as in the case of granites, or artificially, as in the case of metals, glass, bitumen and plastics.

Marbles and slates are virtually non-porous for most purposes. These have been formed naturally due to the application of heat and pressure on other stones which have in the process undergone a metamorphosis.

Non-porous materials which are completely impervious to water penetration are used in those situations where the passage of water must be completely prevented. They therefore constitute many of the materials used for damp proof courses. Some of the non-porous materials may not be completely impervious to water *under pressure,* but may be impervious enough to water vapour. In many constructions it is now necessary to incorporate moisture vapour barriers, so these materials find a useful place. The impervious nature of most of the non-porous materials enables thin sections of materials such as metals, glass and plastics to be used as external claddings for both walls and roofs.

As a group, non-porous materials differ from the porous materials in important ways. Generally non-porous materials are:

1. Dense

Density is primarily influenced by the density of the particles of which the material is composed. (Plastics are often important exceptions.)

2. Strong

Strength is also dependent on the strength of the particles, but in the case of metals the crystal formation or 'grain' is important. There are wide variations under strength, but nevertheless some of the metals, and particularly steel, are exceptionally strong in tension. (See *2.02 Mechanical properties* and C.2.02/1, p. 99.)

3. Impervious

With some exceptions, non-porous materials are impervious to water under normal conditions.

4. Non-weathering

Non-porous materials, although they may be corroded under suitable conditions, are not subject to weathering or the action of salts in the same ways as porous materials.

5. Without surface texture

Surface texture *has* to be applied either by moulding or mechanical means.

6. Good conductors of heat and sound

Non-porous materials tend to permit readily the passage of heat and sound. Because of the former they can be said to favour the formation of condensation.

2.00 strength of materials

introduction

Strength is at once a basic property of all solid materials and one of the most important properties of materials used in buildings. Irrespective of any other property or properties which a material may possess for a particular use, it must, above all else, be able to withstand any loads which may be imposed on it during 'its working life', and which can be reasonably forecast. In this context any loads would also include those imposed by the material's own self-weight. In short, therefore, no material can perform its function properly if, during use, it is unable to carry loads without undue distortion or structural failure.

In very general terms the strength of a material is its actual ability to sustain loads without undue distortion or failure. This ability is dependent on two closely inter-related primary factors. One of these is the strength that is inherent in the material itself and which is measured by its mechanical properties. The other is concerned with the way in which the inherent strength is employed through the size and shape of the material and the method of loading, i.e. the application of a force or forces. The latter factor, i.e. the employment of the mechanical properties of a material, forms the subject of structural mechanics. Thus mechanical properties of materials and structural mechanics are in many ways inseparably tied.

In the design of the structure of a building, i.e. those members such as foundations, walls, columns, beams, floors and roofs which actually contribute to the stability of the building, the close inter-relation of mechanical properties and mechanics is a fairly specialised one due to a large extent to the complexities which arise in practice. However specialised or involved these aspects may be it is usually possible to translate the most complex structural behaviour in terms of the behaviour of members under simple loading conditions. Furthermore, a better understanding of the meaning and importance of the mechanical pro-

perties of materials is obtained if the materials are considered when they are actually loaded. Although there is no intention of discussing structural mechanics in any great detail, it is still necessary to consider those basic aspects which are relevant to simple static loading, and which produce axial tension, axial compression, simple bending, shear and torsion. As already noted, the complex nature of stresses in actual structures may very often be explained or predicted on the basis of materials or members under simple conditions of loading. However, it is important to emphasise that *none* of the considerations given in this study will be sufficient to undertake structural designing. For this standard works must be consulted.

Loading and the effects it has on the mechanical behaviour of materials is obviously of primary importance in any considerations of the basic structure of buildings. However, it does also play an important part in understanding the reasons and causes of cracking of materials in use. In this elements other than the basic structure, such as non-loadbearing partitions, wall and floor finishes, etc., are included. The inherent strength of materials also influences the way in which materials may be used in such operations as bending, shaping and fixing or, on the other hand, the performance of materials when subjected to abrasion and impact as commonly occurs on floor finishes and working surfaces, etc. Finally, strength also plays an important part in the resistance materials will provide to impacts commonly encountered in buildings.

In order to deal with all aspects of the strength of materials it has been convenient to divide the whole part into the following general headings:

1. Elementary considerations of strength

This heading is intended to serve as an introduction to the whole subject.

It deals with methods of loading and the behaviour of materials subjected to loading. In the main an attempt has been made to explain both the structural mechanics and the behaviour of materials by essentially simple means and without getting involved with specific mechanical properties.

2. Mechanical properties

All the essential mechanical properties are included together with values as applicable. In some cases it has been possible to give an indication of some of the uses of these properties and also reasons for variations which occur in different materials.

3. Cracking in buildings

The basic causes of cracking in buildings are discussed in some detail. As cracking is not confined to finishes, considerations of complete elements such as walls, roofs, floors, etc., are included.

4. Strength and the use of materials

Under this heading shaping, cutting and fixing of materials, abrasion and impact damage are considered.

References

BUILDING RESEARCH STATION, *Principles of Modern Building*, Volumes 1 & 2, HMSO, 1961.
HANDISYDE, CECIL, H., *Building Materials: Science and Practice*, Architectural Press, 1966.
LISBORG, NIELS, *Principles of Structural Design*, Batsford, 1967.
MORGAN AND WILLIAMS, *Structural Mechanics*, Pitman, 1968.
PASCOE, K. J., *Introduction to the Properties of Engineering Materials*, Blackie, 1961.
RICHARDS, CEDRIC W., *Engineering Materials Science*, Chapman and Hall, Chapters 3–10 incl. and Chapter 12, 1961.
ROSENTHAL, WERNER, *Structural Decisions* Chapman and Hall, 1962.
RYDER, G. H., *Strength of Materials*. Cleaver-Hume, 1961.

2.01 elementary considerations of strength

The mechanical properties of materials (and their derivatives) are values which result from the testing of samples of materials (or values calculated from test results). As such the values are 'cold' and without meaning. In addition there are a number of terms which are used in connection with both mechanical properties and structural mechanics — the two inevitably overlap. In order, therefore, to attempt to give the properties a little more meaning and to make them a little more understandable, *an elementary consideration of strength* is given in this section. At the risk of over-simplification a number of non-technical terms are used, while at the same time a liberal extension of some technical terms is made.

In an attempt to provide some basis for assessment the following general limitations have been made: (1) Loading of materials is only considered in relation to the slow application of a force. Loading which may occur over a period of time or of a momentary nature will constitute a variation. The extent of such variation will be given under mechanical properties as relevant in *Section 2.02*. (2) All materials are considered to be subjected to what may best be termed 'room temperature' environment. Temperatures above or below this standard will alter the amount of strength involved but will not generally alter the principles being discussed or explained. (3) No material used in building is really pure. In this consideration normal building purity is assumed. Thus any abnormal impurity will cause a change in the strength properties of any material.

Forces and their representation

Forces and strength of materials are inseparably connected. No material 'displays' its strength qualities until it is acted upon by a force. An explanation of forces and the manner in which they act on a material and the manner in which they are influenced by external physical conditions is covered generally in *Part 1.00* and particularly in *Section 1.07*. Here it should, therefore, suffice to reiterate that a

force acting on a body (hereafter termed the 'acting force') always produces a *reacting force* in the body (hereafter termed the 'counteracting force').

Because of the importance of force both in relation to strength and also for structural mechanical reasons, it is normal to represent forces quite simply by means of arrows. The arrows used are intended only to show the direction of the force and do not normally give an indication of the intensity of the force, other than by actually writing the value on or near the relevant arrow stem. (For comparative purposes it is sometimes convenient to use various thicknesses of the stem of the arrow so as to be able to indicate relative intensity.) By using arrows it is also possible to show quite easily the acting and counteracting forces which may be acting on a point.

In practice it is not very often that a force actually acts on a point. It is more usual for the force to act over an area, however small. Some areas, on the other hand, may be relatively small while others may be relatively large. In order to differentiate between the relatively small and relatively large area a simple device is usually employed. For the 'small' area a single arrow would be used. A typical example of a force which would be represented by a single arrow is the force in the rope or wire of a crane lifting a load. Another simple example which is considered to impose *a point load,* are the legs of pieces of furniture supported on a floor. The actual representation of these and other forces is shown in diagram D.2.01/1.

For the large area a number of arrows fairly close together covering the total 'width' of the load is used to simulate what is otherwise known as a *distributed load*. Some distinction has to be drawn between uniformly distributed loads and those which are non-uniformly distributed. For clarity the latter could be considered as a series of point loads or merely shown in triangular or other similar form depending on the non-uniformity. (See diagram D.2.01/1.)

Finally it should be noted that arrows are also used to indicate the

direction of movement. Such movement may be as a result of temperature or moisture content changes. The use of the same 'symbol' for different things can be useful, as the direction of movement can also indicate at the same time the direction of force which may be involved, especially when members are restrained from actual movement. This is clarified under 'Loading'.

Deformation

The term *deformation* has a rather specific meaning when considered in relation to the strength of materials. Here it is used in the physics sense to refer to the *changed shape* of a material and which has occurred as the result of the application on or inducement of a force in a material. Infinite rigidity cannot be found in any material and so all materials are capable of undergoing a change in shape, that is, being deformed. The degree of change will depend on the amount of strength inherent in the material and the intensity of the acting force.

All materials are used in specific shapes and sizes for specific uses and so it is against the particular shape and size that is used in a given situation that the deformation which may result from an acting force must be related. Thus no material which is 'fit for use' in the structural sense can be said to be deformed just because 'it looks' disfigured.

Looked at in another way, every material has an 'original' shape and size and it is against this original shape and size that any deformation must be gauged. Diagram D.2.01/2 shows simple examples of original and deformed shapes.*

It is also important to note that deformation as such does not imply that there has been any structural failure of a material. It only means that there

*It is important to note that it is common to refer to steel reinforcing bars which have been specially processed so as to have a surface pattern, as 'deformed bars'. The term is not used in the strictly structural sense, but mainly to differentiate these bars from ordinary steel reinforcing bars which have no special surface texture or pattern. (Examples of deformed bars are included in *Section 2.03*, under 'Cracking due to externally applied loads', p. 112.)

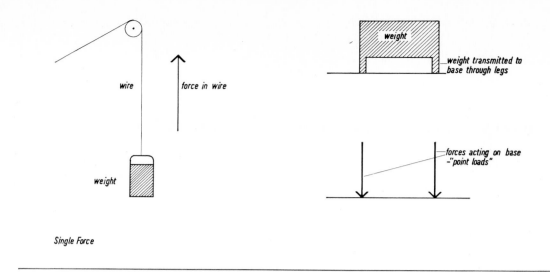

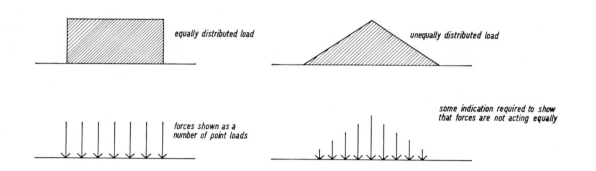

D.2.01/1 *Diagrammatic representation of forces*

has been a change in the dimensions of a member due to an acting force. This is relevant because many materials will, within limits, spring back to their original dimensions when the acting force is removed. Thus they are only deformed while under load. As there are infinite degrees of deformation the precise state that has occurred should be stated.

Loading

The term loading as used in structural mechanics has a fairly restricted meaning although it has many applications.* It simply implies that some weight has been imposed on a structural member or element and may also include the manner in which this weight has been imposed. As load is a weight it is measured in newtons (N). When it is distributed over an area it is

*See British Standard Code of Practice, *Loading*, CP3, Chapter V, 1952, for structural mechanical use. It is important to note that this code was shown to be out of date and in need of revision by the Ronan Point tribunal (Report published in November, 1968) particularly in so far as wind loading on high buildings is concerned. As an interim measure refer to *Wind loading of buildings* 1 & 2, BRS Digests (2nd series) Nos. 99 & 101, HMSO, November, 1968 & January, 1969. (The new CP3, Part 1 *Loading*, 1967 deals only with dead and imposed loads. Wind loads will be dealt with in Part 2.)

measured per unit area (N/m²).† For the purposes of examining and understanding the strength of materials in general and not only the way in which this strength is applied to the basic structure of building alone, it is more convenient to expand the meaning of the term. This may reasonably be done when it is considered that the application of a load on a material is virtually the same thing as saying that a force has been applied. Also forces may act on materials in ways other than by means of simple weights or load. Furthermore, whenever a force is applied to a body some counteracting force is supplied by the body in its attempt to *either* prevent a change in its position or more important, in this context, to prevent its being deformed. Thus, *loading* in the wider meaning which is used here *implies both an acting force* and *a counteracting force*. By using the term in this way it is then possible to include all ways in which forces may be set

†In the British system, units of weight used are mainly tons-force and pounds-force (loosely referred to as tons and pounds) and for distribution, tonf/ft², lbf/ft², etc. It is important to note that whereas in the British system units of mass and weight are for practical purposes interchangeable, in SI it is necessary to multiply mass in kilograms by standard acceleration (9·806 65 m/s²) to obtain weight in newtons (N). See also *Section 1.07*.

up in materials due to the application of external forces by whatever means, and in which the strength of materials plays a part.

There are two distinctly different types of loading, namely *direct* and *indirect*.

1. Direct loading

Direct loading is in many ways the more easily understood and perhaps the more obvious method of loading. In all cases the load can either be seen (physical weights) or felt (wind pressure). Thus, it is in simple terms the imposition of weight. The most elementary case occurs when a material has to support its own weight. Here it is convenient to consider the whole of the material as consisting of a number of layers. Each layer is then supporting the weight of the layer or layers above it or, conversely, each layer transmits its own weight to the one underneath. Thus, the layers at the 'top' support the layers at the 'bottom'. (Top in this context means any position furthest away from the gravitational pull of the earth, while bottom means any position nearest to the gravitational pull.) Diagram D.2.01/3 illustrates the transmittance and support of weight. The 'layer' principle is not restricted to whole materials but is also equally applicable to units of material, such as bricks, etc., which are built up one on top of the other, as will be seen in the photograph. In these examples the material or element remains static because it is prevented from movement by virtue of being supported. Support may be provided in a number of different ways. The most obvious one is the ground on which the foundation, and hence the whole of any building, is supported.

If the support is taken away the force created by the weight will cause the material or element to move. The object or material providing the support is, therefore, itself subject to loading. This is a case of a superimposed load, which is static and is said to be a 'dead load'. Other loads caused by moving objects, such as people moving across a floor, are not static and are said to be 'live loads'. Thus live loads are in some ways forms of vibration, although they are not necessarily dealt with as such.

Pressure due to wind produces a special kind of superimposed load. This load may act in a variety of different ways. In triangulated structures, for example, such as occurs in a pitched roof, the forces will be trans-mitted along the members making up the triangulation. Therefore, the direction of the force is not always downwards, but is governed by the direction of the exerting force and the arrangement of the members forming the triangulation.

On vertical or flat surfaces the situation is similar in many respects to a simple superimposed load. Again the method of transmission of the force through the structure is complex.

2. Indirect loading

Indirect loading is slightly more complicated than direct loading in that the source of the weight or load is not seen or felt. In some ways the directional operation of forces in a triangulated structure already mentioned and other similar structures may in some ways be regarded as indirect loading.

However, indirect loading is more relevant to (and is, therefore, being restricted to) situations where materials are restrained from movement. Because of the restraint, forces are set up within the material very much in the same way *as if* the material had been subjected to a superimposed load. Detailed reasons why there should be

a force set up within a material will be given when stress and strain are considered later (*Section 2.02*). Suffice it to say here that there are many instances in building practice when movement of materials may take place. In all cases where the movement is re-strained, that is, actually prevented from taking place, there is 'induced deformation'. The induced deformation may be initiated by a number of causes, chief of which are: changes in the moisture content of a material; changes in the temperature of the material; and chemical actions.

Both moisture content and temperature changes may result in either expansion or contraction, while chemical action normally results in expansion only.

Under normal unrestrained conditions any material or member subject to these changes will change its shape and form following normal physical laws discussed in *Part 1.00* and no forces will be set up within the material. (Excessively rapid changes may sometimes cause the structural failure of a material, if the rate of change is such that forces are set up within the material and with which the material cannot 'cope'.) However, if the material is, in fact, prevented from having its dimensions changed 'naturally', it counteracts this restriction by having forces set up within itself. In this way it does in a sense use its strength to maintain its rigidity or shape. Here again, whether or not it will eventually deform or rupture will depend partly on the force which is being exerted caused by the change which should and cannot take place and partly by the strength of the restraint placed on the material. In all cases of restraint the member or element actually being restrained will automatically apply a force on the member or element causing the restraint. Thus, the restraining member will also be subject to loading. The application and possible effects of forces in restrained members is illustrated in diagram D.2.01/4.

It is important to note, in principle at any rate, that materials should always be allowed to 'breathe', that is move, if there is a likelihood of *excessive* forces being set up due to indirect loading and which may cause failure of *either* the restrained *or* restraining member. Generally speaking most materials can accommodate small amounts of movement while being restrained. However, each material and condition requires to be examined on its own merits.

All cases of indirect loading are particularly relevant when considering the *cracking of materials*. In many cases cracking results from materials or members being restrained, as shown in *Section 2.03*.

Behaviour of members subject to loading

When considering the behaviour of materials subject to loading it is more

original + load = deformation

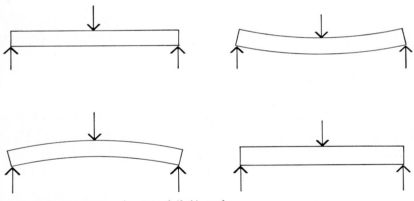

D.2.01/2 *Comparison of original (left) and deformed (right) shapes*

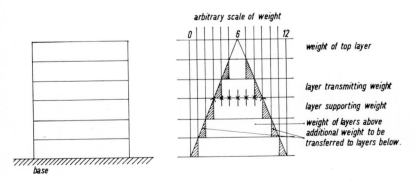

Elevation of Solid Material divided into layers.

Graphical Representation of Weight Distribution.

D.2.01/3 *Transmittance and support of weight in a solid material using the principle of layers*

realistic to consider not the material itself, but rather the material in the form of a member, that is, a material with a shape and size. The application of forces in various ways can then be related to the member.

1. Overall effect of loading

The nature of the counteracting force which a member subject to loading provides is entirely dependent on the direction of application of the acting force (in some degree the method of application is also important) relative to the actual shape and size of the member. In all, five basically different conditions are created in so far as the nature of the counteracting forces which may be set up are concerned within the member as a whole. These forces and the conditions which they create within a member are known as: *tension, compression, shear, bending* and *torsion*.

The application of the acting force relative to the shape and size of a member to produce any one of these counteracting forces is shown in diagram D.2.01/5.

2. Subsidiary reactions

In addition to the overall effect of loading on the member as a whole there are also subsidiary reactions which affect each part of the section of a member. This is accounted for by the fact that, as the application of the acting force does not occur at a point but over an area of the member, there is a subdivision of the acting force into a number of subsidiary forces, that is, the acting force is resolved into other forces. These then are the subsidiary forces which act over the area of the section of the member. In this way the acting force is transmitted throughout the whole of the member, with each subsidiary force counteracted by a force within the member.

Two examples will serve to illustrate the principle at work. Firstly, in bending part of the section is in tension and part is in compression. Secondly, in torsion the forces may be resolved into shear. As a consequence it is possible within certain limitations to consider that an acting force will in effect only produce, as far as each part of the section of a member is concerned, only three counteracting forces: *tension, compression* and *shear*.

At this point it should, however, be emphasised that these three counteracting forces represent simplification of the many complex forces, often 'intermingled' within a member, and the resolution of which requires structural mechanical analysis. Nevertheless these are the basic or elementary forces at work, and as a result are the only ones which are considered throughout this study.

3. Resistance by particles

A member setting up a *tensile* counteracting force is in effect trying to prevent the particles of the material

Brickwork supported on a plinth. An example of a direct application of the layer principle of transferring weight shown diagrammatically in D.2.01/3

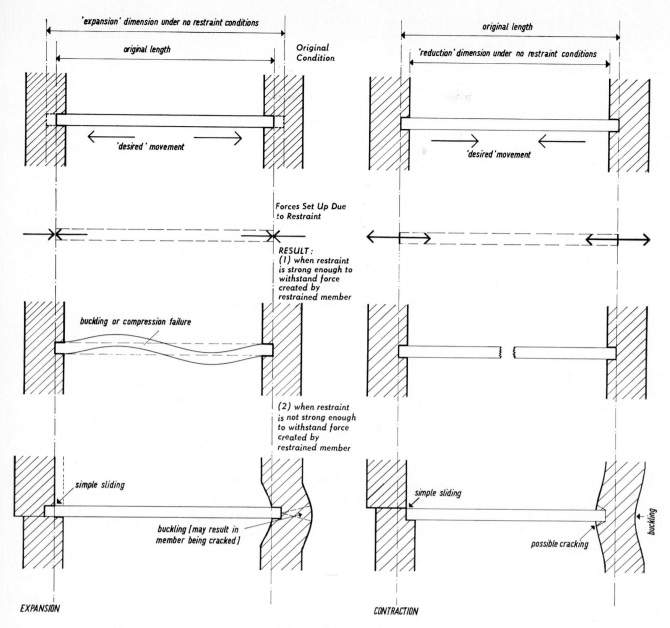

'expansion' dimension under no restraint conditions

original length

Original Condition

'desired' movement

Forces Set Up Due to Restraint

RESULT:
(1) when restraint is strong enough to withstand force created by restrained member

buckling or compression failure

(2) when restraint is not strong enough to withstand force created by restrained member

simple sliding

buckling [may result in member being cracked]

EXPANSION

original length

'reduction' dimension under no restraint conditions

'desired' movement

simple sliding

possible cracking

buckling

CONTRACTION

D.2.01/4 Diagrammatic representation of forces set up due to restraint (expansion and contraction) and two possible failures which may result

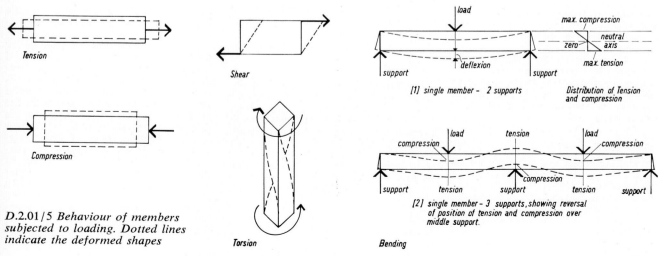

Tension

Compression

Shear

Torsion

load

deflexion

support   support

max. compression

neutral axis

zero

max. tension

[1] single member – 2 supports

Distribution of Tension and compression

compression   load   tension   load   compression

support   tension   compression   support   tension   support

[2] single member – 3 supports, showing reversal of position of tension and compression over middle support.

Bending

D.2.01/5 Behaviour of members subjected to loading. Dotted lines indicate the deformed shapes

of which the member is composed being torn apart. In other words there is resistance to the stretching of the member. On the other hand the *compressive* counteracting force tends to prevent the particles being crushed, that is, prevents shortening of the member taking place.

Thus in general terms the particles of which materials are made are either resisting being torn apart or crushed together. In this, account has also to be taken of the direction in which the stretching or shortening is taking place. In the case of *shear,* resistance to both stretching and shortening is, in fact, taking place at the same time.

As the internal structure of materials, and particularly of the solid matter of which materials are composed, may vary a great deal, it follows that there is bound to be a wide difference of behaviour of different materials due to different structural arrangements. Thus under loading the structural arrangement of the solid particles will play an important part in the strength properties possessed by materials.

Structural arrangement in materials and strength

The actual ability that all the solid particles of which a material is composed may have in resisting being torn apart or crushed together is dependent on the strength of the forces which, in fact, not only maintain all the atoms and molecules of the individual particles but also the groups of particles of any material, in 'fixed' positions. One of the basic characteristics of solids, as explained in *Section 1.03,* is that their particles can only move about a mean position. This characteristic, in fact, differentiates solids from liquids and gases, where the particles are freer to move about.

1. Types of particles in materials

All materials for building are aggregates of many different kinds of solid particles, each different kind of particle in the material having its own particular properties. Thus, the actual proportions of the various kinds of solid particles *together* with their structural arrangement, both individually and as a group, affect the overall strength which a material may offer to being deformed.

As far as the strength properties of the individual particles of any aggregation are concerned, it is possible to divide these into *two* broad groups, namely, crystalline and amorphous (see *Section 1.04*).

(a) *Crystalline solids*

Crystalline solids are generally *anisotropic,* that is, their properties are not the same in all directions. This means that the solid will deform more readily in one direction. Thus, the direction of the application of a force relative to the orientation of a crystal in which

deformation takes place most easily, is important.

(b) *Amorphous solids*

Amorphous solids, however, are *isotropic,* that is, they have the same properties in all directions. And so, the direction of the applied force is not important.

2. Effect of bonding

In any aggregation there may be wholly crystalline, wholly amorphous or a combination of both types of solid particles which make up the actual material. The strength properties of the aggregation do not necessarily follow the same general rules as those applicable to the individual particles. This is due to the fact that there are many different ways in which the individual particles may be bonded one to another.

(a) *Metals*

At one extreme there are the metals which are completely crystalline. The individual crystals (or grains as they are normally termed) orientated at random within the material, are bonded one to another by a secondary crystal structure at the boundaries of the various grains. These grain boundary crystals have considerable strength even in excess of the strength of the grains which they are bonding together. The overall effect of this type of combination, consisting of anisotropic* solid particles, is to make the material as a whole *isotropic.* Thus, the strength properties are the same in all directions. It is the randomness of orientation of the grains which imparts this isotropy, mainly because the grains are all acting in different directions at the same time while under load, and thus are 'cancelling out' the anisotropy of the individual grains.

Another important consideration of the crystal structure of *metals* is the fact that the material as a whole can be said to be, in the context implied here, *homogeneous.* This is important because the material generally has the same resistance to both tensile and compressive forces.

(b) *Granites*

By contrast, in *granites,* which also consist of a crystalline structure, the position is somewhat different. Here the material is *heterogeneous,* as it consists of crystals of different kinds. Thus although the material is itself *isotropic,* it does not have the same resistance in tension and compression. In fact the compressive resistance is much higher than the tensile resistance.

*The fact that there are a number of crystals which are anisotropic does not materially alter the principle being outlined.

(c) *Porous materials*

The more traditional and porous materials, such as *bricks, other clay products, stone and concrete* (and excepting timber), are quite different. These materials may consist of either crystalline or amorphous solids (or a combination of both). There are usually a number of different kinds of solids which have been aggregated. The actual bonding of the various solid particles also takes place in a variety of different ways. Whereas the metals may broadly be said to bond together by cohesion, these porous materials are bonded together by adhesion. Thus, among other things, interlocking plays an important part. In many cases too the matrix, that is, the adhesive material, in which the basic particles are held, may itself be either crystalline or amorphous.

However, the materials are still considered to be *isotropic,* although they do have quite different resistances in tension and compression. As it is generally more difficult to crush than to stretch anything, these materials are on the whole much stronger in compression than in tension. Most other porous materials have similar characteristics.

(d) *Timber*

Timber, essentially a fibrous and, as important, a natural growing material with directional grain, is one of the porous materials which is essentially *anisotropic.* Thus, the strength properties are governed very much by the direction of an applied force which in this case must be related to the fibres of the member—that is, the direction of the grain. Unlike the other porous materials, timber has, subject to the direction of the applied force, almost equal strength in both tension and compression. It must be emphasised that *the direction of the grain* (which should not be confused with those in metals) in any member is important relative to the direction of the applied force.

(e) *Plastics*

Finally, the *plastics* consist essentially of amorphous solids, although there may be some crystallinity which for the purposes required here is of little importance. The materials are all *isotropic.*

Although it is not general policy to include any reference to special loading-, temperature- or time-dependent properties in this section it is important to make some general observations in connection with the plastics. Compared to other materials they are more susceptible to changes in their strength properties under long-term loading; the thermoplastics particularly are prone to a lessening of their strength properties even under moderate increases of temperature. In general, therefore, plastics are far more sensitive to changes in their environmental conditions than most other 'traditional' materials.

The basic mechanisms of elastic and inelastic action

The term counteracting force has been used in a general sense but at the same time it is also in a more specific sense the summation of the mechanisms which are at work whenever a material is subjected to an acting force. None of the generalisations already used explains why it is that materials are actually capable of withstanding the action of acting forces, however small, without, at best, permanent deformation, or, at worst, complete structural failure (or rupture). In addition, all materials may, within limits, be temporarily deformed while subjected to a force, but are capable of returning (sometimes better described as 'springing back') to their original shape and form, once the applied force has been removed.

In this the manner in which the atoms and/or molecules of which the material is composed may take up positions *outside* their equilibrium positions plays an important part.

Of primary importance is the fact that the atoms and/or molecules are *actually* able to take up new positions outside their equilibrium positions, without causing a complete breakdown of a material. And, as important, also the fact that they can, within certain limits, return to their equilibrium positions once the acting force has been removed. In addition, and in the extreme cases of permanent deformation, the atoms and/or molecules are capable of remaining locked in new positions, setting up new equilibrium positions, and in this way still allowing the material, in its deformed state, to retain a good deal of its strength. In cases such as these, the material takes on new strength characteristics. Thus, although the deformed material is not capable of fulfilling its original structural requirements, based on its original shape and form, it is capable of fulfilling structural requirements based on its deformed shape and form. Obviously the deformation implied here means that a material is still structurally intact, with no rupturing of any kind.

The mechanisms which are involved during temporary deformation are known as *elastic action*, while those which take place after the temporary deformation limit has been exceeded and which result in either permanent deformation or rupturing are known as *inelastic action*.

When considering the mechanisms involved in both elastic and inelastic action it is preferable to use as a basis the idealised state of a crystalline structure, such as a metal, where the mechanisms are comparatively simple and operating at their maximum efficiency. Variations which occur in other types of structure, and particularly amorphous solids like plastics where the mechanisms are far more complex, can be related to the basic mechanism as applicable to metals. Slightly different factors are at work

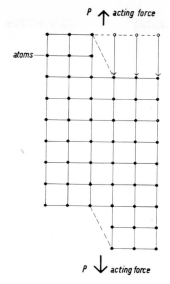

D.2.01/6 *Diagrammatic representation of slip of one section past another in a crystal. Total slip = 2 atomic distances (*based on 'Engineering Materials Science' by Richards*)

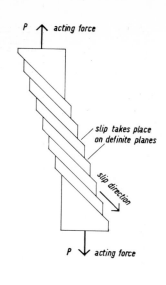

D.2.01/7 *Slip plan and direction of slide in a single crystal. Compare with photograph of slip bands at bottom of page*

in tension and compression. Tension and compression are therefore dealt with separately.

1. Elastic action

(a) Tension

The elongation which takes place when a solid metal bar is subjected to a tensile acting force can be visualised as a simple separation of the atoms in the direction of the acting force. Under normal conditions the bonds between the atoms ensure that the atoms are maintained away from each other in their equilibrium positions. The result of the application of an acting force is to force the atoms out of equilibrium. In the process of the atoms being displaced from their normal equilibrium positions, additional attractive forces are created between the atoms sufficient to balance the intensity of the acting force. Within limits these attractive forces are sufficiently strong enough to allow the atoms to stretch to new positions while the force is applied. On removal of the acting force the atoms are allowed to return to their equilibrium positions. When this happens the bar will have returned to its original shape and size and an *elastic deformation* is said to have taken place. (It may be noted here that the ability of atoms to stretch to

new positions with the attendant attractive forces that are created, is the way in which enough energy is stored by the atoms in order that they may spring back to their original equilibrium positions. The energy required is, in fact, 'taken from' the work done by the acting force. This accounts for what is known as Strain Energy and which is outlined in more detail in *Section 2.02*). This action is the result of the combined actions which take place in the individual crystals of which the material is composed. Each of these crystals has only one definite plane along which the atoms which make up the crystal can move—this particular movement is known as the slipping of the atoms, and the plane along which it takes place is known as the *slip plane*. For movement to take place the force has to be applied with a particular relationship to the direction of the slip plane, as shown in diagrams D.2.01/6 and 7. During slipping, the atoms move to positions previously occupied by other atoms. In this way the basic structural pattern of the crystal is maintained. The actual slipping which takes place is a kind of shearing action as shown in the diagrams. (It should be noted that the different crystal types, that is, face-centred, body-centred and hexagonal, have different directions of slip.)

Photograph shows slip bands on extended copper-aluminium single crystal (Elam)

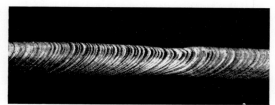

As the aggregation of crystals which occurs in *metals* are orientated at random the result is that the slip planes of the individual crystals are in different directions. Thus when an acting force is applied those crystals whose slip planes suitably related to the direction of the force will begin to slip first (regarded in this context as weak crystals). However, their slip is retarded and restrained by neighbouring crystals which have different directions of slip. The net effect is that a greater force is required to cause the material to slip as a whole, than would be required if all the slip planes had been orientated in the same direction relative to the acting force. One other factor which adds to the force required to cause slip is the fact that the crystal structure at the grain boundaries offer far greater resistance to slip than do those crystals in the interior, i.e. those which are joined together by the boundary crystal structure.

In amorphous materials and particularly *the plastics* a variety of mechanisms are involved. Basically there is also a displacement, but here of both atoms and molecules. During the slipping process the molecules (long chain) do slip past one another, but bonds between the molecules are more often broken as fast as they are re-formed. Under most short-term loading the process is similar to metals.

The complexities which exist in *porous materials* is accounted for by the fact that the individual particles of solid matter cannot 'act together' as in the case of metals. Also the restraining action of different orientation of crystals cannot work in the same way because of the way in which the whole aggregation of solid particles is held together. Elastic action of the various solid particles therefore takes place separately and, generally speaking, because of the overall weakness of bond between them, porous materials are, except for timber, rather weak in resisting tension.

(b) *Compression*

Elastic action in compression in non-porous crystalline metals is exactly the same as in tension except that the whole action takes place in the reverse direction.

In porous materials the action also takes place in the reverse direction. However, these materials, with the exception of timber, are capable of withstanding greater compressive forces, and also possess more elasticity in this condition. This is partly accounted for by the fact that, whereas in tension there is very little to stop slipping from taking place, in compression the physical juxtaposition of all the particles is an aid to providing some measure of restraint. The position is further complicated by the fact that the voids which occur in all porous materials result in the formation of 'walls' within the whole material. These walls then act almost as if they were structural members and their behaviour must be dealt with

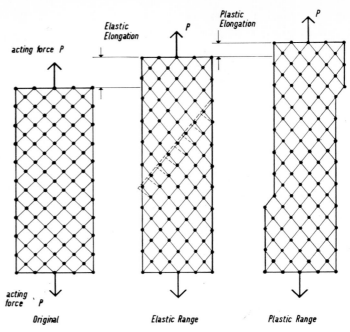

D.2.01/8 *Diagrammatic representation of slip in a single crystal in tension and showing elastic and plastic elongation (based on 'Engineering Materials Science' by Richards)*

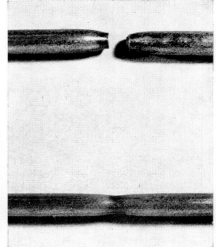

Detail of cup-and-cone fracture in a tensile test specimen of manganese bronze after necking

Above, 'necking' in a steel bar in tension. Fracture, i.e. rupture, has occurred at the 'necking' position of the top bar in tension

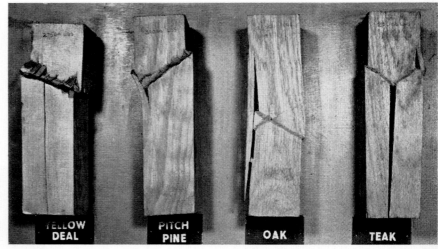

Types of failure in timber when subjected to compression parallel to the grain

accordingly. All these factors do contribute to explain why it is that most of these materials exhibit wide variations in the actual values of their strength properties.

2. Inelastic action

(a) *Tension*

The inelastic action that does occur cannot be idealised in the same way as elastic action. This is due to the fact that although inelastic action eventually leads to rupturing of a material, materials differ quite considerably in their behaviour after the elastic range has been exceeded. (Behaviour which takes place after the elastic range, with rupturing excluded, is known as *yielding*.)

After the elastic range some materials fracture immediately without warning; others yield, that is, the dislocation of the atoms proceeds, albeit at a different rate, before final fracture occurs. Materials which fracture immediately after the elastic limit has been exceeded are said to be *brittle*; those which exhibit the greatest amount of yielding are said to be *ductile*. Materials in between these two extremes may generally be said to have *low-ductility*. Brittleness in materials is due to imperfections and these imperfections actually initiate the fracture.

Ductile materials have an important characteristic, especially in tension. Once the elastic limit has been exceeded the atoms are capable of reforming bonds in their new positions. The elongation which occurs after the elastic range is irrecoverable, once the acting force is removed. (The elastic range is still, however, recoverable.) During this process the material is said to be in a *plastic* condition, and so the deformation which remains after removal of the acting force is said to be *plastic deformation* while the deformed material is said to have a *permanent set*. Thus the material still possesses strength properties because the atoms have remained in new equilibrium positions. (Diagram D.2.01/8.) Once the plastic range has been exceeded rupturing occurs usually after the material has 'necked'—the break occurs at the smallest part of the neck. (Ductility in many metals and particularly copper in the annealed state is utilised when thin wire is required, as the metal is capable of being drawn without rupture.)

In the case of amorphous materials the mechanisms are again more complex. Yielding does take place when the long chain molecules slip past one another. However, reforming of bonds takes place as fast as the bonds are broken with the result that there is no maintaining of strength. Provided the acting force is maintained the molecules continue to slip. This is true viscous flow which is a characteristic of amorphous solids.

(b) *Compression*

In tension, failure of a homogeneous non-porous material occurs because there is a limit to the strength that is available between the atoms. However, in compression, there is theoretically no limit to the repulsive force which may exist between atoms. Thus inelastic action in compression in these materials has to be accounted for by the shearing action which occurs on inclined planes.

Ductile materials, whose bonds can be easily reformed do yield to the same intensity as in tension. In brittle materials, on the other hand, where bonds cannot be easily reformed slip leads to fracture with the bonds permanently ruptured. Fracture may occur along either a single shear plane or a number of small fractures on shear planes in all directions. Fracture usually occurs somewhere between these two.

In porous cellular materials (most materials in this context are cellular because they all contain voids however small) the complexities associated with elastic action are carried through to the inelastic range. Final fracture usually occurs when there is a failure in the cell walls mentioned earlier. Most of the porous materials like brick, stone and concrete are extremely brittle. Fracture, therefore, takes place along slip planes near maximum shear, as in the case of those metals which are also brittle.

2.02 mechanical properties

Stress and strain

Stress and strain are two related phenomena which are involved in elastic action when a member is acted upon by a force. *Stress* is concerned with the manner in which the acting force is transmitted over the section of the member, that is, the internal distributive force, while *strain* is concerned with the deformation caused by the acting force. Both stress and strain are also applicable during any inelastic action but in this case they are not so closely related as during an elastic action.

1. Stress: (f)

Stress is the sum total of all the elementary atomic forces (outlined in *Section 2.01*) which act over the section of a member when an acting force is applied to the member. In other words stress is the counteracting force which is distributed uniformly or in some other way over the area of the section of the member and which is set up to balance the intensity of the acting force. Stress has the same intensity at any plane along the length of the member.

The intensity of stress, commonly known merely as stress, is calculated by taking the intensity of the force (or load) transmitted across *any* section divided by the area of that section, and may be written as:

INTENSITY OF STRESS=

$$\frac{\text{ACTING FORCE (OR LOAD)}}{\text{CROSS SECTIONAL AREA}}$$

It is thus *force per unit area* and the standard SI unit is the Newton per square metre, N/m^2. As this unit is extremely small for structural calculations the accepted unit is MN/m^2 and may be written in the form N/mm^2.*

*In the British system units commonly used are either lbf/in^2 or $tonf/in^2$.
where: $1 lbf/in^2 = 6\ 894 \cdot 76 N/m^2$
$0 \cdot 000\ 145 lbf/in^2 = 1 N/m^2$
$1 tonf/in^2 = 15 \cdot 444\ 3 MN/m^2$
$0 \cdot 064\ 759 tonf/in^2 = 1 MN/m^2$

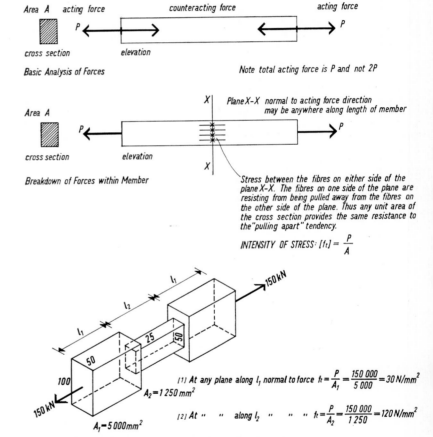

Area A   acting force   counteracting force   acting force

cross section   elevation

Basic Analysis of Forces   Note total acting force is P and not 2P

Area A   Plane X-X normal to acting force direction may be anywhere along length of member

cross section   elevation

Breakdown of Forces within Member

Stress between the fibres on either side of the plane X-X. The fibres on one side of the plane are resisting from being pulled away from the fibres on the other side of the plane. Thus any unit area of the cross section provides the same resistance to the "pulling apart" tendency.

INTENSITY OF STRESS: $[f_t] = \dfrac{P}{A}$

[1] At any plane along l_1 normal to force $f_t = \dfrac{P}{A_1} = \dfrac{150\ 000}{5\ 000} = 30\ N/mm^2$

[2] At " " along l_2 " " " $f_t = \dfrac{P}{A_2} = \dfrac{150\ 000}{1\ 250} = 120\ N/mm^2$

$A_2 = 1\ 250\ mm^2$

$A_1 = 5\ 000\ mm^2$

Example of a Member with different Cross Sections [dimensions in mm].

D.2.02/1 *Illustration of direct tension and intensity of stress*

The normal symbol used to denote stress is *f*.

Direct stresses occur when the section of a member is normal to the plane of the acting force. Thus direct stresses may occur either in tension (f_t) or in compression (f_c). These are explained in diagrams D.2.02/1 and 2.

In the case of shear stress (f_s) the situation is different and a little more complicated. The stress involved is not direct. Here the acting forces are not in the same plane—they are still equal and opposite—as shown in diagram D.2.02/3. One part of the body must, therefore, resist sliding over another part. Thus shear stress, which is only an average, is tangential to the area over which it acts, i.e. the plane is measured parallel to the acting forces. Pure shear exists most commonly in riveted joints. Another factor to be noted is that shear stress is accompanied by an equal complementary shear stress on planes at right angles. These complementary shear stresses play an important part in the failure of anisotropic materials, such as timber which is weak in shear along the grain.

The limit of intensity of stress which a given material can withstand is termed *ultimate stress.* Failure of the material occurs once the ultimate stress has been exceeded. Because of the different mechanisms which may be involved prior to the failure of different materials, ultimate stress may not necessarily, for design purposes at any rate, mean stress just before physical fracture (see *Factor of safety,* p. 108). However, values for ultimate stress can be taken, unless otherwise stated, as the limit of intensity of stress which a given material can withstand.

For design purposes some measure of safety has to be 'built into' the stresses which may be used. These design stresses are known as permissible or working stresses and may be put into a formula as follows:

PERMISSIBLE (OR WORKING) STRESS =

$$\frac{\text{ULTIMATE STRESS}}{\text{FACTOR OF SAFETY}}$$

2. Strain: (ϵ)

Strain is concerned with the alteration of the form and dimensions of a member which result from stress. It is a measure of the deformation produced in a member by an acting force and relates change in form (length, width, depth or volume) with the original form of the member, i.e. prior to loading. It may be written as:

$$\text{STRAIN} = \frac{\text{CHANGE IN FORM}}{\text{ORIGINAL FORM}}$$

and is defined as a *ratio.* It is thus *dimensionless.*

For most practical purposes strain is confined (unless otherwise stated) to changes in *length* only and so may be written as:

$$\text{STRAIN} = \frac{\text{CHANGE IN LENGTH }(\delta)}{\text{ORIGINAL LENGTH }(l)}$$

The methods of evaluating strain for tension, compression and shear are shown in diagram D.2.02/4.

3. Relationship between stress and strain

Elasticity is that property of a material which enables it to return to its original shape and form once the stress causing the deformation has been removed. The maximum stress at which complete recovery of the material can take place is known as the *elastic limit.* Comparative graph C.2.02/1 shows the relationship between stress and strain for both the elastic and inelastic range for a typical ductile metal. (The relationship which occurs in materials with low ductility and those which are brittle is compared with the ductile metal in C.2.02/2.) The graphs are drawn for materials under tension. The principle of the strain slope is generally applicable in compression.

(a) *Elastic range*
Within the elastic range there is a proportional relationship between stress and strain. *Hooke's Law* states *that strain is proportional to the stresses*

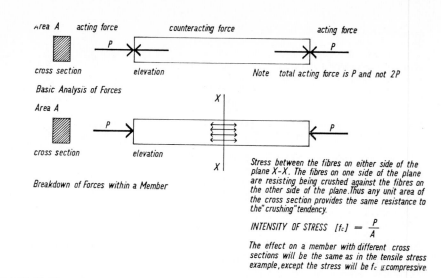

Basic Analysis of Forces

Breakdown of Forces within a Member

Note total acting force is P and not 2P

Stress between the fibres on either side of the plane X–X. The fibres on one side of the plane are resisting being crushed against the fibres on the other side of the plane. Thus any unit area of the cross section provides the same resistance to the "crushing" tendency.

$$\text{INTENSITY OF STRESS } [f_c] = \frac{P}{A}$$

The effect on a member with different cross sections will be the same as in the tensile stress example, except the stress will be f_c ᴇ compressive.

D.2.02/2 Illustration of direct compression and intensity of stress

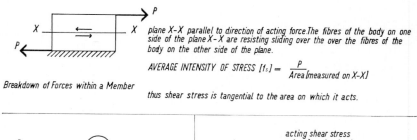

Breakdown of Forces within a Member

plane X–X parallel to direction of acting force. The fibres of the body on one side of the plane X–X are resisting sliding over the over the fibres of the body on the other side of the plane.

$$\text{AVERAGE INTENSITY OF STRESS } [f_s] = \frac{P}{\text{Area}} \text{ [measured on X–X]}$$

thus shear stress is tangential to the area on which it acts.

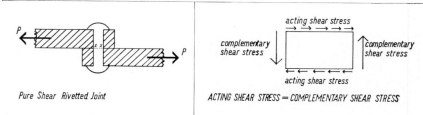

Pure Shear Rivetted Joint

ACTING SHEAR STRESS = COMPLEMENTARY SHEAR STRESS

D.2.02/3 Illustration of simple shear and average intensity of stress

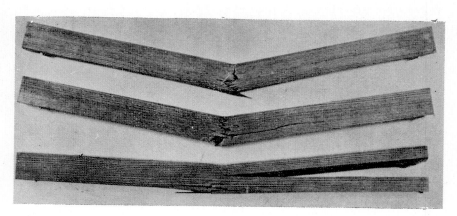

Examples of the shearing that occurs in timber, along the grain, in types of failure that have resulted from static bending and impact bending tests (Courtesy: Forest Products Research Laboratory (Crown Copyright))

H

producing it. This applies up to the 'limit of proportionality' and is true for ferrous metals. However, it is also generally assumed to apply to all other materials. The elastic limit sometimes occurs beyond the limit of pro-portionality, and although Hooke's Law does not apply in this range, materials will nevertheless recover the strain produced by stresses when the stresses are removed.

The Principle of Superimposition states that the resultant strain caused by a number of acting forces will be the sum of all the strains produced by each force.

(b) Inelastic range

Once the elastic range has been exceeded there is no proportional relationship between stress and strain. In fact, in the inelastic range com-paratively small *additional* stresses are required to produce relatively large amounts of strain.

The lack of any proportional relationship between stress and strain in the elastic range does not necessarily imply that a material will not recover elastic strain on removal of the stress causing it. For many materials there is a range between the elastic limit and ultimate stress, known as the *plastic range*. The limit of this range is indicated by point D. On removal of the stress in the plastic range, the material will generally recover the elastic strain, while there will be a certain amount of irrecoverable strain, that is, *permanent deformation* (OG). During unloading the strain slope will follow DG. Any subsequent reloading of the deformed section will give a strain slope GD with D being the new elastic limit. This is also shown dia-grammatically in C.2.02/3. An impor-tant consideration arises here. The deformed section requires the same amount of acting force as the original section to reach its own elastic limit which is higher than that for the original section. This is accounted for by the fact that the deformed section is *smaller* in area (the example shows tension) and hence there is a higher stress in the member. Deformed sec-tions, therefore, have smaller loading capacity when compared to the original section. For this reason among others it is generally agreed that no material should, for safety, be strained beyond its elastic limit.

In most ductile metals as yielding progresses an ever-increasing stress is required to produce further yielding. This is due to the dislocations which occur in the crystals whereby the metal offers increasing resistance to further deformation. This phenomenon is known as *strain-hardening* (sometimes also *work hardening*) and takes place when the metal is cold. The effect of strain-hardening is an increase in the strength but a decrease in the ductility of the metal. In industry this charac-teristic is used to strengthen ductile metals during cold working processes as shown in diagram D.2.02/5.

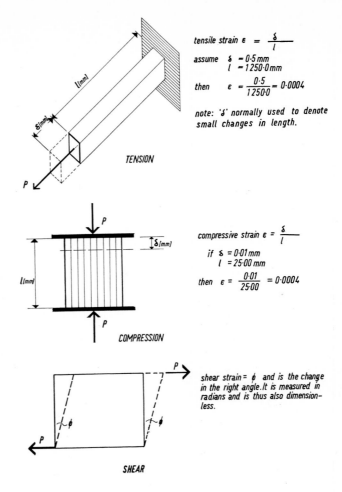

tensile strain $\epsilon = \dfrac{\delta}{l}$

assume $\delta = 0.5\,mm$
$\quad\quad\quad l = 1250.0\,mm$

then $\epsilon = \dfrac{0.5}{1250.0} = 0.0004$

note: 'δ' *normally used to denote small changes in length.*

TENSION

compressive strain $\epsilon = \dfrac{\delta}{l}$

if $\delta = 0.01\,mm$
$\quad\quad\; l = 25.00\,mm$

then $\epsilon = \dfrac{0.01}{25.00} = 0.0004$

COMPRESSION

shear strain $= \phi$ *and is the change in the right angle. It is measured in radians and is thus also dimension-less.*

SHEAR

D.2.02/4 *Illustration of the calculation of tensile, compressive and shear strain*

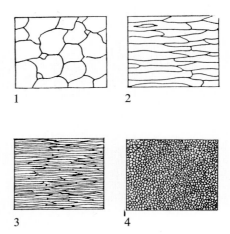

D.2.02/5 *The effects of cold working on the grains of a pure metal. 1. Original grain structure. 2. Grain structure after moderate deformation by cold working. 3. Grain structure after more severe deformation by cold working. 4. Recrystallized grain structure after hot working*

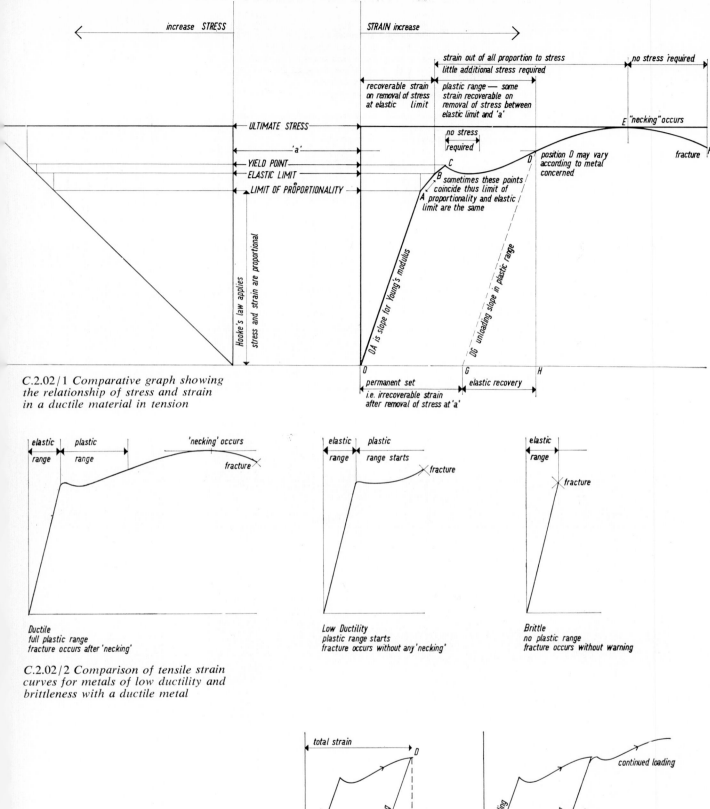

increase STRESS

STRAIN increase

strain out of all proportion to stress
little additional stress required

no stress required

recoverable strain
on removal of stress
at elastic limit

plastic range — some
strain recoverable on
removal of stress between
elastic limit and 'a'

ULTIMATE STRESS

E "necking" occurs

'a'

no stress
required

fracture F

YIELD POINT

position D may vary
according to metal
concerned

ELASTIC LIMIT

C

LIMIT OF PROPORTIONALITY

B sometimes these points
coincide thus limit of
proportionality and elastic
limit are the same

A

Hooke's law applies
stress and strain are proportional

OA is slope for Young's modulus

DG unloading slope in plastic range

O   G   H

permanent set

elastic recovery

i.e. irrecoverable strain
after removal of stress at 'a'

*C.2.02/1 Comparative graph showing
the relationship of stress and strain
in a ductile material in tension*

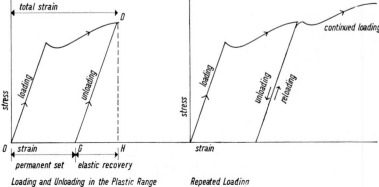

elastic
range

plastic
range

'necking' occurs

fracture

Ductile
full plastic range
fracture occurs after 'necking'

elastic
range

plastic
range starts

fracture

Low Ductility
plastic range starts
fracture occurs without any 'necking'

elastic
range

fracture

Brittle
no plastic range
fracture occurs without warning

*C.2.02/2 Comparison of tensile strain
curves for metals of low ductility and
brittleness with a ductile metal*

total strain

D

stress

loading

unloading

O   strain   G   H

permanent set   elastic recovery

Loading and Unloading in the Plastic Range

continued loading

stress

loading

unloading

reloading

strain

Repeated Loading

*C.2.02/3 Stress and strain relationship
in tension for loading and unloading
in the plastic and repeated loading*

99

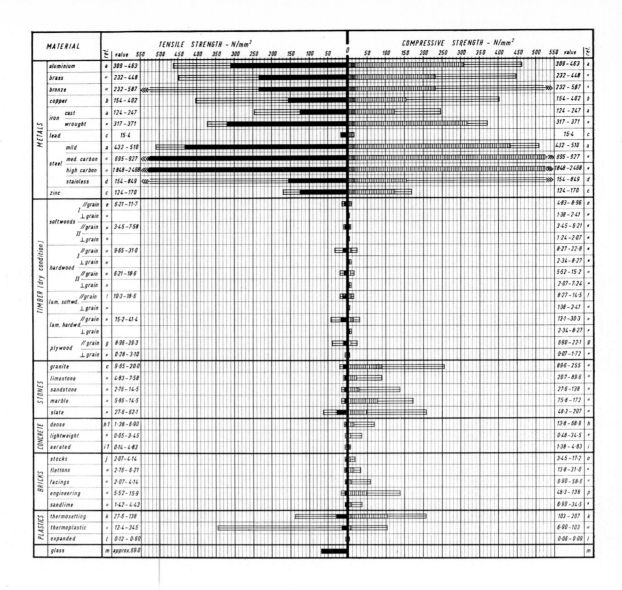

MATERIAL		ref.	value (Tensile Strength N/mm²)	Compressive value	ref.
METALS	aluminium	a	309–463	309–463	a
	brass	"	232–448	232–448	"
	bronze	"	232–587	232–587	"
	copper	b	154–402	154–402	b
iron	cast	a	124–247	124–247	a
	wrought	"	317–371	317–371	"
	lead	c	15·4	15·4	c
steel	mild	a	432–510	432–510	a
	med. carbon	"	695–927	695–927	"
	high carbon	"	1848–2468	1848–2468	"
	stainless	d	154–849	154–849	d
	zinc	c	124–170	124–170	c
TIMBER (dry condition)	softwoods I //grain	e	6·21–11·7	4·83–8·96	e
	I ⊥grain	"		1·38–2·41	"
	II //grain	"	3·45–7·58	3·45–6·21	"
	II ⊥grain	"		1·24–2·07	"
hardwood	I //grain	"	9·65–31·0	8·27–22·8	"
	I ⊥grain	"		2·34–8·27	"
	II //grain	"	6·21–18·6	5·52–15·2	"
	II ⊥grain	"		2·07–7·24	"
lam. softwd.	//grain	f	10·3–18·6	8·27–14·5	f
	⊥grain	"		1·38–2·41	"
lam. hardwd.	//grain	"	15·2–41·4	13·1–30·3	"
	⊥grain	"		2·34–8·27	"
plywood	//grain	g	8·96–39·3	6·90–22·1	g
	⊥grain	"	0·28–3·10	0·07–1·72	"
STONES	granite	c	9·65–20·0	89·6–255	c
	limestone	"	4·83–7·58	20·7–89·6	"
	sandstone	"	2·76–14·5	27·6–138	"
	marble	"	5·86–14·5	75·8–172	"
	slate	"	27·6–62·1	48·3–207	"
CONCRETE	dense	h1	1·38–6·90	13·8–68·9	h
	lightweight	"	0·05–3·45	0·48–34·5	"
	aerated	i1	0·14–4·83	1·38–4·83	i
BRICKS	stocks	j	2·07–4·14	3·45–17·2	o
	flettons	"	2·76–6·21	13·8–31·0	"
	facings	"	2·07–4·14	6·90–58·6	"
	engineering	"	5·52–15·9	48·3–138	p
	sandlime	"	1·42–4·43	6·90–34·5	"
PLASTICS	thermosetting	k	27·6–138	103–207	k
	thermoplastic	"	12·4–345	6·90–103	"
	expanded	l	0·12–0·60	0·06–0·09	l
	glass	m	approx. 69·0		m

C.2 02/4 Comparative chart of tensile and compressive strengths of various materials

Notes: 1. All values are stresses at breaking except timber where working stresses are given. 2. Tensile stresses for timber, stone and brick are in bending. 3. Compressive stresses of the metals are taken to be the same as tensile stresses, although this may not be strictly true in all cases

REFERENCES:
(a) 'Properties and strengths of materials', by J. A. Cormack and E. R. Andrews
(b) Copper Development Association
(c) Civil Engineering Reference Book—Volume 1
(d) Firth-Vickers Ltd.
(e) Forestry Research Products Bulletin No. 47
(f) Forestry Research Products Special Report No. 15
(g) Forestry Research Products Bulletin No. 42
(h) BRS Digest 5 (second series)
(h1) Taken as 1/10 of (h)
(i) BRS Digest 16 (second series)
(i1) taken as 1/10 of (i)
(j) BRS Special Report 21
(k) 'The Properties and Testing of Plastics Materials' (Lever and Rhys)
(m) 'Glass, in Architecture and Decoration' (McGrath and Frost)
(o) National Building Studies Bulletin No. 3
(p) National Building Studies Bulletin No. 4

C.2.02/5 Comparative chart of I/E for steel and aluminium, which shows the deformation in each material assuming the same load and section. Values are relative units

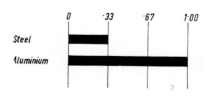

1. *Wrought brass . . .*

2. *hot rolled at 694 degrees C . . .*

3. *reduced 60 per cent by cold rolling*

4. *recrystallized by annealing
one hour at 599 degrees C*

Elastic constants

Elastic constants are relationships between stress and strain or longitudinal and lateral strain, and which, therefore, determine the deformations produced by a given stress acting on a particular material. Although these constants are used mainly in structural design they are also useful in determining the stress created in materials which are restrained from movement.

Whereas stress and strain are evaluated from physically measured values, i.e. load, extension, contraction, cross sectional area, the elastic constants are calculated from the evaluated values.

1. Modulus of elasticity (Young's Modulus (E))

The modulus of elasticity or Young's modulus (E) as it is more commonly known is the ratio of the direct stress to the strain produced by that stress, and may be written as:

$$\text{YOUNG'S MODULUS } (E) = \frac{\text{STRESS } (f)}{\text{STRAIN } (\epsilon)}$$

and is expressed in N/mm^2. (The standard SI unit is N/m^2 but see *Intensity of stress* and related footnote for the equivalent in the British system on page 96.)

This modulus applies only within the limits of Hooke's Law and, therefore, is constant for a given material. Furthermore, it *is assumed* to be the same in either tension or compression.

Young's modulus represents the stress required to cause unit strain. Comparison of the values of (E) for various materials will indicate the relative amount of deformation that will occur assuming the *same* load and the *same* section of the various materials. As an example compare steel and aluminium.

The value of E for steel is $207 \times 10^3 N/mm^2$ and for aluminium is $69 \times 10^3 N/mm^2$. The ratio between these two is $3:1$. This means that *section for section,* for the same deformation, steel requires three times the load as aluminium. It follows that *load for load* and *section for section,* aluminium will deform three times as

Illustration of the fact that the structure of a wrought metal need not be changed by hot working but is strongly influenced by cold working. Note that microstructures, 1, 2 and 4 are alike except for incidental difference in grain size (Photomicrograph at ×75 reproduced at $\frac{2}{3}$ size) (Courtesy: American Brass Co.)

much as steel. This is shown in the comparative chart C.2.02/5.

E values for a selected range of materials is given in comparative chart C.2.02/6. In some materials like concrete there may be considerable variations in the elastic limits with corresponding variations in the modulus of elasticity. In these cases *mean values* are usually used. For design purposes other factors such as creep have to be taken into consideration and so in some cases, concrete is again an example, *effective* moduli of elasticity are used.

The use of the E value for determining the stresses created when a member is restrained from movement is given in diagram D.2.02/6. In the example given there will be no failure of the steel beam as the compressive stress caused by the restraint is *below* the permissible stress for steel.

2. The modulus of rigidity (C)

Young's modulus is the ratio of stress and strain in tension and compression. The ratio that exists in shear is known as the Modulus of Rigidity (C) and may be written as:

MODULUS OF RIGIDITY (C) =

$$\frac{\text{SHEAR STRESS}}{\text{SHEAR STRAIN}}$$

and is also expressed in N/mm². This modulus also only applies within the limits of reliability of Hooke's Law. Moduli of rigidity of some materials are given in comparative chart C.2.02/7.

3. Poisson's ratio (l/m)

For most purposes strain is normally considered in relation to the length of a member (longitudinal strain). In addition to this longitudinal strain there is also a lateral strain on both dimensions of the section. As an example, and as shown in diagram D.2.02/7, in tension a bar will increase in length but at the same time will be reduced in its sectional dimensions. Within the limit of proportionality it has been shown that the lateral strain is proportional to the longitudinal strain and is of the opposite type. This ratio, known as Poisson's ratio, may be written as:

POISSON'S RATIO (l/m) =

$$\frac{\text{LATERAL STRAIN}}{\text{LONGITUDINAL STRAIN}}$$

as produced by a single stress. As both the strains are dimensionless, the *ratio* is also *dimensionless*.

Originally Poisson determined from theoretical considerations the particular value $\frac{1}{4}$ for isotropic material. Experiment has shown, however, that metals do not depart far from the true value. Nevertheless there are different values for different materials ranging from $\frac{1}{3}$ to $\frac{1}{4}$, with a value of $\frac{3}{10}$ taken for metals. (India rubber has a value of $\frac{1}{2}$.)

An example of the use of Poisson's ratio is given in diagram D.2.02/8.

C.2.02/6 Comparative chart of Moduli of Elasticity (E) of various materials

REFERENCES:

(a) 'Materials and Structures' by E. H. Salmon
(b) Copper Development Association
(c) Civil Engineering Reference Book—Volume 1
(d) Forestry Research Products Bulletin No. 47
(e) Forestry Research Products Special Report No. 15
(f) Timber Development and Research Association
(g) 'The Chemistry of Cement and Concrete' by F. M. Lea
(h) BRS Digest (2nd Series) No. 16
(i) BRS Special Report No. 22
(j) 'The Properties and Testing of Plastics Materials' by A. E. Lever and J. Rhys
(k) Airscrew-Weyroc Ltd.

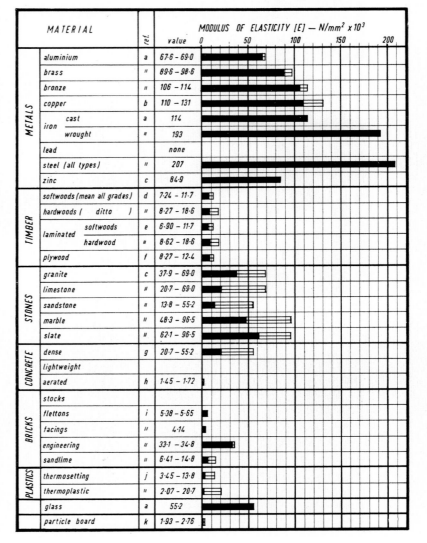

	MATERIAL	ref.	value
METALS	aluminium	a	67·6 – 69·0
	brass	"	89·6 – 98·6
	bronze	"	106 – 114
	copper	b	110 – 131
	iron cast	a	114
	iron wrought	"	193
	lead		none
	steel (all types)	"	207
	zinc	c	84·9
TIMBER	softwoods (mean all grades)	d	7·24 – 11·7
	hardwoods (ditto)	"	8·27 – 18·6
	laminated softwoods	e	6·90 – 11·7
	laminated hardwood	"	8·62 – 18·6
	plywood	f	8·27 – 12·4
STONES	granite	c	37·9 – 69·0
	limestone	"	20·7 – 69·0
	sandstone	"	13·8 – 55·2
	marble	"	48·3 – 96·5
	slate	"	62·1 – 96·5
CONCRETE	dense	g	20·7 – 55·2
	lightweight		
	aerated	h	1·45 – 1·72
BRICKS	stocks		
	flettons	i	5·38 – 5·65
	facings	"	4·14
	engineering	"	33·1 – 34·8
	sandlime	"	6·41 – 14·8
PLASTICS	thermosetting	j	3·45 – 13·8
	thermoplastic	"	2·07 – 20·7
	glass	a	55·2
	particle board	k	1·93 – 2·76

MODULUS OF ELASTICITY [E] — N/mm² × 10³

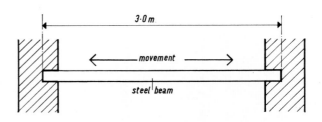

D.2.02/6 Calculation of stress caused by restraint using E value

Restrained expansion = 1·5mm

E for steel = 200×10^3 N/mm²

Permissible compressive stress for steel = 140 N/mm²

Stress produced: $fc = \epsilon$ (strain) $\times E$

$$= \frac{1·5}{3000} \times \frac{200\,000}{1}$$

$$= 100 \ N/mm^2.$$

C.2.02/7 Comparative chart of Moduli of Rigidity (c) of various materials. (Average values only given)

REFERENCES:
(a) 'Strength of Materials' by G. H. Ryder
    (Clever-Hume—third edition)
(b) 'Materials and Structures' by E. H. Salmon
    (Volume 1—Longmans)

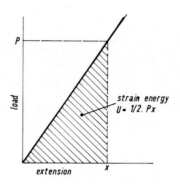

Material	Ref.	Av. value	MODULUS OF RIGIDITY [C] $N/mm^2 \times 10^3$
Brass	a	379	
Bronze	a	448	
Cast iron	a	414	
Copper—hot rolled	b	386	
hard drawn wire	b	483	
Duraluminium	a	262	
Glass	b	221	
Mild steel	a	793	
Nickel chrome steels	b	793	
Timber	a	10·3	

D.2.02/7 Below, an illustration of lateral contraction which occurs when a member is extended, i.e. during tension, for use in determining Poisson's Ratio. In compression there is a lateral extension

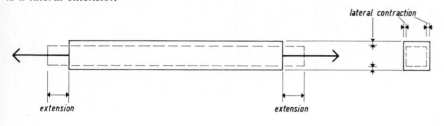

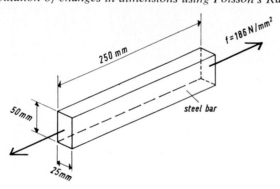

D.2.02/8 Calculation of changes in dimensions using Poisson's Ratio

D.2.02/9 Force and extension graph showing the work done by a force in straining a member

Use of Poisson's Ratio
$E = 207\,000\ N/mm^2$
$l/m = 0·3$

Find changes in all dimensions:

(1) *Longitudinal strain* $= f/E$
$$= \frac{186}{207\,000} = 0·9 \times 10^{-3}$$
∴ *250mm length increases by* $0·9 \times 10^{-3} \times 250 = 225 \mu m$

(2) *Lateral strain* $= l/m \times f/E$
$= 0·3 \times 0·9 \times 10^{-3} = 0·27 \times 10^{-3}$

 (a) *25mm side decreases by*
   $0·27 \times 10^{-3} \times 25 = 6·75 \mu m$

 (b) *50mm side decreases by*
   $0·27 \times 10^{-3} \times 50 = 13·50 \mu m$

Note: All values are for tension. For compression everything is reversed, i.e. increases become decreases

Strain energy and resilience

In non-technical terms *resilience* is often understood to mean the power of a strained body to 'spring back' on the removal of the acting force causing the straining. The term is widely used in connexion with floor finishes and other materials used for surfaces and which may be required to spring back to their original shape and form after being deformed by an acting force—in many cases a momentary one.

In technical terms, however, *resilience* is concerned with the *amount of energy stored in a material*. The stored up energy does in fact cause the material to spring back after a straining force has been removed.

When a member is being strained the acting force is doing work. The energy expended and which is measured by the work done (i.e. acting force × change in dimensions and expressed in m/N) in producing the strain is stored in what is known as strain energy in the strained material. If the strain is elastic the stored up energy re-appears with the removal of the acting force and causes the material to return to its original shape and form. If, on the other hand, the strain is inelastic, part of the stored up energy is used to overcome the forces of cohesion between the particles and causes them to slide over one another. The energy so expended appears as heat, with the remainder restoring the elastic strain.

Strain energy (U) is only concerned with the work done by a force in straining a member and is calculated from a force and extension graph as shown in diagram D.2.02/9. This diagram indicates the tensile loading condition, but the principle is also applicable to other forms of loading. Other factors are involved in the inelastic range.

The strain energy per unit volume of material is the resilience of the material. Thus account is taken of stress and the volume, i.e. the dimensions of a member and which is reduced to the formula

$$\text{RESILIENCE} = \frac{f^2}{2E}$$

for tension and compression. In principle the calculation is the same for other forms of loading.

The greatest amount of strain energy which can be stored in a material without permanent strain is called its *proof resilience*. The value of proof resilience is generally at the elastic limit. Some variations do occur in different materials.

Time- and special loading-dependent properties

The theories, mechanisms and basic mechanical properties of materials associated with stress and strain are all based on what may best be termed the steady state of loading under more or less controlled conditions. Values of either stress or strain are obtained from measurements taken while a sample of material is under controlled conditions

of loading at room temperature. The load is applied gradually while in most cases the sample is allowed to rupture. (It is normal for a number of tests to be undertaken so that average values may be obtained.)

Under conditions of use materials will behave in much the same way as occurs during the sample testing *provided* the loads are applied at a constant and gradual rate. In actual practice materials are seldom if ever subjected to any form of controlled loading. The rate and type of load may vary considerably, while, above all else, materials will be subjected to loads over a considerable period of time. Other factors such as changes in temperature may also operate during the period of use. Under these changed conditions differences in behaviour result which also lead to changes in the strength properties of materials—normally a lessening of the strength properties. The change in the strength properties have to be taken into account when permissible stresses and other design criteria are determined.

The main properties to be considered in connection with these changes are *creep, fatigue* and *impact*.

1. Creep

Creep has been defined as 'the time-dependent part of strain resulting from stress'.* It is thus *additional* deformation which takes place in materials subjected to a constant load over a period of time.

In mechanical engineering it was found that metals tended to undergo an additional deformation at high

*American Society for Testing Materials (ASTM) definition.

temperatures without an increase in load. Creep was, therefore, associated with high temperature environments. Subsequent research showed that creep was also associated with room temperature environments. Lead is an example from the metals which undergoes quite considerable creep at room temperatures as is shown in the comparative graph C.2.02/8. Temperature has to be related to the melting point of a material. (Lead has a comparatively low melting point.) Asphalt is a common building material which is subjected to creep at comparatively low 'high' temperatures, and as a result requires 'support 'to control the creep. Lead also requires frequent support to prevent 'sagging' which in this context is another way of saying creep.

Other materials such as plastics, concrete and even timber to some extent, have been found to be subjected to creep at normal room temperatures.

(a) Types of creep

There are two types of creep, namely transient and viscous creep. All are measured in a similar way to strain. Creep is sometimes referred to as creep strain.

(i) *Transient creep.* Transient creep is associated with the elastic range in materials and is the initial creep that takes place. One of its chief characteristics is that the amount of strain is rapid at first, gradually slowing down until some fixed value is reached.

In crystalline solids such as the *metals*, there is a slight additional strain which occurs under constant load and is known as the elastic after-effect. This is due to a number of reasons, chief of which are the heat losses and gains which take place

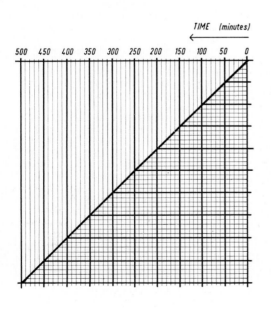

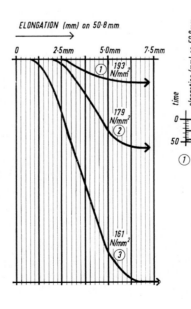

C.2.02/8 *Comparative graph showing the creep of lead at room temperature under three different intensities of loading. (Based on a graph in 'The Introduction to the Properties of Engineering Materials' by K. J. Pascoe, Blackie, 1961)*

during straining. Many metals are capable of *strain hardening* which means a higher yield stress and consequently the elastic after-effect is insignificant. Elastic after-effect always forms part of the transient creep. In most metals, however, the transient creep is so small when compared to other creep deformations, as to be of little practical significance.

The situation in the amorphous materials and particularly the *thermoplastics* is quite different. Here the transient creep contributes a major part and is entirely made up of elastic after-effect. This is particularly so when there is no strain hardening in the material. (Few of the plastics are capable of strain hardening.)

The complex process which is at work during the creep of *concrete* is becoming more fully understood. It is generally believed that under ordinary compressive stresses creep is made up entirely of transient creep, when the strain approaches some final value after a period of time. Of the many mechanisms that are involved the following appear to be the most important:

While subjected to external pressure there is a flow of absorbed water out of the cement gel; the voids in the material tend to close up; there is plastic or viscous flow in the hardened cement paste; there is plastic deformation in the aggregate.

(ii) *Viscous creep.* In the thermoplastic or amorphous polymers viscous flow is the normal deformation which takes place in the inelastic range. Once the elastic range has been exceeded the molecules continue to slip over one another, breaking bonds as quickly as they are reformed, with no strain hardening. This is true viscous flow. (Use is made of this property when thermoplastics are extruded and moulded.)

In the crystalline materials viscous creep is generally complicated as strain hardening is just balanced by the effects

Creep of a lead pipe due to inadequate support for exposure on a South elevation

of heat. In the plastic range there is an increase in the yield stress with every increment. However, the yield stress is also lowered by thermal softening. The cycle proceeds in this way, the slipping being still the mechanism involved. The softening which occurs takes place mainly through an annealing process. During this stage the atoms become far more mobile and in fact can 'get round' obstructions far more easily. In addition to the slip of the atoms there may also be a slip of the grains of the metal.

Finally, in other amorphous solids like *glass* and *asphalt*, viscous creep is like the flow of liquids. In the case of asphalt, as already mentioned, comparatively small increases in temperature (above that necessary for the solid state) result in viscous creep.

(b) *Stages of creep*
Sustained creep eventually leads to fracture of a material. The total time from the initial creep to final fracture is normally divided into three stages, as shown in diagram D.2.02/11 and which are as follows:

(i) *Primary creep* which is the stage during which most of the transient creep takes place. There is a rapid increase followed by a gradual slowing down.

(ii) *Secondary creep* follows with the strain continuing at a more or less constant creep rate. This occurs once the transient creep has reached a constant value.

(iii) *Tertiary creep* is the final stage before fracture occurs when there is again a rapid increase in the creep strain.

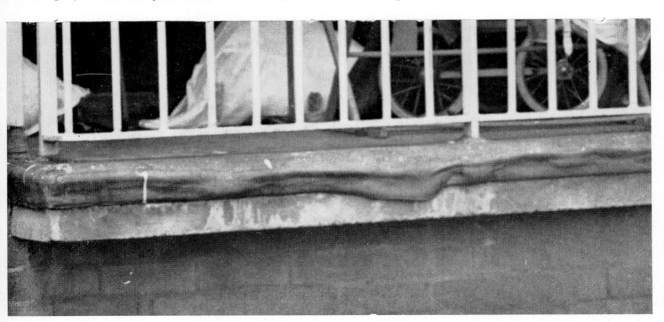

Creep in asphalt due to insufficient support required for thermal exposure

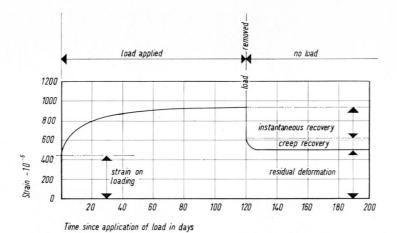

D.2.02/10 *Graph illustrating creep recovery of a mortar specimen stored in air at R. H. 95 per cent subject to a stress of 14·8N/mm² (2,150lb/sq in) and then unloaded. (From 'Properties of Concrete' by A. M. Neville, Pitman)*

These three stages do not always occur. In many cases, and particularly where brittle fracture occurs, the third stage may not occur.

(c) Creep recovery

In materials such as *concrete* where creep plays rather an important part, particularly in the early life of the material, creep recovery is significant. After the removal of a sustained load there is an immediate decrease in strain by an amount equal to the elastic strain at a given age of the concrete. This elastic strain is generally lower than the elastic strain on loading. Following this immediate recovery there is a further but gradual decrease in strain which is known as creep recovery. An example of creep recovery in a mortar specimen is shown in the graph D.2.02/10. From this it will be seen that there is still some deformation which means that the reversal of creep is not complete.

(d) Stress relaxation

Creep may be viewed in a completely different way. Instead of a constant load producing an additional deformation over a period of time, the effects of subjecting a material to a constant strain over a period of time will be

to produce a reduction in the intensity of stress, otherwise known as stress relaxation. This stress relaxation takes place as a result of the creep potential of the material. An example of stress relaxation in concrete is given in the comparative graph C.2.02/9. This particular aspect of creep is rather important when the probability of materials cracking under restrained conditions is analysed.

(e) Creep and design

With the *metals* creep is taken into account in what are known as creep strength and creep rupture strength. Various methods are used in assessing these properties. In the case of the non-metals, such as *plastics* and *concrete*, creep is taken into account by the use of apparent or effective moduli of elasticity. These are defined as the ratio of the stress to the total strain that has developed after a given time.

2. Fatigue

Materials subjected a large number of times to fluctuating or repeated loads (as may be caused by vibrations) may break suddenly without the permanent deformation which would normally signify impending fracture, although the material could sustain an even greater load if this was applied at a steadily increasing rate. As an example, a sample of steel (0·5 per cent carbon, 5 per cent nickel) has an ultimate tensile stress of 834N/mm². It could, therefore, be loaded in tension to 618N/mm² without fear of fracture. If this load is applied repeatedly, it is found that fracture may occur after about 10^4 loadings. Or an even lower load of 463N/mm² may fracture the specimen if applied 10^5 times. This phenomenon is known as fatigue.*

Unlike creep, *fatigue* is an effect of the *repetition of loads* and not simply an effect of time. In the case of metals

on which the greater amount of research has been done it has been found that the behaviour of materials subjected to fatigue is distinguished by three main features, namely: (1) loss of strength; (2) loss of ductility and (3) an increased uncertainty in both strength and service life. All these stem from the fact that all materials contain some impurities and are thus not strictly homogeneous. Under repeated loading the effect of the impurities is emphasised in much the same way as in the case of brittle fracture. There are, therefore, similarities between fatigue and brittle fracture. Fatigue is initiated in materials by small cracks that occur during the initial loadings.

Fatigue is important in materials other than metals, and research is naturally now being undertaken with other materials and particularly concrete and the plastics.

As a general guide it has been found that materials, such as *steel*, with fairly constant Moduli of Elasticity are satisfactory provided their elastic limit is not exceeded during the loadings.

With materials, such as *concrete*, where the elastic limit may vary, the situation is slightly more complex, and the materials may fracture at stresses below the effective modulus of elasticity. In cases such as these and because of the absence of any firm guidance samples of materials should be subjected to the relevant tests if there is any danger of fatigue developing as the result of vibrations.

Fatigue plays a more important part in the wider fields of engineering than it does in building practice. In buildings it is generally considered that it is unlikely that structural elements, as against finishes, will be weakened by vibrations caused by machinery and traffic. However, it should be noted that the effects of vibrations on buildings are as yet inconclusive. Changes in attitude in structural mechanics with the tendency to reduce the assumed imposed loads and increase permissible stresses, point to the possibility of fatigue becoming a subject for greater consideration in building practice in the future than it was in the past.

3. Impact

Whereas fatigue is concerned with the repeated application of a load on a material, *impact* is concerned with the *sudden application of a load* on a material. Any sudden application of a load results in stresses that are momentarily higher than those due to the same static load.

Whether or not a material is likely to fail as the result of an impact load depends very much on its ability to absorb the kinetic energy of the impacting body. It is generally true that the greater the ability to absorb the less likely the material is to fail. The ability to absorb the kinetic energy is related to the amount of deformation a material can withstand without breaking. On the whole, ductile materials are capable of absorbing

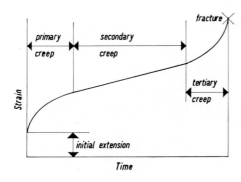

D.2.02/11 *Idealized creep curve for test at constant load illustrating the three stages of creep*

*Example taken from Pascoe, K. J., *Introduction to the Properties of Engineering Materials*, Blackie & Son Ltd., 1961.

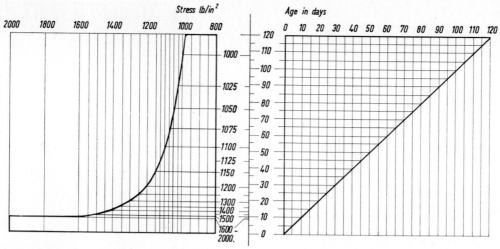

C.2.02/9 Relaxation of stress under a constant strain of 360×10^{-6}.
(Based on graph in 'Properties of Concrete' by A. M. Neville, Pitman)

and storing more energy than brittle materials.

In general, impact is important in such structures as bridges, cranes, etc. Except in special circumstances, when machines may produce special dynamic effects, impact is not important in buildings.*

Ductility

Ductility has already been mentioned. It is an important property and is mainly related to the metals, although other materials, such as plastics, may also display this property.

Ductility is defined as the capacity of a material to be drawn out plastically before breaking. Brittleness is the opposite of ductility.

Measurement of ductility may be done by one of two quantities:

*The unimportance of impact in buildings is confined to the strength of materials insofar as loadbearing elements are concerned. Impact is, however, of some importance when considering damage to isolated elements and corners of elements in buildings. This aspect is covered in *Section 2.04.*

(1) Percentage elongation: This is the total increase in gauge length at fracture expressed as a percentage of the original length.

(2) Percentage reduction in area or contraction. This is the reduction in cross sectional area at the neck expressed as a percentage of the original area.

The latter quality is usually considered to be the better measure of ductility as it is independent of the gauge length.

Comparative chart C.2.02/10 illustrates the ductility of various metals as measured by percentage elongation.

Hardness

Hardness is essentially concerned with the surfaces of materials and is the direct result of the interatomic forces acting at the surface. Technological hardness is defined as the resistance of a material to permanent deformation of its surface.

Because of the close connection between technological hardness and the

resistance of precious stones to surface scratching and wear (abrasion), mineralogists were the first to be concerned with this aspect of materials. Metallurgists later became interested with the development of special metal alloys which could be hardened to increase their abrasion resistance. The term was thus carried over to metals.

Although the surface hardness of a material is the direct result of interatomic forces acting at the surface, it does not always follow that the surface layer will be the same as the body of the material. Materials, such as surface-hardened steel, are specifically manufactured to possess a different surface layer. Nevertheless, even in materials without special surface treatments, the surface layer is only a few atoms thick, and thus relatively unimportant in technological hardness. Methods of measuring hardness soon penetrate this thin layer and thus it is the hardness of the bulk of the material which is measured. For this reason hardness tests are considered important in addition to the fact that there is usually a relationship between hardness and other properties of materials. In many cases hardness does give some indication of overall strength. This is useful because, generally speaking, hardness tests are comparatively simply and easily carried out.

Various methods are used to determine deformation of a surface. Among these scratching, mechanical wear, indentation or cutting are used. It is common to find tables of the results of indentation tests. Of these tests the diamond-pyramid hardness test (common type known as the Vickers hardness test) uses a diamond pyramid tester and measures the indentation produced by the diamond; the Brinell hardness test uses a specially hardened steel ball and measures the diameter of the indentation, and the Rockwell hardness test measures the depth of the indentation. The indentations are all related to the load applied and accordingly different scales of hardness are available.

C.2.02/10 Comparative chart of the ductility of various metals measured by percentage elongation

REFERENCES:
(a) *Civil Engineering Reference Book—Volume 1*
(b) *'Properties and Strength of Materials' by J. A. Cormack and E. R. Andrews*

MATERIAL		ref	value	ELONGATION % 0 10 20 30 40 50 60 70
Aluminium & alloys		a	10-21	
Brass 70/30 cast		'	55	
	drawn/annealed	"	60-65	
Bronze cast		"	10-15	
Cast iron		"	neg.	
Copper annealed		"	55	
	hard	"	15	
Lead extruded		"	65	
	rolled	"	50	
Steel mild		b	20-35	
	med. carbon	"	25	
	high carbon	"	18	
	nickel chrome	"	12-21	
Wrought iron		a	25	
Zinc rolled		"	30-60	

In addition to indicating the overall strength of a material, hardness is also useful in assessing the wearing qualities of materials. The formulation of precise values has been somewhat retarded by the practical variations which always occur particularly in elements such as floors where comparative values would be extremely useful.

Factor of safety

Mention has already been made of the fact that when use is made of the mechanical properties of materials in any structural design calculations, it is common, in building practice at any rate, to use permissible or working stresses rather than ultimate stresses. By so doing some measure of safety is incorporated. The relationship between the actual working stresses produced and the maximum stress the material is capable of taking without failure is known as the Factor of Safety. This may be written in formula form as:

$$\text{FACTOR OF SAFETY} = \frac{\text{ULTIMATE STRESS}}{\text{WORKING STRESS}}$$

A number of different criteria will influence the precise factor of safety applicable to any given material and the use to which it is put. Not least among these are social and economic forces. In addition the type and rate of loading together with the precise shape and size of material used relative to the acting force also play an important part. It is important to note that new ways of using materials or new techniques of building may show that existing criteria used for loading may be quite inadequate. Although the progressive collapse of the system-built point block of flats at Ronan Point in East London early in 1968 was shown to be due to a gas explosion, the tribunal in its report drew attention to the out-datedness of wind loading data particularly for high buildings. A few years earlier there had been the collapse of cooling towers at the Ferrybridge power station, also due to the action of wind. The effects of disasters such as these are bound to influence many of the criteria, including factors of safety used in the design and construction of buildings.

Important as all these are, there are, however, three basic criteria which essentially determine factors of safety for materials used in buildings. These are:
(1) The extent and accuracy of the knowledge available of the properties of a material; (2) The degree of regularity of the quality of a material; (3) The degree of variation in the properties of a material due to site or factory workmanship.

The more accurately these can be defined the smaller the factor of safety can be. To illustrate the wide variations that still do occur it may be noted that factors of safety may range from

Illustration of the bent forms possible in a laminated timber structure and a detail of the laminations

as low as 1·5, in the case of steel, to as high as about 10 in the case of brickwork.

The reason for these variations may be better understood if each of the three criteria is looked at individually.

1. Knowledge

Many of the mechanical properties of materials can nowadays be determined with a great deal of accuracy. However, it is in the application of these properties to everyday problems when the limitations of theoretical knowledge are apparent. Much of this theory is naturally enough based on many assumptions, but fortunately the great body of theory which now exists has been shown to agree with experimental results within reasonable margins of error. Nevertheless, new problems are continually being presented and many of these cannot always be dealt with on a mathematical basis. Accordingly problems such as these must be solved after experimental methods have been investigated. Recently a number of different complex structures have been finally determined after testing models. This technique is becoming more widely used.

Developments such as these also lead

to changes in attitudes to some aspects of mechanical properties themselves and which subsequently influence accepted factors of safety. A case in point is the definition of ultimate stress in the context of factors of safety. At one time it was assumed that ultimate stress would be deemed to have occurred just prior to fracture. However, as in the case of mild steel, it has been shown that failure can be said to occur at yield point. Thus for purposes of calculating factors of safety ultimate stress must be interpreted as yield point. By taking yield point as meaning ultimate stress it has been possible to reduce the factor of safety. Factors of safety against yield in mild steel and reinforced concrete are, therefore, between 1·8 and 2·0 instead of 3·5.

2. Quality

The regularity of the quality which can reasonably be expected in materials of the same type are greatly influenced by the degree of control which can be maintained during manufacture. In this the quality of the raw material is also very important.

With naturally occurring materials such as timber and stone the degree of control is outside human limits. These materials do on the whole display wide variations in their properties. Consequently it is not uncommon to find that high factors of safety are employed. On the other hand, careful selection of the actual pieces of material to be used often results in higher permissible stresses being safely used. *Timber* illustrates this point quite well. Normally the stresses used for unselected timber assume that the timber is the weakest of its kind. However, it is possible by careful selection of the actual pieces of timber which are going to be used, to eliminate those with defects which in fact are known to cause weakening. This has led to what is known as stress grading of timber, when limitations as to the maximum defects allowable are laid down. Another method which is commonly employed and which derives in principle from plywood manufacture, is that of laminated timber construction. Here, by cutting the timber into comparatively thin pieces and glueing these pieces together, it is possible to eliminate some of the inherent defects in timber. This method of using timber has other advantages in that

timber members built up in this way may be more easily and conveniently bent into shapes for specific structural uses.

Quite considerable control is exercised in the manufacture of *clay products.* However, wide variations are still encountered, particularly in bricks which are important structural units. These variations are partly due to difficulties in being able to control the properties of the basic raw material, i.e. the clay. *Concrete blocks* are usually capable of higher control. Bricks and blocks may, of course, suffer during actual site use.

Most of the *metals* are generally manufactured under a high degree of control. The processes used also make it possible for the raw materials to be suitably screened. In addition, the manufacturers ensure that testing is carried out regularly through all stages. For building purposes the quality of metals, particularly those for structural purposes, is generally assumed to be constant. Accordingly factors of safety for metals are generally much lower than for other traditional materials.

3. Variations

The degree of variation in the properties of materials which may occur due to site or factory workmanship depends, as in the case of quality, on the degree of control which can be effected. *Concrete,* and particularly that made on the site, is one material which does suffer quite seriously from lack of proper control at all stages. For this reason factors of safety for the material are comparatively high and fall somewhere between the metals and the naturally occurring materials. *Brick and block work* are also likely to be affected by site usage.

Other processes such as drilling, screwing, nailing, shaping, etc., are also likely to have some effect on the properties of various materials. It is usually impossible to make general rules for each case which may arise. Thus the effects of these processes must be considered as they arise. The only general statement that can be made is that factors of safety may have to be substantially increased where workmanship is likely to affect adversely the properties of materials.

2.03 cracking in buildings

General considerations

1. Significance

Cracks in building materials and including particularly the elements of which they form part is probably one of the most common, and in some senses the most tiresome, failure encountered in building practice. Slight cracks are usually only unsightly and, as important, unacceptable to occupants or owners but excessive cracking may have deleterious results leading to serious structural weakening.

As a principle it is always good practice to make every possible attempt to reduce cracking to the absolute minimum particularly as cracks, however small or apparently insignificant, are often likely to provide capillary paths for water penetration. In such cases the penetration of water may result in further cracking taking place or it may result in other hidden materials corroding or being otherwise adversely affected. In addition cracking can result in a loss of efficiency of the building through air infiltration, increased heat loss, and reduced sound insulation. The occurrence of cracks in buildings, whether initially or during use, usually imposes extra expenditure on maintenance. In cases of serious structural weakening the cost of rectifying the failure could be considerable.

2. Structural weakening

All kinds of cracks that may develop in materials can all be accounted for as a failure in the particular material to resist the induced stresses which have been imposed on it at any given time. In general it is normally the failure of the material to resist the tensile stresses imposed. From the structural point of view, the extent of the reduction in strength which may be caused by cracking will depend on the *extent* of the cracking which, in fact, has taken place. It is for this reason that slight cracks (the term slight is in this context relative to circumstances) are not normally regarded as serious as they do not necessarily result in a significant loss of stability.

However, it is important that any determination of whether cracks in any particular circumstance are serious or otherwise must be based in the first instance on the relationship between the actual strength of the material in question and its size and shape relative to the imposed stresses. On the other hand, account must also be taken of loss of efficiency of the building in other ways (see '1. Significance', above) when determining the seriousness of cracks.

3. Occurrence

(a) *Materials commonly affected*

Although cracking may take place in any kind of material it is most commonly found to take place in the wet trade processes in buildings such as concrete, brickwork, plastering, rendering, screeding, and particularly in those in which cement has been used. The

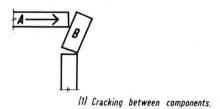

[1] *Cracking between components.*

[2] *Cracking within components.*

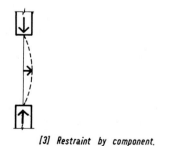

[3] *Restraint by component.*

D.2.03/1 *Illustrations of three common conditions resulting in cracking (Based on BRS Digest 75 (2nd Series))*

use of cement does require certain basic precautions to be taken in order to reduce the possibility of cracking taking place, due particularly to drying shrinkage. The common occurrence of the failure of cement-based products can therefore usually be attributed to the fact that the proper precautions have *not* been taken. Other factors such as precautions required for proper adhesion also play an important part. A further point which in part also accounts for the comparative ease with which these, and other brittle materials, appear to crack is that they possess, relatively speaking, very little tensile strength.

In composite materials, such as brickwork, the position is slightly more complicated by the fact that the maximum tensile strength which may exist will be determined by either the strength of the individual materials (in this case the bricks and the mortar) or by the strength of the adhesion which is effected between the individual materials. The same kind of situation, in principle at any rate, will occur with plastering, rendering, painting and any other process in which adhesion plays a part.

(b) *Basic mechanisms*

Movements of one kind or another are basically responsible for the development of cracking. The combined effect of the extent of the movement and the extent to which materials are restrained will influence the degree of cracking. The forces that may be set up due to restraint (expansion or contraction) are shown in diagram D.2.01/4. The diagram also shows that failure may occur either between or within components.

Diagram D.2.03/1 illustrates the three common conditions for cracking: (1) is a typical example of cracks occurring between components. The cyclic (thermal) movement of block A permanently displaces block B so as to produce a crack in the structure. Neither A nor B may necessarily fail. The movement of B could be progressive if debris gains ingress into the crack. In this case movement is largely in the direction of the forces applied, and is very often (as shown) at right angles to them. It may be noted here that movement of only 0·03mm in 6·1m can produce a bulge of about 25·4mm, as for example in cladding units subjected to vertical compression; (2) is a typical example of cracking within components when the strength of the material is much more directly involved. The effects of restraint are significant, and damaging stresses should be kept to a minimum; (3) illustrates that restraint is supplied by the component itself when *differential* movements occur in the component. Such movements may occur as a result of drying from one face only, or of different temperatures on opposite faces. In such cases distortion and often cracking then follow.

4. Basis for consideration

As a general basis for considering the causes of cracking in buildings it is convenient to divide the movements by which stresses may be set up in materials and which may result in cracking taking place into the following headings:

(i) *Externally applied loads.* This is concerned with direct loading of structural and other elements which results in deflection taking place.

(ii) *Restraint of internal movements* caused by either temperature or moisture changes in materials. This is indirect loading.

(iii) *Momentary loading* as caused by vibrations and which may effect the fatigue properties of materials.

Before each of the above three causes are dealt with in detail it is worthwhile noting *some* of the similarities which exist among these three and which effect in principle the manner in which the possibility of cracking may be reduced in practical terms. In all cases it is not normally possible to prevent entirely the cause of the stresses. The stresses involved are always associated with the material or element 'wanting to move'. A reduction of induced stresses particularly can often be effected by actually allowing the material or element to move, that is to deform, at least to some degree—it is not always practical to allow the maximum movement to take place. It is for this reason that some 'elbow room', that is the provision of some space in which the movement can take place, should be aimed for if the likelihood of cracking is to be reduced.

(iv) *Chemical reactions* such as sulphate attack, corrosion of metals and carbonation.

(v) *Physical changes* such as ice or crystalline salt formation and loss of volatiles.

In these two cases there is no question of providing space for movements to take place. The solution here is basically to prevent the reaction or change from actually taking place. In the case of physical changes this is not always possible with the result that materials which are more likely to resist changes have to be selected.

(vi) *Movements* which may occur *in soils.* This is a rather specialised cause and can be related to both externally applied loads (i) above and movements caused by temperature and moisture changes (ii) above, although other factors are also involved.

5. Principal causes and effects

Table 2.03/1 contains by way of a summary of this section the principal causes and effects of movements responsible for cracking. In the main examples are used to explain cause and effect of each aspect.

6. Assessment in practice

In view of the fact that cracking may result from *any* one of the six causes outlined above, it is important before each is covered separately, to

Table 2.03/1 Principal Causes and Effects of Movements responsible for Cracking

Cause	Effect	Duration	Examples of Materials affected
1. EXTERNALLY APPLIED LOADS 1.1 Dead and imposed loading within design limits 1.2 Structural over-loading	Normally insignificant Excessive deflection and distortion		
2. RESTRAINT OF INTERNAL MOVEMENTS 2.1 Temperature changes 2.2 Moisture content changes 2.21 Drying 2.22 Wetting 2.23 Drying alternating with wetting	Expansion (with temp. increase) and contraction (with temp. decrease) Shrinkage Expansion Expansion and contraction	Intermittent diurnal, seasonal Mainly short-term, due to loss of initial moisture Short-term, due to take-up of moisture Seasonal	All; see C.2.03/1 Mortar, concrete, sand-lime bricks, unseasoned timber Ceramic products Poorly protected joinery, shrinkable clay soils
3. MOMENTARY LOADING Vibration from traffic, machinery and sonic booms			Authenticated cases of damage are rare. Developing situation needs to be watched
4. CHEMICAL REACTIONS 4.1 Corrosion 4.2 Sulphate attack 4.3 Carbonation	Expansion Expansion Shrinkage	Continuous Continuous Continuous	Metals Portland cement and hydraulic lime products, e.g. concrete and mortar Porous Portland cement products, e.g. lightweight concrete, asbestos cement
5. OTHER PHYSICAL CHANGES 5.1 Ice or crystalline salt formation 5.2 Loss of volatiles	Expansion in building materials; Frost heave in soils Contraction	Intermittent, dependent on weather conditions and moisture content of materials/soils Short-term or long-term	Porous natural stones and other porous building materials (bricks, mortars); Soils Mastics
6. MOVEMENTS IN SOILS 6.1 Loading 6.2 Mining subsidence, swallow holes, landslips, soil creep, earthquakes	Settlement Settlement	Extent of settlement varies with seasons	Silts and peaty ground particularly susceptible

note, that in practice, cracks usually result from a *combination* of some of the main causes operating at one and the same time. It is for this reason that it is not always possible to assess precisely the exact cause or causes of cracking *after* they have actually occurred.* Nevertheless, each of these main causes must be considered separately, as in each case there are particular precautions which may be taken, in order to attempt to reduce the possibility of cracking taking place.

This generalisation cannot, of course, apply to each and every situation which may arise in practice, and so each situation must be assessed on its own merits so that it is possible to determine which of the six causes are likely to apply. Having made such an assessment it is then important to try to evaluate, either by calculation or experience, as applicable, the exact nature of practical precautions which should be taken. In this respect there are still very few methods available by which the likelihood of cracking may actually be calculated. Many calculations that could be applied are mostly related to complete structural failure, that is fracture.

Cracking due to externally applied loads

Cracking which may result due to the application of external loads is closely associated with the elastic deformations, and to some extent those deformations caused by creep, which occur in all structural members subjected to loading. Most, although not all, cases of cracking occur in members, such as beams and slabs, subjected to bending. In these cases the amount of deflection which may take place will strongly influence the amount of cracking which may result. Structural calculations all take into account the elastic and creep behaviour of materials, and so a certain amount of deformation is therefore actually allowed to take place. Thus the deflection of members has to be expected. This is an extremely important consideration. The amount of deflection (in terms of measurement) will vary according to the load and span of a particular member—allowable deflexion is normally quoted as a ratio of the span—and is limited to that which occurs at midspan. Method of loading and the rigidity of the structure are other considerations which also have to be taken into account. However, very broadly speaking, greater deflexion can be expected with long spans relatively heavily loaded, than with short spans lightly loaded.

Deflection due to loading may cause cracking of *either* the structural member itself *or* of any other material (particularly applied finishes such as

*This study is concerned with prevention rather than with cure. Where, however, it is necessary to repair cracks, the nature of the cause of the cracks will determine the best method to use to effect the repair. Determination of the cause and in particular whether it is likely to re-occur is important.

112

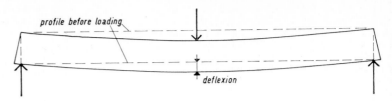

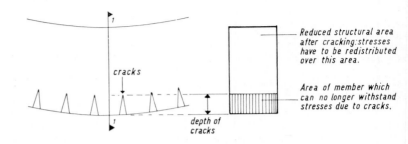

Elevation of Structural Member

Detail A

Section 1-1

Reduced structural area after cracking:stresses have to be redistributed over this area.

Area of member which can no longer withstand stresses due to cracks.

D.2.03/2. The effects of excessive deflection of a simply supported beam

Some available types of specially twisted and indented reinforcing bars, generally now referred to as 'deformed bars'

Below, cracking due to excessive deflexion of a reinforced concrete beam under test. Compare with diagram D.2.03/2

plaster, tiling, etc.) and elements such as partitions which may be closely attached or otherwise connected to a structural member subject to deflection.

1. Structural members

If cracking is to occur in structural members subjected to bending, then this will usually occur in those parts where tension occurs. Diagram D.2.03/2 illustrates a simply supported beam which has been loaded and which has deflected. The tension occurs at the bottom of the beam. (In continuously supported beams there will be reverse bending over the supports in which case there will be some tension at the top of the beam and which will occur over the supports.) When cracks develop in the tension zone there is likely to be a reduction of the structural area of the member as shown in the diagram. The precise size of the cracks will influence very much the manner in which the stresses will have to be redistributed over the reduced effective structural area in order to resist the loads applied on the member.

The possibility of cracking occurring in structural members has particular significance in composite structures such as *reinforced concrete*. The prevention of cracking in these cases is very much a matter for structural mechanics and the actual design of the size and shape of the members. However, the significance of cracks in reinforced concrete work is outlined here very briefly.

The steel in a reinforced concrete beam, for example, is there primarily to resist tension, although the concrete is capable of withstanding some of the tensile stresses that develop. The amount contributed by the concrete is relatively small. The steel reinforcement does not actually prevent cracking, but rather helps to mitigate the effects of the cracking. And this within limits. During loading the steel and the concrete work together to resist the tensile stresses. Thus, once cracking has occurred the steel must then provide the tension previously developed in the concrete. The steel bars also, in effect, tie the concrete together on the opposite faces of each crack. Under these circumstances there is a tendency for the concrete to slide along the bars. The actual width of the crack is determined by the extent of movement which takes place and this in turn is dependent on the stress in the steel and the degree of bond between the bars and the concrete. Advantage may be taken of steels with higher strengths than ordinary mild steel, and in order to increase the bond between this special strength reinforcement and the concrete, the bars are given special surface characteristics either by simply twisting the bar or by forming them with projections or indentations. Examples of these bars, commonly known as 'deformed bars' to distinguish them from ordinary bars, are shown in the photographs.

2. Other closely associated materials and elements

(a) *Directly applied rigid finishes—ceilings*

Rigid plaster and other similar finishes which may be applied *directly* to the underside of structural members such as beams and suspended concrete floor or roof slabs are likely to crack comparatively easily and when these, i.e. the beams or slabs, are subjected to *excessive* deflection. (The deflection may not be excessive for the member but may be for the finish.) The reason for cracking will be the same as that illustrated in diagram D.2.03/2 mentioned before. In this case, in addition to the cracking of the finish, there may also be a loss of adhesion between the finish and the background and which in turn may aggravate the cracking.

Isolation of the plaster from its background so that the latter is free to move without deflecting the plaster or causing a loss of adhesion, is the only method of avoiding cracking of the plaster. Normally this implies some form of suspended ceiling, in which case the suspension system must provide the requisite amount of 'spring' for the deflection of the structural member. At the same time there should not be any physical connection between the plaster and surrounding vertical surfaces of walls or beams. An alternative to this would be to select a finish which is not rigid but which is resilient enough to take up the movement of the deflecting structural member without cracking.

(b) *Directly applied rigid finishes—floors*

With rigid floor finishes such as tiling on suspended concrete floors either cracking or a loss of adhesion may occur due to deflection of the slab. Diagram D.2.03/3 illustrates a floor continuous over supports and where ordinary and reverse bending occurs. In the case of the ordinary bending high compressive stresses are developed in the tiling and this may lead to a failure of the bond between the tiles and their base. The tiles may then lift.

Where reverse bending occurs the tension created may also result in a loss of bond and lifting of the tiles. (The photographs (p. 114) illustrating the lifting of pavement slabs and a welded steel gas main are included to draw a parallel with the lifting of floor tiles due to surface compression. The lifting has been caused by surface compression due to mining subsidence which, when compared to buildings, produce exaggerated conditions, showing the effects of the compression very well.) Some cracking of tiles may also occur. Where a loss of bond does occur it is important to note that this may not have been caused entirely by the deflection of the slab but more likely due to the combined effect of deflection plus movements due to moisture or thermal changes or to vibrations. (See example 3(f) under *Moisture movements,* page 32.)

Floating floors are sometimes used in order to avoid cracking due to deflexion. This type of solution is, however, more often used in connection

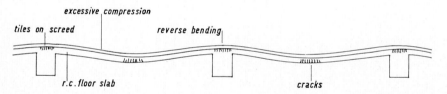

Section through continuous floor slab showing deflexion under load

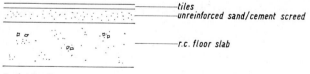

Typical Detail

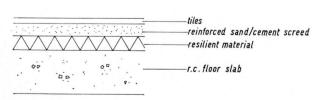

'Floating' Floor

D.2.03/3 *Deflection in a continuous reinforced concrete floor slab with reverse bending over supports and details of typical and floating floors*

K

with the reduction of the transmission of impact sound. A detail showing the principle of the floating floor is included in diagram D.2.03/3.

(c) *Partitions—framed buildings*

In framed buildings, partitions built tight up against the underside of a beam may crack when the beam deflects. Diagram D.2.03/4 illustrates a typical case, and also shows a method for isolating the partition from the beam, in order to allow the movement caused by deflection to take place. (Isolation could obviously be effected by simply stopping the partition before it reached the beam. For sound and fire reasons this is not always practical.) A resilient material is used between the underside of the beam and the top of the partition, because such a material will not transfer all of the load caused by the deflection to the partition, while at the same time it has sufficient springiness to allow continual 'up and down' movement as and when this occurs.

As the resilient material is used to isolate the two elements, it follows that no other material, and especially applied finishes such as plaster, should be allowed to span over the resilient material, and thereby effecting a connection. (Within certain limits rigid sheet materials may span over the resilient material provided their fixing system incorporates a method of accommodating movement and without transferring any significant load to the partition.)

If a cover strip is to be provided to hide the gap created, then this strip should only be fixed to one or other of the elements (*either* the beam *or* the partition, but not both). If the principle of discontinuity is to be carried to its logical conclusion, then *even* a paint finish should not be applied so as to form a continuous film over the partition, cover strip and beam. The paint film will not enable any significant load to be transferred from the beam to the partition, but it will nevertheless crack, due to its own weakness, at or near the junction of the cover strip and partition, or cover strip and beam, when movement takes place.

Cracking due to restraint of thermal and moisture movements

As this section is generally only concerned with the principles which are relevant to the causes of cracking, the mechanisms and the extent of both moisture or thermal movements in various materials are not covered here at all. These aspects are dealt with in detail in *Part 3.00* for moisture movements and *Part 4.00* for thermal movements. However, for convenience, movements in selected materials are given in the comparative chart, C.2.03/1.

Despite the fact that these move-

114

Two examples illustrating lifting caused by surface compression. The top picture shows pavement slabs and the bottom a welded steel gas main. In both cases the surface compression has been caused by mining subsidence (Crown Copyright)

D.2.03/4 *Illustrations showing reasons for the cracking of a partition in a framed building due to deflection with detail of possible method of allowing for a movement in the frame*

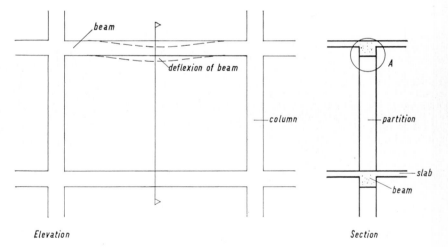

Elevation

Section

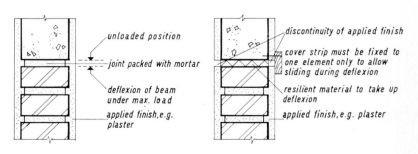

Cracking likely

Solution to reduce the likelihood of cracking

Detail at A

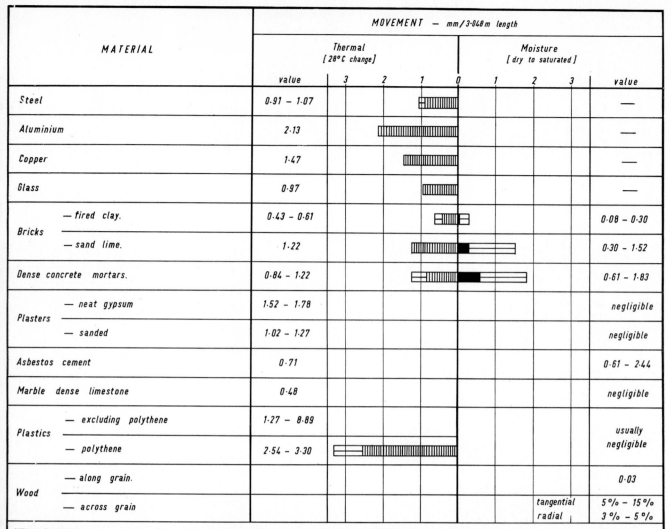

MATERIAL		Thermal [28°C change] value	3	2	1	0	1	2	3	Moisture [dry to saturated] value
Steel		0.91 – 1.07								—
Aluminium		2.13								—
Copper		1.47								—
Glass		0.97								—
Bricks	— fired clay.	0.43 – 0.61								0.08 – 0.30
	— sand lime.	1.22								0.30 – 1.52
Dense concrete mortars.		0.84 – 1.22								0.61 – 1.83
Plasters	— neat gypsum	1.52 – 1.78								negligible
	— sanded	1.02 – 1.27								negligible
Asbestos cement		0.71								0.61 – 2.44
Marble dense limestone		0.48								negligible
Plastics	— excluding polythene	1.27 – 8.89								usually negligible
	— polythene	2.54 – 3.30								
Wood	— along grain.									0.03
	— across grain							tangential	5% – 15%
									radial	3% – 5%

MOVEMENT — mm/3·048 m length

NOTES: 1) The 28°C temperature range may be greatly exceeded in practice. Thus a black panel, insulated at the back, can reach 71°C. Colour, orientation, thermal conductivity and insulation all play a part. (See 4.00 Heat and its effects).
2) The initial moisture expansions of fired clay products are omitted – for details see 3·03 Moisture content.
3) The initial drying shrinkage of Portland cement products are omitted – for details see 3·03 Moisture content.
4) See 3·03 Moisture content (particularly CC. 3·03/5) for movements related to selected timber species.

C.2.03/1 *Moisture movement in selected materials*

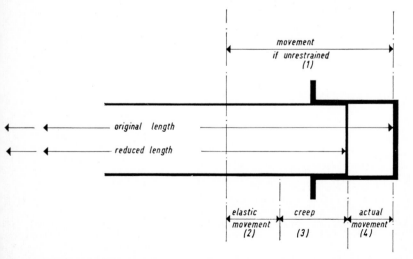

D.2.03/5 *Factors influencing stresses due to temperature or moisture changes (Courtesy: 'Principles of Modern Building', Vol. 1, 3rd Edn., HMSO, 1959 (Crown Copyright))*

ments are apparently unrelated, it is nevertheless convenient to consider them under the same heading, because in both cases any restraint to movement results in stresses being induced in materials or elements. Excessive stresses may result in cracking taking place.

This section covers aspects of stress inducement as related to both types of movements first, and then deals separately with selected aspects of each.

1. Stress inducement

(a) *Material as a whole*

Under 'Loading', in *Section 2.01*, a simple example is given of the acting forces, that is the stresses, which are induced in a material or member which is restrained from movement due to changes in moisture or temperature (diagram D.2.01/4). The magnitude of these stresses which are induced will, in fact, depend on four factors:*

(i) The magnitude of the movement in the material if unrestricted; (ii) the modulus of elasticity of the material; (iii) the capacity of the material to creep or flow under load; (iv) the degree of restraint to the movement of the material by its connection to other elements in the structure.

The interdependence of these factors is illustrated in diagram D.2.03/5. This shows that the unrestrained movement is equal to the sum of the actual movement, the elastic movement and the creep. Of these three it is only the actual movement which *physically* takes place. This movement is inversely proportional to the restraint. Elastic movements and creep are movements which do not physically take place, but are so called because they are the movements which would normally take place if the member was subjected to an externally applied load and free to move. Under conditions of restraint, therefore, and because this movement (another word in this context for strain) does not take place stresses are either created (for elastic movement) or relaxed (for creep). The elastic movement is proportional to the induced stress and inversely proportional to the modulus of elasticity. The creep on the other hand increases with the induced stress and depends on the time during which movement takes place.

This theoretical consideration cannot, unfortunately, be applied easily in practice to make an actual quantitative assessment of the liability of a building component to crack due to induced stresses. The reason for this is that change in any of the first three factors mentioned above is often accompanied by *compensating changes* in the others and by changes in the strength of the material. As an example, a concrete mix with a high water/cement ratio has greater unrestrained shrinkage movement than a mix with a low water/cement ratio. The additional water in the mix has the effect of reducing the modulus of elasticity which allows a larger elastic movement for a given stress. At the same time there is an increase in creep which in turn reduces the degree of elastic movement necessary. Thus, for a particular degree of restraint the induced stresses due to shrinkage are less than with concrete mixes having lower water/cement ratios. However, there is still a tendency for greater shrinkage cracking with wet mixes (that is high water/cement ratios) because they have reduced tensile strength.

In the wet trade processes generally, further complications arise in connection with shrinkage cracks. Reinforcement of a material serves to act as a restraint and so stresses are induced. However, the reinforcement does help to distribute the shrinkage cracks so that these become *much finer* than they would have been in the unrestrained material.

Principles of Modern Building, Vol. 1 (3rd Ed.), Chapter 2.

116

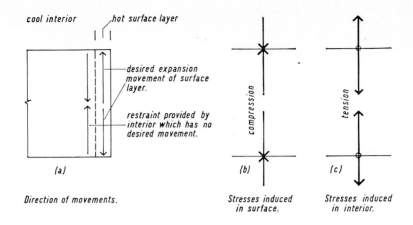

(a) Direction of movements.

(b) Stresses induced in surface.

(c) Stresses induced in interior.

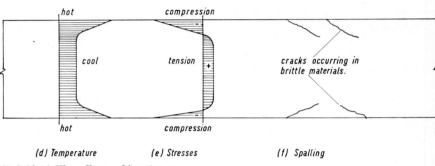

(d) Temperature (e) Stresses (f) Spalling

D.2.03/6 *The effects of heating a material*

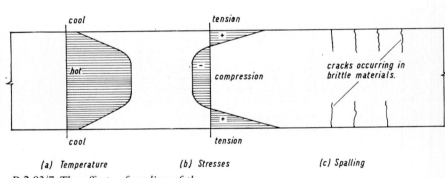

(a) Temperature (b) Stresses (c) Spalling

D.2.03/7 *The effects of cooling of the surface of a material*

Because of the difficulties connected with induced stresses no precise recommendations have been put forward for reducing cracking due to induced stresses in materials. It has been suggested (*Principles of Modern Building*, Vol. 1, p. 22) that it is probably reasonable to assume that the likelihood of serious cracking can be reduced by: (1) avoiding materials that, when unrestrained, deform considerably as a result of moisture or temperature changes; (2) avoiding unnecessary restraint to shrinkage or expansion of the material; (3) using materials or combinations of materials in a building element in such a way that the extensibility (i.e. the total elastic and creep deformations before cracking occurs) is as large as possible.

(b) *Surface/Interior movements*

There is another aspect of stress inducement due to restraint which can occur in materials. This is related to the differential movement which may occur between the surface and the interior of a material. The effect of heating or cooling a material is the best example to take in order to explain how stresses may, in fact, be induced.*

(i) *Heating the surface*

Heating of the surfaces of a material results in a temperature gradient being set up across the material as shown in

*Richards, Cedric W., *Engineering Materials Science*, Chapter 12.5, 'Thermal Stresses', 1961.

diagram D.2.03/6 (d). The surface of the material, being hotter than the interior, will want to expand, but this expansion will be restrained by the interior, as shown in (a). The result of this restraint is to induce a compressive stress (b) in the surface and a tensile stress (c) in the interior. This is shown graphically in (e). If the material is ductile and the stress high enough, it will yield and in so doing the stress will be relieved. Under conditions of high temperature the stress distribution will be zero, as yielding will take place at lower stresses than usual. Brittle materials, on the other hand, may fail by compression in the surface, in which case there will be a shearing failure on planes at 45 degrees, known as spalling and shown in (f).

(ii) Cooling the surface

Cooling of the surface of a hot material will produce the reverse effect when there will be tensile stresses in the surface and compressive stresses in the interior as shown in diagram D.2.03/7 (a and b). As in the case of heating, ductile materials will relieve the stresses on yielding, but brittle materials may crack. Because there is tension in the surface, the cracks will occur at right-angles to the surface instead of 45 degrees.

(iii) Exfoliation

From these two examples it will be seen that as a general rule the hot region is in compression while the cool region is in tension. Materials such as the *sedimentary stones,* which are classed as brittle, consist of layers of material and may fail due to a shearing action that takes place at the junction of the surface and the interior, when there is differential movement due to heating or cooling. In such cases the surface virtually 'peels off'; the process being known as exfoliation.

(iv) Differential drying shrinkage

The general principles applicable to the heating and cooling of materials are, within certain limits, also applicable to differential drying shrinkage which may occur in the wet trade processes such as *plastering, rendering, screeding* or *concreting.* If the surface layers dry out before the interior, then the surface will act as a restraint to the shrinkage which must still take place in the interior. The movement directions will be the same as for heating of the surface (diagram D.2.03/6 (a)), except that the desired movement will occur in the interior. Nevertheless, the stress situation will be the same, and the surface will be subjected to compression while the interior to tension. As in the case of heating, and as the materials referred to in this context are brittle, cracking of the surface may occur. This is partly why it is so important that drying shrinkage is very carefully controlled by also ensuring that the drying takes place relatively slowly and, as important, evenly. It should, however, be noted that there are other equally important considerations such as the amount of water used in making the mixture and the effects of compaction (this would include trowelling of surfaces) which also influence the degree of possible shrinkage cracking. For this reason, the carrying out of careful drying-out precautions alone are not sufficient if shrinkage cracking is to be reduced.

When a restraint is provided to drying shrinkage of the surface layer then the stress situation is similar to the cooling shown in diagram D.2.03/7. For this analogy to be complete and also to be related to practice, the surface layer must also include in its meaning a whole material as in the case of plastering where restraint is provided by the background.

2. Thermal movements

Buildings are continually exposed to changes in their thermal environment and so problems associated with thermal movements are perennial. This particular aspect is important when solutions for reducing the possibility of cracking are considered. As the exterior of buildings present, on the whole and particularly in traditional terms, the greatest exposure to seasonal variations in temperature, it has been customary to consider this aspect only. It is, however, now relevant to note that significant changes in temperature may also occur inside buildings. In many cases such exposure may only be localised. Nevertheless, it is still important that these situations are taken into account. The general principles of detailing various parts of a building to accommodate movement and thereby reducing the possibility of cracking are given here for the exterior of buildings, as there is greater experience with this aspect. These principles are, however, equally applicable to those circumstances inside buildings where there may be significant changes in temperature.

In addition to the four factors upon which stress inducement is dependent (outlined earlier), account must also be taken of the *rate* at which changes in temperature take place and this in turn must be related to the thermal conductivity of materials. In general, it is reasonable to assume that small gradual changes in temperature are likely to produce far smaller stresses than large rapid changes in temperature. It is for this reason that the gradual seasonal variations which normally take place over a period of a year are less important than the

Crazing of the surface of a precast concrete cladding panel. The main cause of crazing, which is a very variable phenomenon in concrete products, is believed to be differential moisture shrinkage between the surface layers and the adjacent layer underneath. The fine cracks, usually confined to the surface only, may occur during the initial curing period or after exposure to the weather. The latter sometimes after many years. Crazing appears to be more susceptible in those products which have a very fine and smooth surface, as this requires fine aggregate and surface trowelling, which results in a different material in the surface as compared to the interior which is coarse. The differences in composition and characteristics usually lead to differences in moisture movements as between the surface and the interior. Although the cracks may be analogous with diagram 2.03/7, in section, the actual surface 'pattern' is not predictable

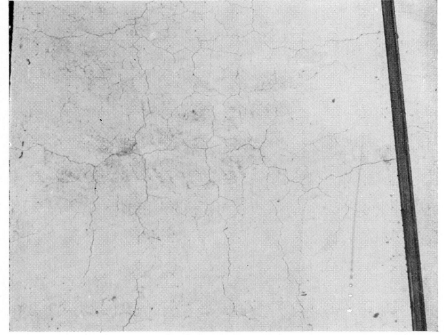

rapid changes which can take place in summer even in this country within a day and perhaps within 7 to 8 hours. This does not imply that gradual changes must never be taken into account. The extent of the likely movement is always one of the main factors to be considered.

Techniques of using materials for fairly large elements such as walls, floors and roofs do incorporate, in theory at any rate, some measure of allowance for movement of the individual units which make up the element. Practical procedures and methods however often reduce considerably this allowance. For example, *small unit materials* such as *bricks* do have theoretically any number of joints (particularly the verticals) which should be able to take up movement of the individual units. However, good practice requires that all joints, including the verticals, should be well filled. This automatically restricts the amount of movement possible for the individual units. This restriction can also be further increased as the strength of the mortar used is increased. (Traditional lime mortars, usually soft, do provide more freedom of movement than strong cement-based mortars. Despite this apparent advantage, other requirements have accounted for the rapid discontinued use of mortars consisting only of lime and sand. For details of mortar mixes see *3.04 Exclusion* under 'Joint design'.)

Sheet materials provide another example, but in this case of *a large unit material*. As a group these materials have greater potential movement by virtue of the size of units normally used. However, a fair amount of movement may be allowed especially when they are *suitably* fixed to a background by means of screws or similar devices which require pre-drilled holes (the diameter of the holes being slightly larger than that of the fixing device), and also when adhesives which maintain a certain amount of resilience are used. Such movement as may be allowed for in this way may be completely prevented from taking place if adjoining sheets are tightly butted to one another, or if some form of cover strip rigidly connects the two adjoining sheets. The fixing and jointing of large unit materials such as precast stone or concrete panels need careful design and execution, if allowance is to be made for the considerable movement that may take place while still preserving other functions of the fabric. Brittle materials, and here *glass* is particularly relevant, may crack if there is insufficient allowance for movement. *Ductile sheet materials* (mainly metals), on the other hand, may only buckle if there has not been sufficient room for their expansion—they may, however, also cause cracking of adjoining elements.

Some of the more serious cases of cracking due to restraint of thermal movement in most traditional building

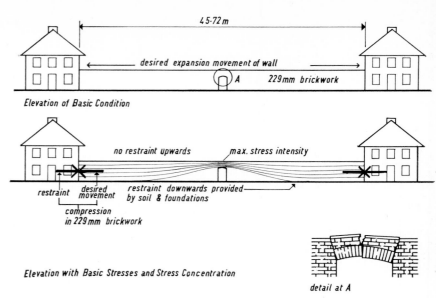

Elevation of Basic Condition

Elevation with Basic Stresses and Stress Concentration

detail at A

D.2.03/8 *Damage to brickwork under conditions of restraint due to thermal expansion. Example shows cracking of restrained member (Courtesy: 'Principles of Modern Buildings', Vol. 1, HMSO, 1959 (Crown Copyright))*

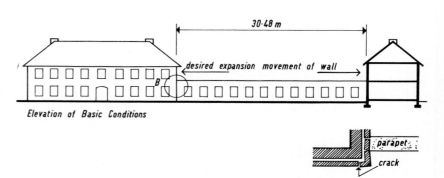

Elevation of Basic Conditions

Plan at B

D.2.03/9 *Damage to brickwork under conditions of restraint due to thermal expansion. Example shows cracking of restraining member (Courtesy: 'Principles of Modern Building', Vol. 1, HMSO, 1959 (Crown Copyright))*

Cracking of part of a garden wall without expansion joints and over 75m long due to thermal movement

appear to occur in structures as a whole, and particularly when these are over 30·48m long. (It has been *generally* assumed that 30·48m is the maximum length that can be allowed, in this country, without making suitable provision for expansion. This general rule is not universally applicable. In long brick walls for example, expansion joints should be provided capable of accommodating an expansion of 9·5mm in 12m.) The following examples (taken mainly from BRS experience) illustrate the causes of cracking which have resulted from restraint of thermal movements in a number of different situations. The failures shown here occur as a result of expansion, but this does not rule out the possibility of failure during contraction which does also occur in practice. In the diagrams accompanying the examples possible solutions are given as applicable—the allowances that should be made for expansion in finishes and other applications are given in *4.00 Heat and its effects*.

(a) Failure in walls

(i) *Garden wall*. The 229mm garden wall restrained from movement at each end (D.2.03/8) was exceptionally well built with cement mortar and with every joint filled. On expansion compressive forces are induced within the wall. Because of the opening in the wall the intensity of stress varies and reaches a maximum over the opening, as shown. The effect of this is to create a weak point in the wall and this occurs over the opening. There is no restraint to movement upwards (the ground and foundations will prevent any downward movement in this situation) and so the wall has opened up over the opening, i.e. the weakest point as shown in detail A. In so doing the stress has been relieved at the expense of structural weakening of the wall! This particular crack opened up at mid-day and closed again in early morning.

(ii) *External cavity wall*. Unlike D.2.03/8 in D.2.03/9 there is no particular concentration of stress in any part of the restrained wall, and so it does not have any inherent weak point. (It is the same as the previous example in that it was well built with cement mortar and with each joint filled.) On expansion the restrained wall (which has induced compression) exerts a thrust on the walls offering the restraint. As the latter is not strong enough to resist this thrust, a crack has been formed down the front of the weakest of the restraining abutments—in this case the outer leaf of a cavity wall, as shown in detail A. This particular example is significant enough to emphasise the caution which needs to be taken in using as a precedent *apparently* similar traditional constructional forms which have not failed. The restrained wall is exactly 30·48m and thus theoretically within the limit in which no special expansion provision is usually thought necessary. More important, however, is the fact

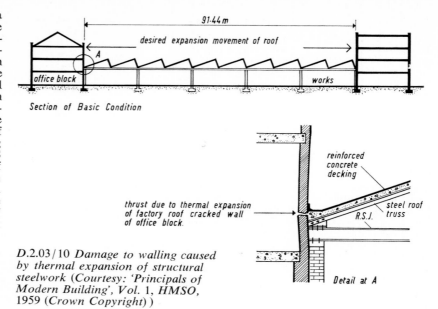

Section of Basic Condition

thrust due to thermal expansion of factory roof cracked wall of office block.

D.2.03/10 *Damage to walling caused by thermal expansion of structural steelwork (Courtesy: 'Principals of Modern Building', Vol. 1, HMSO, 1959 (Crown Copyright))*

Detail at A

that similar simple structural forms resembling the example shown in outward appearance have been in existence for centuries. However, these traditional buildings did not incorporate strong cement mortars nor thin external walls in cavity construction.

(iii) *Restrained steel roof*. The reason for failure of the wall in D.2.03/10 is similar to the last example—the restrained member was stronger than the member offering the restraint. In this case the thrust on the wall has been caused by the thermal expansion of the structural steelwork, for which no adequate provision for movement was made.

(b) Failures with rigid flat roofs

In general, flat roofs are far more highly exposed to natural thermal changes—solar radiation by day and cold skies by night—than vertical elements such as walls. There is, therefore, a differential in movement between horizontal and vertical elements that can further be influenced by differences in coefficients of thermal expansion in the materials making up these elements. In addition, there is a significant differential in the movement of the exposed surface and interior of a flat roof, with the exposed surface being continuously subjected to thermal changes which tend to be both rapid and of considerable magnitude. For these reasons, and because flat roofs are usually restrained to some extent by their supporting structure, it is the latter which normally cracks as the result of thermal movement in the roof. Failure of the supporting structure is likely to be particularly severe when a rigid roof system is used due mainly to its rigidity. Rigid roof systems include concrete whether cast *in situ* or precast.

As in all cases of thermal movement, the effect of thermal changes when rigid roof systems are used is largely dependent on the *rate* with

which the changes occur. The structure can generally accommodate movements when they occur uniformly and at a slow rate through gradual movements at the joints or through creep. It is, therefore, the sudden movement (a rapid rise or fall in temperature) which causes the damage. However, differential movements are also likely to cause considerable damage to the building as a whole. In this the time-lag in the response of different parts of a building to thermal changes is significant. In addition, because of differences between the coefficients of thermal expansion of different materials, the structure has less time to accommodate these differential movements when there is a rapid change in temperature.

When different parts of a roof (or different parts of a building) are heated at a different rate and to different temperatures, the resultant differential temperature variations lead to stresses that may become very high, particularly when changes take place rapidly. This is a particularly complex and potentially dangerous situation. For example, there will be a rapid and daily swing in temperature in a rigid roof slab when, during a run of hot summer days it is subjected to a maximum temperature at noon and a minimum temperature at night. In addition to daily repetitions of high differential deformations in the roof and the walls, there will be stresses within the roof itself due to uneven temperature distribution within it. Consequently a relatively flexible roof system is less likely to cause damage as it can deform by buckling and bending and therefore cannot exert an appreciable force on its own supporting structure or on the walls.

Although particular emphasis has been given above to the deleterious consequences of rapid thermal changes, it is important to note that the amount of movement, with the range of temperatures found in Britain from winter to summer, is sufficient to cause very troublesome cracking, *if* the roof is not properly protected. A concrete roof, for example, can undergo a movement of about 8·33mm in every 15m.

In concentrating on the thermal movement of the roof slab itself, it is easy to forget about the movement of the actual roof covering, that is the waterproofing membrane. Whereas failures of the slab are relatively uncommon, though by no means impossible, this is not necessarily true of the roof covering, which in addition to being weaker than the slab is far more severely exposed. Consequently it is easier for the covering to fail by tearing or cracking. When this happens, there is a danger of water finding its way into the structure and causing damage—see *3.04 Exclusion* for a detailed consideration.

(i) *Typical conditions.* It is always important to establish the direction in which the maximum movement of the roof slab is likely to take place. Whether completely unrestricted or *uniformly* restrained, the maximum movement will take place along the longest dimension. Thus in a square roof, the magnitude of movement will be the same in both directions. However, in order to predict how cracking is likely to be distributed, it is necessary to take into account the effects

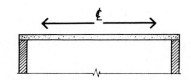

[A] UNIFORM EXPANSION OUTWARDS FROM CENTRE.

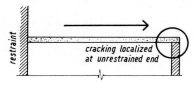

[B] RESTRAINT BY ABUTMENT.

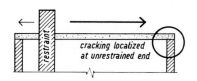

[C] RESTRAINT BY PROJECTIONS – lift shafts, stairs wells.

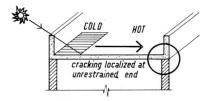

[D] RESTRAINT BY AREAS SHADED FOR LONG PERIODS.

D.2.03/11 *Illustration of conditions that may result in restraining of a rigid flat roof*

120

of non-uniform restraint. Four typical conditions are shown in diagram D.2.03/11. (A) represents either a completely unrestrained or uniformly restrained condition of a simple symmetrical roof, in which movement takes place uniformly from the centre outwards. Under restrained conditions, cracking may take place anywhere along the perimeter, subject to the ratio between the length and width of the roof which will influence the magnitude of movement in any one direction.

(B), (C) and (D) represent some possible conditions of non-uniform restraints. In the diagrams 'restraint' is used to signify the greatest restraint, and with this as a basis, it will be seen that movement can only take place in one direction, that is away from the restraint with the result that cracking will be localised at the unrestrained end. It should be noted that in (C) in particular it has been assumed that the projection is asymmetrical. Thus if projections such as lift shafts, stair wells and the like, fix the roof slab symmetrically, then the condition would be the same as in (A).

(ii) *Effect of structural type.* Basically a roof slab subjected to increases in temperature not only spreads outwards but also tends to bow upwards from the centre due to the higher temperature of the outer surface, as shown diagrammatically in diagram D.2.03/12. The combined effects of these two movements results in local cracking in the structural or non-structural elements in contact with the underside of the slab and at the end of the slab, that is the enclosing perimeter. The forms of cracking are however different in framed and unframed buildings, with the effects being more disfiguring in framed buildings. Diagram D.2.03/13 illustrates some of the basic differences.

In the *unframed building* (A), the tops of walls running *in the direction* of the long axis exhibit *shear cracking,* whereas the walls *at right angles* to the long axis of the roof (and furthest from the restrained parts of the slab) are *cracked by*

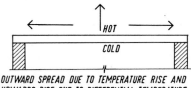

OUTWARD SPREAD DUE TO TEMPERATURE RISE AND UPWARDS RISE DUE TO DIFFERENTIAL TEMPERATURE IN SLAB

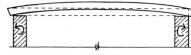

DIAGRAMMATIC REPRESENTATION OF SPREAD AND BOW.

D.2.03/12 *Illustration of outward and upward movements in a flat roof slab and their possible effects*

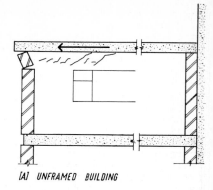

[A] UNFRAMED BUILDING

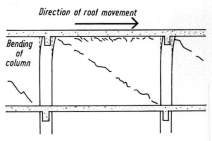

[B] FRAMED BUILDING

D.2.03/13 *Forms of cracking in unframed and framed buildings due to thermal movement (Courtesy: BRS Digest 75 (2nd Series) and 'Principles of Modern Building', Vol. 2, HMSO, 1959)*

rotation of the part in contact with the underside of the slab.

In the *framed building* (B), the beams too tend to bow upwards and may take part of the walls with them, giving rise to localised cracking at the top of the walls. In addition walls and partitions may be distorted as a whole. Those *parallel* to the movement of the roof show a diagonal fracture, that is *shear cracking,* running downward from the top corner where the pressure is applied as shown in the diagram. More simple horizontal breaks as in unframed buildings but often further down the wall occur in walls *across the line* of movement. This is because the wall is bent by being connected to the columns that themselves deflect.

Two examples of shear cracking in unframed buildings are illustrated in diagrams D.2.03/14 and 15. The cracks have occurred mainly because of the differential movement between the roof and the walls. It is important to note that in both cases the greatest thrust occurs at the ends of the buildings, that is away from the restraint. The fact that the cracks have taken place roughly at an angle of 45 degrees suggests that some form of shearing action has taken place. This may be explained by the fact that in these cases the walls provide the restraining force opposite to the expansion movement in such a way that a typical shear condition is created. Although cracking can take place in framed buildings as outlined above, it may be noted that in such buildings the frame, because it is

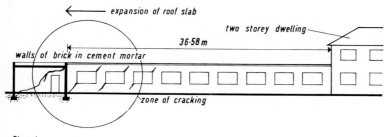

Cracking of a wall in an unframed building due to thermal movement of a rigid concrete flat roof as illustrated in D.2.03/12 (A) (Crown Copyright)

D.2.03/14 Cracking of external walls due to expansion of roof slab in a single-storey building. Roof slab: hollow tile reinforced concrete. Notes: (1) Cracks opened up to 4·76mm at hottest time of day. Closed again in early morning and on dull days. (2) Ends of buildings seem to have tilted without cracking under effects of thrust from roof slab (Courtesy: 'Principles of Modern Building', Vol. 1, HMSO, 1959 (Crown Copyright))

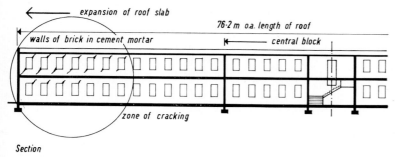

D.2.03/15 Cracking of external walls due to expansion of roof slab in an institutional building. Roof slab: hollow tile reinforced concrete. Note that cracks diminish towards the middle of the building (Courtesy: 'Principles of Modern Building', Vol. 1, HMSO, 1959 (Crown Copyright))

rigidly connected with the roof, allows the expansion to be generally distributed uniformly in each bay of the walling. This of course is not the case in an unframed building with the result that the most important site of trouble is usually the junction of the roof slab with the walls.

(iii) *Precautions.* Precautions to reduce the likelihood of cracking may be considered from three points of view. In practice a combination may be used depending on circumstances. Firstly, to restrict the amount of movement either by suitable reflective and insulation treatments or by reducing the length of the slab, that is splitting the slab and the structure into smaller units and using expansion joints (see (d) later). Secondly, to reduce the amount of restraint by allowing the slab to move which necessitates the use of sliding joints (see (c) later and diagram D.2.03/16). This may be done in unframed buildings. Thirdly, to ensure that the structure is designed to accommodate the stresses that will be induced by restraint of thermal movement. This could be done in framed buildings.

(c) *Internal wall/roof failure*

Differential movement (diagram D.2.03/16) may also occur between a roof slab and *internal* walls or partitions. The occurrence of cracking does not appear to be restricted to any particular kind of building and has been known to occur in both framed and loadbearing constructions. The cracks, usually horizontal, form at the top of the wall or partition just below the underside of the slab. Repeated attempts to repair cracks of this kind have usually been unsuccessful—the cracks open every summer. The section through the partition illustrates the type of failure that occurs. Possible methods of avoiding the trouble are given in the details.

Detail A is for a non-loadbearing partition and detail B for a loadbearing wall. The principle involved in both cases is to allow the roof slab to be able to 'slide over' the partition or wall, without, so to speak, taking either with it during movement.

In the case of the non-loadbearing partition (Detail A) it is possible to allow the roof to slide by actually stopping the partition below the underside of the slab and so forming a physical gap. Applied finishes, such as plaster, must not be continuous over the wall and the soffit of the slab. Discontinuity of the finish on both surfaces must be such so as to allow the slab to slide. To prevent sound leakage through the gap over the partition a cover mould is provided. This must only be fixed to the partition (fixing to the slab would only restrain sliding) with felt used between the top of the mould and the underside of the slab to provide a positive seal and also to allow sliding.

In the case of the loadbearing wall (Detail B) it is not possible to create any gap between the top of the wall and the underside of the slab. The solution is then to insert a material (in practice it is placed before casting the slab) such as a thin sheet of metal —lead is often used in cases like this —or other thin rigid material between the top of the wall and the underside of the slab. By so doing the slab is then free to slide over the wall. The principle of detailing any applied finish such as plaster is the same as for the partition. Although a cover mould is not essential for preventing sound leakage, it is usually provided if there is to be an applied plaster finish to either wall, slab or both, in order to mask the discontinuity gap which must be provided.

(d) Expansion joints

The details given in (c) above are those which would normally have to be employed when there is likely to be *excessive* movement in the roof slab. The extent of the movement in the slab will be determined, among other things, by the temperature rise, thermal properties and length of the slab as noted previously (b) (iii). For relatively small expanses, say under 30·48m, the best safeguard to prevent excessive heat absorption by the slab, is to provide a white reflective surface to the roof finish, as such a surface does serve to reflect much of the solar radiation. (The use of insulation in addition to the reflective surface will help to reduce the temperature rise in the slab but will also tend to raise the temperature of the waterproofing membrane. This problem is covered in *Part 4.00.*). With large expanses of roof, say over 30·48m long, it is necessary, in addition to the provision of the reflective surface, to physically split the structure (either partially or completely depending on circumstances) into smaller units and to provide expansion joints between each unit. The provision of expansion joints immediately raises difficulties in detailing so that complete weathertightness, and particularly the exclusion of water, is ensured.

There are basically two methods by which expansion joints may be provided in a structure (see D.2.03/17):

(1) By forming a continuous expansion joint in the roof, walls, floors and other elements. To be effective the structural break must be complete. This means that there must be no rigid connections between the parts or elements that have been split. The principle of discontinuity previously outlined must also apply to finishes.

(2) By arranging the roof slab so that it is capable of sliding over its supporting walls and by breaking the slab only with an expansion joint. Here again the break must be complete if it is to be effective, with the principles employed in detail B of diagram D.2.03/16 applicable.

The principles which should be employed in detailing to ensure weathertightness are illustrated in the details. A note on the resilient

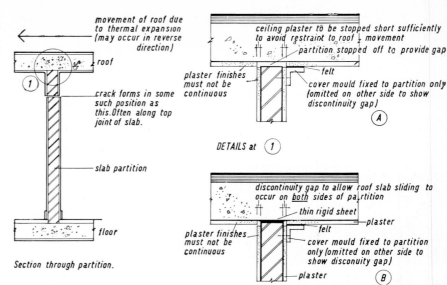

Section through partition.

D.2.03/16 *Section through internal partition, illustrating cracking of partition at or near junction of roof slab resulting from expansion of roof slab. Details show principles to be adopted in non-loadbearing partitions (A) and loadbearing partitions (B) (Courtesy: 'Principles of Modern Building', Vol. 1, HMSO, 1959 (Crown Copyright))*

materials generally shown in the expansion joints is necessary. A resilient material is not strictly necessary for expansion alone (if not properly used or if too rigid it may cause a certain amount of restraint) but it is usually necessary to avoid problems associated with water while at the same time it does facilitate the casting of *in situ* concrete.

It may be noted here that in recent years there has been a significant rise in the use of *mastics* as gap-fillers in all kinds of joints in an attempt to solve the problems associated with both thermal expansion (and contraction) and water penetration. Selection of a mastic that will meet both requirements can be difficult in view of the large range of materials now available (see *3.04 Exclusion* under 'Joint design'). For thermal movements, it is important to select a mastic which not only does not harden but also retains its elasticity after repeated expansion and contraction. In this account must be taken of the fact that no mastic has yet been shown to retain these or other properties permanently, so provision for replacement must be considered, in addition to ensuring that the material is protected as much as is reasonably possible. (Protection, particularly from solar radiation, helps in general to prolong the life of mastics.)

(e) Glazing failures (special glasses)*

Although all glasses expand with increases in temperature, special glasses such as coloured glass (particularly black), heat absorbing glass

*See Markus, T. A., 'The glass curtain wall 2, heat transmission', *The Architects' Journal*, Nov. 21, 1957, pp. 783–84: 'The fracture of glass by solar radiation', *Glass and Windows*, Bulletin No. 4 (Pilkington Bros. Ltd.) August, 1964; 'Glazing and fixing of glass for buildings', *British Standard Code of Practice*, CP152, 1966.

and clear glass with applied colour or with a dark background in close proximity, expand considerably more particularly in those situations where the glass is likely to be heated strongly by the absorption of solar radiation. It may be noted here that in some circumstances, special glasses may be heated to temperatures as high as 93°C even in temperate climates and so appreciable movements between glass and surround can be expected whatever the type and finish of the surround. Thus, whereas ordinary glasses should have an edge clearance (between the edge of the glass and the surround) of between 2 and 3mm (depending on the type of surround and glazing compound used), greater clearances are required for special glasses (not less than 3mm all round when the longer dimension does not exceed 760mm and not less than 5mm all round when the longer dimension exceeds 760mm).

In addition to the thermal expansion problem for which adequate clearance should be provided as stated above, special glasses may crack due to excessive edge cover by the glazing bead, fillet of glazing compound or rebate used for fixing the glass. The cracking occurs because the glass behind the edge cover is shaded from direct radiation thus giving rise to a temperature differential (usually considerable as glass is a poor conductor of heat) between the centre of the glass and the perimeter edge which in turn results in tensile stresses in the edge. The tensile stress is proportional to the difference in the temperature between the edge and the centre of the glass.

The reason for the setting up of tensile stresses in the perimeter is similar to the effects of cooling the surface of a material discussed under *Stress inducement* (p. 115 and

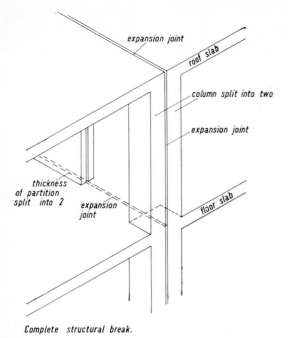

expansion joint

roof slab

column split into two

expansion joint

thickness of partition split into 2

expansion joint

floor slab

Complete structural break.

EXPANSION JOINTS

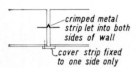
crimped metal strip let into both sides of wall

cover strip fixed to one side only

specially made p.v.c. extrusion for casting into concrete

resilient material

provision for sliding

VERTICAL

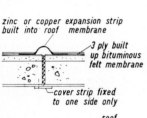
zinc or copper expansion strip built into roof membrane

3 ply built up bituminous felt membrane

cover strip fixed to one side only

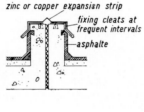
zinc or copper expansion strip

fixing cleats at frequent intervals

asphalte

special metal form

cover strip fixed to one side only

roof

floor

HORIZONTAL

D.2.03/17 *Expansion joints. Examples illustrating complete structural break and principles of detailing vertical and horizontal joints*

Left, an expansion joint filled with a mastic. Note the detail for the cill which has been designed to allow for movement and also to prevent water penetration. Right, watertightness of a mastic filled expansion joint can be impaired if the mastic is liable to deteriorate as in this example. Mastics must, therefore, be carefully selected for the exposure condition, failing which constant replacement will be necessary

Above, an example of a positive break between a boundary wall and the main wall of a building. Below, continuous expansion joint in a reinforced concrete column. The principle of discontinuity has not been entirely followed with the result that the render filling with a V-groove has cracked when movements have taken place

COLD

HOT

desired expansion movement of centre of glass

restraint provided by perimeter edge

Centre of glass absorbs heat from solar radiation and tries to expand outwards.

Edge covered by beads, fillets of glazing compound or rebates is shaded (i.e. cooler) and provides restraint

desired expansion movement of centre of glass.

RELATIVE MOVEMENTS OF CENTRE OF GLASS AND PERIMETER EDGE.
Note: Centre of glass = exposed portion.

RESULTANT TENSION IN PERIMETER EDGE.

D.2.03/18 *Diagrammatic illustration of thermal stress in a pane of glass due to shading of the edges*

diagram D.2.03/7). For convenience the present problem is illustrated in diagram D.2.03/18. When heated the centre of glass will try to expand but this expansion will be restrained by the cool edges.

Glass is extremely strong in compression but relatively weak in tension. However what is more important is that the tensile stresses due to the temperature differential occur in that part of the glass, namely the edge, which is in any case weakened by minute 'flaws' caused when the glass is cut to size. More serious flaws it should be noted are caused by knocks and abrasions and by 'nipping off' a piece of glass to reduce its size. The flaws determine the limiting tensile stress of the glass while failure occurs by the enlargement of an existing flaw into a crack.

In order to minimise the risk of cracking, *it is recommended* (CP 152 : 1966) that the edge cover to special glasses should *not exceed* 10mm all round, except where toughened glass is used. Additional precautions include: adequate allowance for movement (see above); clean cut edges; avoid using glass with nipped or damaged edges; setting or location blocks should be used whatever the size of glass to ensure that equal cover is provided on all edges, and, a non-setting glazing compound should be used with all absorbent rebates and grooves treated with a sealer and not merely primed.

(f) Cladding failures

There have been some failures of claddings such as granite facings, reconstructed or natural stone and precast concrete panels fixed to concrete frames, due to the cladding bowing outwards and moving away from the frame. The cladding is restrained by the background to which it is fixed and very often at top and bottom even if only by the cladding itself. Consequently differential movement between the cladding (the surface exposed) and the background (the interior) under conditions of restraint results in the cladding moving outwards in order to relieve the compressive stresses induced. Such stresses may be induced by the restraint at top and bottom or by restraint caused by the fixings to the background. The former is analogous to the expansion condition shown in diagram D.2.01/4 (page 91) and the latter to the effects of heating the surface of a material, shown in diagram D.2.03/6 (page 116). Normally it is not possible to adopt a less rigid method of fixing to the background and so some form of expansion joint is advisable.

It should be noted here that a similar type of failure may occur as a result of moisture movements, particularly if the background shrinks appreciably during drying out (see *3. Moisture movements*, below).

124

3. Moisture movements

(a) General considerations

Moisture movement is by definition the dimensional change, i.e. expansion or contraction which takes place in materials when there is a change in their moisture content—increases in moisture content result in expansion while decreases in contraction. As moisture movement can only take place in those materials which are capable of absorbing or giving off moisture, it is confined, unlike thermal movements, to the porous materials (*Section 1.12*). As in all properties of materials some porous materials are capable of greater amounts of movement than others. The degree of movement in various materials is given in *3.03 Moisture content*. Suffice it to mention here the two main factors upon which the extent of movement are dependent. Firstly, the structure of the material and, secondly, the concentrations of moisture in the environment of the material—under this must be included the amount of wetting which a material may be subjected to by soaking or by exposure to rainwater. In general, high concentrations of moisture will increase the amount of movement, while low concentrations will reduce the amount of movement. At the same time materials containing high concentrations of moisture are likely to undergo considerable amounts of movement if the moisture concentration of the environment is lowered and particularly when evaporation is increased by increases in the thermal environment and/or increases in the ventilation rate. Rapid changes in moisture content of materials often results in cracking because the materials cannot adapt themselves, in the structural sense that is, quickly enough. Restraint may in many instances aggravate the position.

(i) *Types of movement.* A distinction has to be drawn between *two types of moisture movement,* each of which has its own characteristics and which occur at different times during the life of a material, namely irreversible and reversible moisture movements.

Irreversible moisture movement, as the name implies, is that movement which only takes place once. The stage during which this movement, which is a shrinkage or contracting movement, occurs, is when the quantities of water present in all porous materials are evaporated or otherwise removed in order to make these materials suitable for building. During the life of the material there may be alternating increases and reductions in moisture content which result respectively in expansion and contraction. The movement which takes place after the material has dried out is the *reversible moisture movement.* Diagram D.2.03/19 shows graphically the difference between the two types of movement. From the diagram it

Cracking of sand-lime brickwork caused by changes in moisture content. Note: Although the cracking is generally confined to the mortar joints there are some instances where the bricks have cracked (Courtesy: Building Research Station (Crown Copyright))

will be seen that irreversible moisture movement is not the complete amount of movement which takes place on drying out, but the difference between the maximum amount on drying out and the maximum (expansion) that may subsequently occur.

Many porous materials used in buildings undergo their irreversible moisture movements away from the building site, sometimes under highly controlled conditions. If the problems associated with drying-out shrinkage are to be taken into account fully then it is important that it is known whether or not materials have completed their irreversible movement *before* they are built into a structure. All *clay products* which are fired at fairly high temperatures may be reasonably assumed to have completed their drying-out shrinkage. Although the same may apply to *seasoned timber,* it must be remembered that the seasoning of timber may be accurately defined in terms of moisture content—low moisture contents are obtainable by artificial seasoning. The relatively large reversible moisture movements possible with timber are far more important than whether or not the timber has completed its irreversible movement.

By far the greatest caution has to be observed with *precast cement-based products,* whether or not these are manufactured on or off the building site. The reason for this is based on the fact that most of these products require comparatively long controlled drying-out periods (to prevent excessive shrinkage cracking) while they may look dry *before* complete maturity and thus before complete irreversible movement has, in fact, taken place. None of these products should, therefore, be positioned in buildings under conditions of restraint until they have matured. The initial drying-out shrinkage probably contributes more to cracking than subsequent reversible movements. Important as the initial shrinkage may be, it is nevertheless important that the reversible moisture movements are not neglected as these may also result in cracking taking place under conditions of restraint.

As in the case of thermal movements it is the *exterior of buildings* which are by and large subjected to the greatest changes in moisture content and which result in reversible moisture movements taking place. In this country *porous walling materials* are subjected to long periods of almost complete saturation during the winter months. Hot sunshine, winds and low humidity during the summer allow the walls to dry out quite considerably. Thus, external walls are subjected to extreme seasonal variations in moisture content. When considering porous walling materials and their moisture changes it is important to note that, to all intents and purposes, they may be regarded as impervious when covered by impermeable applied finishes such as bitumen and paints.

The condition of *internal walls* is quite different and on the whole the amount and rate of moisture content changes in materials is usually, by comparison with external walls, fairly small. With *internal components* it is usually the *initial drying-out shrinkage* which accounts for the greatest amount of movement which results in cracking. The drying shrinkage cracking is often accentuated in new buildings when the heating system is run to capacity in order to secure rapid drying out.

(ii) *Problems with timber.* As already noted, *timber* presents rather a special problem as regards moisture movement in general and reversible moisture movement in particular. Reversible moisture movement may result in cracking of *either* the timber itself *or* of other closely related elements and particularly applied finishes such as plaster and paint. Furthermore, many of the moisture movements in timber result not so much in cracking as in distortion of the material. This, plus the fact that

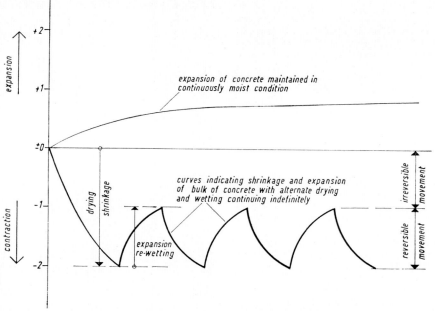

Top picture shows cracking of paint due to excessive moisture movements of timber background. Lower picture shows lifting of parquet flooring due to increase in size of blocks consequent upon an increase in moisture content (Courtesy: Building Research Station (Crown Copyright))

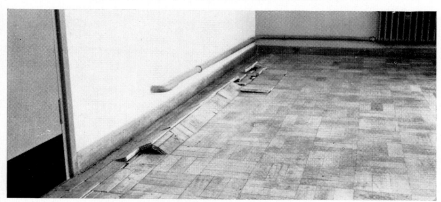

D.2.03/19 Illustration of irreversible and reversible moisture movements in concrete. (Courtesy: L. J. Murdoch, 'Concrete Materials Practice', 3rd ed., Edward Arnold)

movements are, when compared with other materials, so much larger in timber, makes it more convenient to deal with this particular material in more detail under *3.03 Water and its effects*. By so doing moisture movements in the other porous materials may then be dealt with on a more general basis, without each time having to pay regard to the exceptions which invariably are necessary with timber.

(iii) *'Step pattern'* cracking. In the *larger elements* such as loadbearing walls and non-loadbearing partitions, which are restrained from movement, the type of failure which results can usually be attributed to the failure of the material in *tension*. This occurs particularly when restrained members are contracting, and is thus relevant during shrinkage cracking. Because of the tensile induced stresses involved, cracking tends to be in a vertical direction —in walls or partitions built of small units the cracking may take place along vertical and horizontal joints thus producing a *'step pattern'*.

The contraction which occurs in walls of small units is often due to a combination of *both* irreversible (in the mortar joints) *and* reversible (in the bricks or blocks) movements. (The amount of movement in the bricks or blocks may be considerably reduced by ensuring that these materials are as dry as possible before laying and furthermore that they are maintained dry after laying by suitable protection from the weather and until the building is made weathertight.)

(iv) *Mortars/plasters/renders/screeds.* The importance of using and maintaining bricks or blocks in a dry condition before and after laying is better associated with attempts at reducing the drying shrinkage cracks in the *mortar*, in addition to the overall drying shrinkage of the walling element. The principles involved for mortar and bricks or blocks is also applicable to other finishes and elements such as *plasters*, *renders* and *screeds* which are cement based. All these cement-based, wet-trade processes should be restrained by adhesion to non-shrinkable backgrounds. When the adhesion is consistent and good, cracking should then be well distributed. In addition to this the background must be strong enough to provide the necessary restraint. The familiar 'map pattern' cracking illustrated in diagram D.2.03/20 is typical of drying shrinkage cracking in external renderings—cracking of *dense* cement-sand external renderings are a commonly reported failure. (On shrinking a strong cement render has been known to exert sufficient force to tear off the surface layer of rather poor brickwork.) It is always better to try to ensure that shrinkage cracks are *as fine as possible*. This is usually best obtained by ensuring that the cracks are well distributed rather than

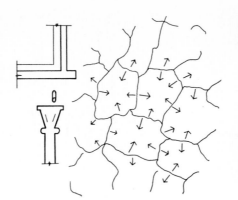

D.2.03/20 *'Map pattern' cracking in external rendering due to moisture movement (shrinkage) (Based on BRS Digest 75 (second series)). The photograph shows this type of cracking in external dense cement/sand rendering. This commonly reported failure typical of drying shrinkage in rendering should not be confused with the pattern associated with sulphate attack—see D.2.03/28 and associated photograph (Courtesy: BRS (Crown Copyright))*

Cracking of making good to fairfaced concrete due to poor adhesion and excessive drying shrinkage of the applied render

Left, vertical cracking in an external wall between the lintel to the ground-floor opening and the cill of the first-floor window above due to moisture movements. Right, 'step pattern' cracking due to moisture movements which has been made good

126

Conditions likely to cause cracking

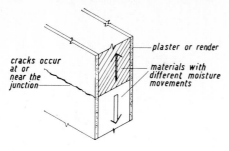

cracks occur
at or
near the
junction

plaster or render

materials with
different moisture
movements

Possible solutions

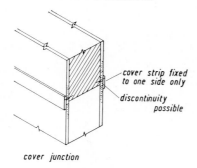

cover strip fixed
to one side only

discontinuity
possible

cover junction

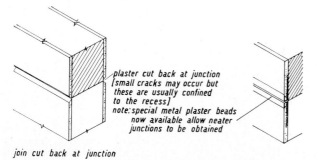

plaster cut back at junction
[small cracks may occur but
these are usually confined
to the recess]
note:special metal plaster beads
now available allow neater
junctions to be obtained

join cut back at junction

Conditions likely to cause cracking

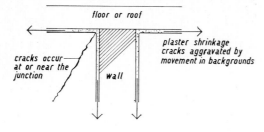

floor or roof

cracks occur
at or near the
junction

plaster shrinkage
cracks aggravated by
movement in backgrounds

wall

Possible solutions

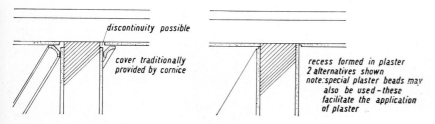

discontinuity possible

cover traditionally
provided by cornice

recess formed in plaster
2 alternatives shown
note:special plaster beads may
also be used - these
facilitate the application
of plaster

D.2.03/21 *Conditions likely to cause cracking of adjoining or abutting
materials with different moisture movements, with possible methods to
reduce the likelihood of cracking*

localised. With *plasters, renders and
screeds* it is always a wise precaution
to avoid covering excessively large
areas without definite breaks in the
material, i.e. a form of expansion
joint. Normally the thicker the
material the smaller the area between breaks should be. No specific
guidance can be given on this point.
Much still depends on experience.

(v) *Control in massive elements.*
Control of shrinkage cracking in the
more massive elements such as *concrete* is usually effected by the reinforcement. The distribution and design
of the reinforcement requires careful
consideration especially as the arrangement of reinforcing, for structural
reasons, may not necessarily suit the
arrangements required to control
cracking. Finally, and by no means
least, drying shrinkage of all cement-
based products is greatly dependent on
the control of quality of the mixes
which may be effected.

(vi) *Differential movements.* Before
considering the problems of moisture
movement in large walling elements,
it is convenient here to draw attention to the possibility of cracking
occurring at or near the junction of
materials with different moisture movements which either abut or adjoin one
another. Invariably the plaster at or
near the junction of the two materials
cracks. Similar cracks also occur
very often at the junction of walls and
ceilings when the plaster is continuous.
(In traditional work these cracks were
always hidden by the cornice.)

Differential movement may also
occur between two adhering materials,
or between two elements of different
materials as for example a finish and
its background, or a panel in a frame.
In cases such as these, if the background or the frame shrinks appreciably then the finish or the panel will
be subjected to *compression*. In order
to relieve the compressive stresses, the
finish or the panel will tend to bow
outwards and this may lead to cracking. The condition will be even more
severe if in addition the finish or the
panel expands—see examples (d) and
(e) later.

The basic conditions which are
likely to lead to the cracking are
illustrated in principle in diagram
D.2.03/21. Also illustrated are possible solutions to avoid the cracking
occurring. This type of cracking is
usually associated with rendering or
plastering which has been applied
continuously over the materials with
the different movements. As an
example plaster or render is very
often applied continuously over
adjoining or abutting brick and concrete. The likelihood of cracking actually occurring will depend primarily
on the relative differences of the
moisture movements of the two
materials, and also on the ability
of the applied finish to accommodate the actual movement which
will take place. In many cases the cause
of the cracking can be attributed to the

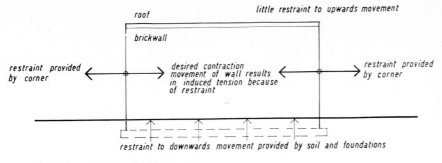

A Elevation of rectangular building showing induced tension in external wall due to restraint of shrinkage

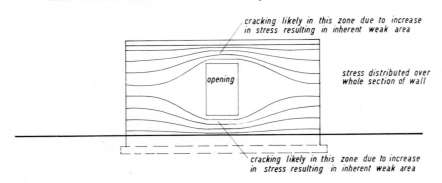

B Stress concentration due to opening in wall creating inherent weak areas

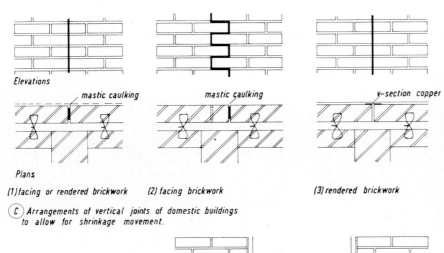

Elevations

mastic caulking   mastic caulking   v-section copper

Plans

(1) facing or rendered brickwork   (2) facing brickwork   (3) rendered brickwork

C Arrangements of vertical joints of domestic buildings to allow for shrinkage movement.

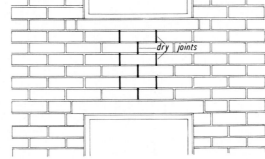

D Dry joints left to accommodate shrinkage movement

D.2.03/22 *Conditions likely to cause cracking of external walls due to moisture movements, together with possible methods to avoid the likelihood of cracking (Courtesy: 'Principles of Modern Building', Vol. 1, HMSO, 1959 (Crown Copyright))*

fact that one of the materials has not fully completed its initial movement (other movements, particularly of the backgrounds, may also be involved). In principle, the possible solutions are all based on effecting discontinuity of the applied finish, i.e. forming a physical break. As mentioned previously, if cover moulds are to be used to hide the discontinuity gap in the render or plaster, then it is logical to ensure that other applied finishes, such as paint, should not be applied continuously over the cover mould.

Attempts are sometimes made to distribute the cracking by applying expanded metal at the junction of the two materials. As yet no guidance has been given as to the extent of expanded metal that should be used over the two materials. Success with expanded metal varies a great deal.

(b) Small unit walling

In the two examples that follow the problems and possible solutions of cracking in traditional small unit walling elements are considered. The principles outlined may, within certain limits, be applied to other similar types of construction or otherwise similar conditions.

(i) *External walling elements.* Most external walling elements are more or less free to move in an upwards direction only. Horizontal movement is restrained by the corners, or other abutments, of the building, while any downwards movement is restrained by the soil and foundations. (See diagram D.2.03/22.) Under these conditions of restraint, shrinkage of the wall as a whole results in induced tension stresses (A). Cracking will, as already mentioned, tend to be in a vertical direction. When there are openings, such as doors and windows, in the wall, then there will be stress concentration, i.e. increase in intensity, in the wall above or below the opening (B). This then produces an inherent weak point. Thus, in practice, cracking usually runs from ground floor sills to the damp proof course, and from upper storey sills to lintels of storeys below. Examples are given in the photographs (p. 126).

In cases such as these it is obviously not possible to reduce the restraint at the ends of the building. Alternative methods must, therefore, be adopted which will reduce the induced stresses. One alternative is to break the wall up into smaller panels, but using continuous vertical joints (C).

In all cases it is necessary to ensure that there is no wind or rain penetration through the movement joint. In facing work the joint may be caulked with a mastic.* In rendered work a strip of damp proof course felt

*Deterioration of the mastic will affect adversely the weather tightness of the joint. It is, therefore, important that mastics are carefully selected relative to the particular exposure condition anticipated. In many cases the life of the mastic can be lengthened by suitably protecting the material from exposure to the deteriorating elements which normally would include sunlight.

may be set vertically in the gap as the wall is being built and the rendering brought up to the projecting felt on both sides of the joint. Absolute rain and wind exclusion will, however, be given by a V-section copper strip fixed to the wall to bridge the gap, with the limbs subsequently embedded in the rendering (C.3). Finally, a vertical break may be made at the midpoint of windows between sills and lintels, leaving the dry joints to be mortared up and pointed later when the structure has ceased to shrink (D).

It should be noted here that attempts have been made to use reinforcement in the bed joints close to openings in order to reduce shrinkage cracking. This does prevent the cracks from becoming wide and unsightly. As before, little is yet known about the optimum amount of reinforcement required, while the durability of the reinforcement (usually a ferrous metal) is likely to be poor in so exposed a position as a mortar joint. Durability is further reduced when cracking occurs.

(ii) *Internal partitions.* With internal partitions and particularly those built of lightweight concrete, where moisture movements may be relatively large, conditions of restraint may be imposed by the surrounding structure, such as walls and columns into which the partitions may be toothed or otherwise firmly tied. (See diagram D.2.03/23.) Some restraint may also be provided by floors and ceilings. Thus, unlike external walls there is unlikely to be any freedom from an upwards movement. However, the induced stresses will still be tensile during shrinkage and roughly the same as the last example. (The longest dimension normally dictates the direction in which the stresses will be the greatest.) Cracks will again be in a vertical direction, although this may also be in a stepped pattern. It is not uncommon to find that a partition has cracked into more or less equal divisions. Where door or other openings occur, there is immediately an inherent weak point, and so cracks run from the corner of the opening upwards to the ceiling.

Unlike the previous example the theoretical solution is to reduce the amount of restraint. In practice this may be difficult to achieve. One obvious solution would be to create a physical break, i.e. a movement joint, between the partition and the surrounding structure. This may not always be possible as some tying of the partition to another element may be necessary to maintain structural stability of the partition. One way out of this problem is to use ties which are capable of allowing some movement —there are ties, usually of the softer metals, which are specially twisted or otherwise formed to allow some movement. Whatever solution may be attempted, it is still important that there should always be some form of *discontinuity* in any applied finishes.

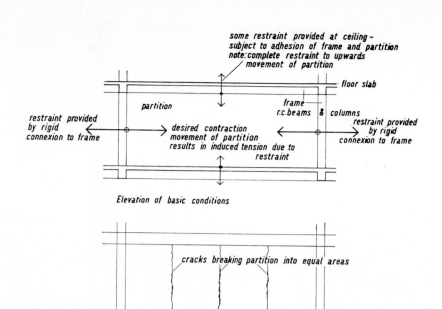

Elevation of basic conditions

cracks breaking partition into equal areas

Elevation showing one possible result of induced tension

crack in either one or both positions

Elevation showing effect of opening in partition

D.2.03/23 Conditions likely to cause cracking of partitions in a framed building

(iii) *General points.* Some general points arise out of these two examples. In all cases account has to be taken of the relative movement of both units and the mortar—the relative strength of the mortar and the units will also be important. Where it is considered that cracking cannot be completely avoided it is desirable that such cracking as may occur should be well distributed—on the whole small cracks in the mortar are less noticeable and unsightly and usually less deleterious than cracks through the units. Units known to have relatively high moisture movements should be stored and maintained in dry conditions until the building is made weathertight.

It has been stated (*Principles of Modern Building,* Volume 1) that generally shrinkage cracking is important only because of its effect on appearance and that is does not materially affect structural stability nor exclusion of rain in cavity construction. As true as such generalisations may be for external walls, it is nevertheless to be remembered that cracks can provide points for water penetration, the effect of which very often leads to further cracking either by chemical or physical action. Furthermore, making good after the first

summer of a new building—the time when shrinkage cracks usually manifest themselves—is not always practical or convenient. Cracks in internal walls or partitions, it should be remembered, may increase sound transmission quite considerably.

(c) *Large unit walling*

Slab and sheet materials such as storey-height panels, wood-wool slabs, building boards, and even paper and textiles present different problems from those encountered in masonry construction. One of the main differences arises out of the different method of fixing of the large units. There is also the larger amount of movement per unit. Many methods of fixing the large units usually allow these materials to have their movement concealed or restrained so that there is at least no opening-up at the joints.

(d) *Moisture expansion—brickwork*

Generally speaking clay bricks do not undergo significant moisture expansion. However, kiln-fresh bricks, that is bricks that have not been out of the kiln for more than a week, may expand considerably when they take up moisture during laying. This expansion has been sufficient to cause cracking in some instances. A basic precaution, therefore, is to ensure that bricks are not used straight from the kiln and that they have been stored for at least a week before being used.

(i) *Short returns.* New walls may be damaged by moisture expansion if they have short returns as shown in diagram D.2.03/24. The damp-proof course can act as a slip joint thus allowing the brickwork to expand with no significant restraint. In this way the brick return in the wall is rotated.

(ii) *Combined with drying shrinkage of concrete.* Diagram D.2.03/25 illustrates the combined effect of drying shrinkage of *in situ* concrete columns and the moisture expansion of the infilling brickwork. The latter is put into compression and the resulting stresses are relieved by outward bowing of the brickwork. The size of the force involved may be gauged by the fact that the intermediate concrete nib has been pulled away.

(e) *Clay tile flooring*

Failures of clay floor tiling in which the tiles either arch or ridge (see photographs) are often due to differential movement between the tiles and the base—tiles may also, but less commonly, fail due to deflection of the base as outlined previously in 2 (a). Restraint is provided by the adhesion of the tiles to the base by cement : sand beddings and at the perimeter where the tiles adjoin walls or columns. Failures are characterised by the fact that the tiles separate cleanly away from the bedding.

Some tiles expand significantly early in their life (the expansion reduces with time). However, it is usually the newly laid screed (sometimes the concrete base as well) that shrinks considerably, thus giving rise to an appreciable differential movement. Thermal movements may also cause similar failures. Often drying shrinkage and thermal movement may act together so that the stresses set up by one and then augmented by the other produce lifting. The combined effects of moisture and thermal movements usually manifest themselves when new tiling is laid on an old base or when tiling has behaved well for many years.

In order to minimise the risk of lifting, the *first precaution* that should be taken is *to prevent bonding* between the bedding and the base so that relative movement between them is *not restrained*. This may be accomplished by one of three laying techniques: (1) Laying the bedding of cement : sand mortar on a separating layer as shown in diagram D.2.03/26, ensuring that adjacent sheets are lapped sufficiently to prevent any key between the bedding and base. The separating layer may be of any material that avoids a bond being formed between the bedding and the base. The bedding itself should not be

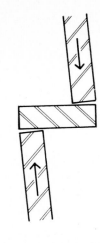

D.2.03/24 Cracking in short return to brickwork due to moisture expansion (Based on BRS Digest 75 (second series)) as illustrated in the photograph left (Crown Copyright)

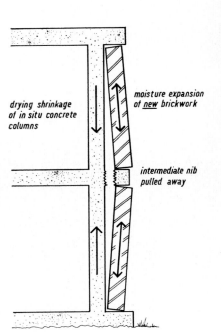

drying shrinkage of in situ concrete columns

moisture expansion of *new* brickwork

intermediate nib pulled away

D.2.03/25 Cracking of concrete nib due to combined effects of drying shrinkage of in-situ concrete columns and moisture expansion of new brickwork (Based on BRS Digest 75 (second series)) illustrated in the photograph above (Crown Copyright)

Arching of clay floor tiles (Crown Copyright)

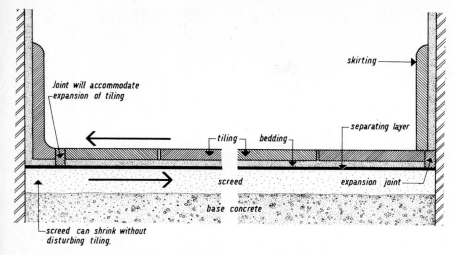

[1] BETWEEN TILING AND SKIRTING.　　　　[2] BETWEEN TILING AND WALL.

D.2.03/26 *Two alternative methods of incorporating expansion joints in clay tile flooring (Based on BRS Digest 79 (second series))*

Ridging of clay floor tiles (Crown Copyright)

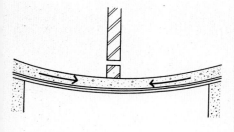

D.2.03/27. *Cracking due to the deflexion of a concrete floor slab that has been accentuated by the inclusion of shrinkable aggregates in the concrete (Based on BRS Digest 75 (second series)). Photograph shows the cracks this produced in a partition (Crown Copyright)*

thicker than the tile or 19mm (whichever is the least thickness) and wherever possible should be as *thin* as is required to provide a level floor. A thickness of 13mm is common but a thinner bed of 9·5mm is possible on a smooth base—a thickness of 19mm may be necessary where there is heavy traffic. (2) Laying on a *thick bed* of a *semi-dry* mix of cement and sand (not richer than 1 : 4) with no separating layer. The mix is packed on to the base to a thickness of not less than 19mm but which may be 76mm— a thickness of 38mm produces good results. The area of bedding placed in one operation should allow grouting and tiling to be completed while the bedding is still plastic. The surface of the compacted bedding should either be spread with a 1 : 1 cement : sand grout or slurry, or, dry cement may be trowelled into the semi-dry mix before bedding the tiles. The tiles are normally laid dry and are tapped into the grout. It should be noted that the surface of the base may require damping to reduce suction. (3) Using a '*thin bed*' (adhesive) fixing conforming to British Standard CP212, laid in accordance with the manufacturer's instructions and at a thickness *not exceeding* 4·8mm. Although in this method the tiling is bonded to the base, the bedding material is sufficiently resilient to tolerate some slight movement between tiling and the base without ill effect.

The *second precaution* that should be taken is to *provide expansion joints* with suitable compressible material around the perimeter and at abutments with columns, machine bases, etc. They may, as shown in diagram D.2.03/26, be formed between tiling and coved skirtings or against walls. In the latter case the skirting laps over the tiles and conceals the expansion joint. It is important to note that where the area of flooring is large, *additional* expansion joints should be provided at intervals of *not more than* 7·62m across *both* the length and the width of the floor.

(f) *Drying shrinkage and deflection— floors*

Normal deflection in suspended concrete floors slabs due to their self-weight and superimposed loads can occasionally be increased by drying shrinkage in an asymmetrically reinforced slab. In the example given in diagram D.2.03/27 shrinkage has been accentuated by the inclusion of *shrinkable aggregates* in the concrete (see *3.03 Moisture content*). Cracking has occurred due to the resulting additional deflection which has removed support from the foot of the partition wall above. In cases like this many factors, including poor design and bad workmanship may be collectively responsible for the cracking.

Cracking due to vibrations

At the outset it is necessary to state that the likelihood of vibrations causing cracking or serious structural damage to buildings is still a matter of some speculation while authenticated cases of damage are rare* However, in many ways it is not unnatural to find that fears have in the past been expressed—today they continue to be expressed—of damage to buildings caused by vibrations from both external and internal sources. Although most people believe that vibrations are capable of damage because they can be felt, this does not detract from the fact that vibration is immediately associated with fatigue. The effect of fatigue has had widespread attention in other fields of engineering but as yet there is no evidence to suggest that fatigue is significant in buildings. A number of different factors may, however, make this an important aspect in the immediate future. Among these are the considerable increases in the sources of vibrations both externally—road, rail and air traffic—and internally—many different kinds of machines and particularly various types of equipment—and the modern tendencies to reduce assumed imposed loads while at the same time increasing permissible stresses. Furthermore, because there are so many other causes of cracking in buildings, there is no conclusive evidence that some cracks can be attributable *solely* to vibrations. Excepting those buildings which have to be specially designed to withstand expected earthquakes or tremors, it is surprising how remarkably well many buildings have withstood slight tremors

without serious damage. On the whole vibrations appear to be more important for their effects on human sensitivity than on buildings as a whole. In many instances attempts to reduce sound transmission due to vibrations for human comfort reasons, do indirectly mitigate the possibilities of cracking due to the vibrations.

The difficulties of assessing whether vibrations are likely to cause cracking in buildings is associated with the fact that there is no universally accepted criterion that may be used to compare the effects of vibrations of differing amplitudes and frequencies. Difficulties are also encountered with other related factors such as the additional stresses set up by vibration; the possibility of resonance; the size of the building; the type of construction; and the fatigue properties of materials.

As far as can be determined most failures which it would appear reasonable to associate with the effects of vibrations occur in finishes such as plaster, particularly on ceilings, where the damage is in any case comparatively minor. Loosening of tiles and cracking of glass have also sometimes been considered as having resulted from vibrations. Other minor forms of cracks have also been known to occur in the immediate vicinity of machines and other pieces of vibrating equipment.

It is not always possible nor practical to completely eliminate vibrations. The most obvious, and perhaps most desirable, method is to deal with the problem at source, i.e. in the design of the equipment itself. Where this is not possible some method of isolation

Cracking due to sulphate attack

Below, cracking due to corrosion of steel reinforcement in projecting nib of a reinforced concrete beam

Bottom picture, cracking of glass due to corrosion of steel frame

*See *Vibrations in buildings,* BRS Digest (1st Series) No. 78, HMSO, June, 1965; *Cracking in buildings,* BRS Digest (2nd Series) No. 75, HMSO, Oct., 1966, reprinted 1968.

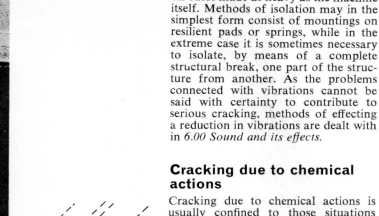

D.2.03/28 Cracking of rendering due to sulphate attack. In the photograph above note that the rendering is cracking horizontally—typical for sulphate attack. Compare with map pattern cracking due to moisture movement D.2.03/20 (Crown Copyright)

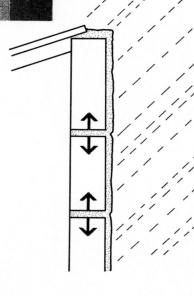

D.2.03/29 Lifting and cracking of concrete ground floor slab due to sulphate attack. Note cracking caused to brickwork (Based on BRS Digest 75 (second series)). The photograph shows severe cracking of a concrete floor laid directly on burnt colliery shale hardcore due to sulphate attack (Crown Copyright)

is often the most effective, although vibrating machines may be mounted on bases made as heavy as the machine itself. Methods of isolation may in the simplest form consist of mountings on resilient pads or springs, while in the extreme case it is sometimes necessary to isolate, by means of a complete structural break, one part of the structure from another. As the problems connected with vibrations cannot be said with certainty to contribute to serious cracking, methods of effecting a reduction in vibrations are dealt with in *6.00 Sound and its effects*.

Cracking due to chemical actions

Cracking due to chemical actions is usually confined to those situations where materials, likely to undergo an action, are embedded in other materials, such as reinforcement in concrete, balustrade, railing and staircase fixings; hidden behind other materials, such as may occur in fixing systems used for sheet materials, large panels, etc., or even in glazing; or behind (sometimes within, too) finishes such as plaster, render, screeding, etc., which are adhered to backgrounds. In all cases the restraint imposed on the materials is an essential part of their proper performance. Apart from carbonation when shrinkage takes place, the more important chemical reactions such as sulphate attack and corrosion of metals, are associated with expansion. Thus, when seeking solutions to the problem of expansion and subsequent cracking which may result, it is not possible to find methods of allowing for the expansion. In practice nearly all of the chemical actions which take place require, among other things, the presence of water. Thus, once all other precautions related to the correct choice of material in a given situation have been taken, it is important that every care should be taken to prevent the ingress of moisture to the hidden positions. Precautions which will reduce cracking due to other causes are, therefore, important as cracks do provide moisture paths.

The whole problem of chemical action in building materials is covered more fully in *Part 3.00* (*sulphate attack in Section 3.06* and corrosion of metals in *Section 3.07*), when the likelihood and susceptibility of materials to chemical action is discussed. Some photographs showing cracking due to chemical actions are included here as a reminder, while diagrams D.2.03/28 and 29 illustrate two examples of sulphate attack.

Cracking due to physical changes

Most of the movements already discussed are in fact physical changes of one kind or another. However, there are three physical changes, namely frost action, crystallisation of salts

133

and loss of volatiles that are better included on their own.

1. Frost action

As in the case of chemical actions, frost action is more fully considered in *Section 3.08*. However, it is convenient to note here that most of the cracking due to frost action commonly occurs externally and is usually only associated with porous materials. By and large the cracking that may result is insignificant when compared to the cracking which may result from thermal and moisture movements. In most cases frost action manifests itself in the breaking away of the surface layers of materials. Pointing in brickwork often suffers very badly. At the same time frost action may aggravate cracks caused through other agencies.

It will be seen later that there are many factors such as pore arrangement; temperature gradient; and conditions of freezing which influence the likelihood of frost action taking place. Whether or not materials will actually crack depends on their strength. In this connexion it should be noted that some materials have been found by experience to be more resistant to frost action than others. In this consideration must be included mix design for mortars, plasters, concrete, etc. Thus where conditions of frost can be anticipated, it is important that suitable frost resistant materials are selected.

Finally, a problem closely associated with winter building and the wet trade processes. Water freezing within these materials before they have set properly does lead not only to cracking of the immature material but also to its structural weakening. Under severe conditions of frost special and sometimes elaborate methods of insulation and protection are required.

Frost action in soils may sometimes also be responsible for cracking of the structure of a building—see *3. Freezing of the soil* under 'Cracking due to soil movements', below.

2. Crystallisation of salts

Crystallisation of salts is covered in full in *Section 3.05*. Suffice it to say here that salts generally crystallise out at or near the surface of porous materials such as bricks and natural stones and cracking is normally confined to the surface of the material. Deposits of *soluble* salts at or near the surface of a porous material as the result of evaporation of water in which the salts are dissolved, is usually known by the term *efflorescence*.

3. Loss of volatiles

Loss of volatiles is associated with mastics and other materials used for sealing joints, glazing, etc. Generally speaking, exposure to direct solar

134

Failure of bricks of low frost resistance in a retaining wall (Crown Copyright)

radiation is usually responsible for the loss of the volatile material. Such loss results in the cracking of the sealing material—see photographs of expansion joints (p. 123). The precautions that should be adopted are included in *3.04 Exclusion* under 'Joint design'.

Cracking due to soil movements

As soils of various kinds have to support the entire load, i.e. both dead and imposed, of buildings—the support of buildings on solid rock is not considered here—it follows that any movement which may occur in the soil will have some effect on the stress distribution of both foundations and superstructure*. Movements will result in some distortion of either foundation, superstructure or both. Subject to the stress redistribution which takes place and which must be related to the type of foundation and superstructure involved, the distortions may at best result in cracking of partitions or finishes and at worst complete structural collapse.

Although the interaction of soil, foundation and superstructure present a complex system there are two alternative basic principles which apply when dealing with this complex system. (1) To ensure that there is as little

*See *Soils and foundations:* 1, 2 & 3, BRS Digests (2nd Series) Nos. 63, 64 and 67, HMSO (Oct., 1965; Nov., 1965; Feb., 1966 respectively); *Cracking in buildings,* BRS Digest (2nd Series) No. 75, HMSO (Oct., 1966.)

movement as possible in the soil once it has been loaded. (2) To ensure that the building as a whole, i.e. foundation and superstructure, is specifically designed to accommodate movements which it is known are likely to occur. The solution to both of these problems requires specialised knowledge firstly of the soil—a subject usually covered under soil mechanics—and secondly of structural mechanics. It is not proposed to deal with either of these subjects in detail, but rather to consider and note the main points in so far as they are relevant to the likelihood of cracking taking place.

In the context of being the main supporting element of buildings, soils constitute some of the most fundamental and in many ways most important materials to be considered in practice. Most soils consist of solid particles of varying shapes and sizes, with water and, to a lesser extent, air filling the spaces between them. Their characteristics, behaviour and general properties are in many ways quite different from those of normal building materials. However, an important similarity between soils and naturally occurring materials used in buildings does exist. Like these materials, soils of the same type may differ quite considerably in their properties. Further more, there are a number of different types of soils each with their own properties. For convenience soils are divided into two broad groups: (1) cohesive soils which consist chiefly of the silts and clays and whose strength is largely dependent on the amount of

Property	Cohesive soils	Non-cohesive soils
Strength	Strength derived from power of cohesion of the particles. Strength does not necessarily increase with increase in depth below surface	Strength derived from internal friction between particles which increases under load. Strength increases with increases in depth below surface
Voids	High proportion of voids	Low proportion of voids
Cohesion	Marked cohesion	Negligible when clean
Compressibility	Very compressible	Only slightly compressible
Reaction to compression	Compression takes place slowly over a long period See diagram D.2.03/18	Compression takes place almost immediately See diagram D.2.03/18
Permeability	Practically impermeable	Permeable

Note: Account should be taken of the ranges which exist between the two extremes quoted above.

Table 2.03/2

Particle size of various types of soil	
Gravel	Particles larger than 2·00mm
Sand	Particles between 2·00mm–0·06mm
Silt	Particles between 0·06mm–0·002mm
Clay	Particles smaller than 0·002mm

Note: There are many systems for grading particle size. The above grading is the MIT System adopted in BSS 1377:1948 page 40.

C.2.03/2 Comparative chart of safe bearing capacities of various types of soil.
Important note: The values should be regarded as approximate guides only as similar soils vary from one another with no marked definition while there may be disagreement on the meaning of terms such as 'hard', stiff and 'soft' as applied to clays or 'compact', 'loose' and 'uniform' as applied to sands

REFERENCES: Values from 'Foundation Design Simply Explained', by John Faber and Frank Mead (Oxford University Press—1961)

	TYPE OF SOILS	SAFE BEARING CAPACITY (kN/m²) Value 0 200 400 600
Non-cohesive soils	Well-graded sands & sandy gravels (compact)	429 – 643
	Well-graded sands & sandy gravels (loose)	215 – 429
	Uniform sands (compact)	215 – 429
	Uniform sands (loose)	107 – 215
Cohesive soils	Very stiff & hard shaley clays	429 – 643
	Stiff clays (sandy or not)	215 – 429
	Firm clays (sandy or not)	107 – 215
	Soft clays & silts	54 – 107
	Very soft clay & silts	Nil

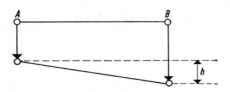

D.2.03/30 Angular distortion. Used in connexion with soil movements (From BRS Digest 63 (second series))

water they contain (clay notable); and (2) non-cohesive soils which consist chiefly of the gravels and sands and whose strength is dependent on the relationship of the closeness of the packing of their particles to the size of the external force. The relative properties of these two groups are given in table 2.03/1, while table 2.03/2 indicates the grading of particle size in each group. The chart C.2.03/2 illustrates the approximate loadbearing capacities of the various types.

In common with the differences in properties which can be expected when dealing with soils, it is also important to note that on any building site it is quite likely that *variations* in the properties of the soil will occur. In addition to this there may be a number of different types of soil especially at different levels below the surface. Because these and other variations may exist, it is always important that a thorough site exploration is undertaken prior to the design of foundations and superstructure.

Damage due to differential movement is not simply dependent on the amount of movement that takes place but on what is known as 'angular distortion' relative to the type of construction. 'Angular distortion' is a measure of the differential movement, defined as h/AB (diagram D.2.03/30) where h is the differential vertical movement and AB the distance between two points (the span). Brickwork and plaster show the effects of differential movement quickly and from the limited data available the onset of cracking can be associated, according to BRS, with an angular distortion of about $1/300$. This is equivalent to a differential movement of 9·5mm over a span of 3·0m. Warehouse and factory buildings of framed construction can usually tolerate larger angular distortions but at about $1/150$ structural damage may be expected unless the joints have been specially designed to tolerate them.

Movements which occur in soils and which influence the likelihood of cracking may be divided into the following general headings: (1) settlement due to the building load; (2) changes in the moisture content of the soil; (3) freezing of the soil; (4) vibrations and other causes.

1. Settlement

One of the primary functions of a foundation is to transfer the total load of a building on to the soil. This load transfer should be as even as possible while it should be spread over sufficient area of the soil for safe bearing. Thus the area required for the distribution of the load will be dependent on the safe bearing capacity of the soil. This deals with one basic problem. The next problem is how does the soil behave once it has been loaded?

(a) 'Normal' conditions

In general all soils will compact or *consolidate*, i.e. there will be a downwards movement, commonly known as settlement, on being loaded. The load on the soil, as applied through the foundations, increases both water and soil pressures. Water is squeezed from between the solid particles and driven to areas where the water pressure is less. The soil particles on the other hand are forced closer together. Consolidation continues until the water pressure has fallen to its original value and the forces between the particles have increased by an amount equal to the newly applied load. The total settlement will be dependent on the type of soil and the imposed load. In addition to this there is the *time* aspect of settlement. The imposed load on a soil is generally increased as construction proceeds. There is, however, a marked difference in behaviour between sandy and clay soils as is illustrated in diagram D.2.03/31. From this it will be seen that the duration of movement in sandy soils relative to the imposed load is short, i.e. each increment of load causes the total settlement of the soil for that load. Thus there is no further settlement once the total load has been imposed. Clay soils on the other hand do not react immediately to the loading increments and thus settlement proceeds for a considerable time after the final load has been imposed. Foundations on sandy soils settle quickly once the load is applied because the soil particles and thus the pore spaces are large which in turn allows rapid water movements. Clay soils on the other hand offer considerable resistance to the expulsion of water and thus settlement caused by consolidation can continue for years after construction. It may be noted here that if the process is reversed (as might happen if the load on the soil is reduced by excava-

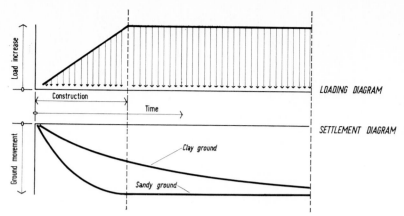

D.2.03/31 *Time and load dependent building settlements liable to occur on sandy and clay soils. (Based on 'Some Principles of Foundation Behaviour', by A. W. Skempton, RIBA Journal, November, 1942)*

tions) swelling of the soil occurs as water tends to move towards the unloaded areas. Shrinkage and swelling may often act simultaneously.

Because of the natural variations which occur in all soils, it is likely that there will not be the same total settlement everywhere. This is then one cause for differential settlement occurring, and it can occur even when the building load has been evenly distributed. If, on the other hand, the building load is not evenly distributed then the amount of differential settlement will increase. Although it is usually impossible to eliminate differential settlement completely, due to the nature of soils, it is always wise to ensure that at least the building load is distributed as evenly as possible.

The *type of foundation* required to ensure even distribution of the building load will depend not only on the type of soil but also on the disposition of loadbearing elements. Some common forms of foundations are:

(1) *Strip foundations* where the loads are transmitted to the foundation by walls and where special soil conditions do not exist. The depth of foundation will depend on the properties of the soil at any depth. Thus where soil conditions are good these may be both narrow and shallow; on poor soil they have to be wider and sometimes deeper, with transverse reinforcement used to spread the load over sufficient area.

(2) *Isolated pad foundations* often support framed buildings where the loads are transferred by columns. As there is no connection between the pads special account has to be taken of differential settlement.

(3) *Raft foundations* are used with all types of load transmissions on poor sites with weak soils in order to spread the load over a large area.

(4) *Piled foundations* may be necessary on extremely weak soils when it may be necessary to transfer the load to a lower stratum.

The time aspect of settlement already noted does not influence eventual differential settlement nor the precautions which should be generally adopted. However, knowledge of this aspect is useful when any assessments of the possibility of the worsening of any trouble in a new building have to be made.

(b) *Special conditions*

The considerations given above are intended to apply to what can only be loosely termed 'normal conditions'. The effect of moisture content, freezing, vibrations or washing away of the soil are, therefore, excluded as they are covered separately later. On the other hand, *serious settlement* may occur in those areas which suffer from *mining subsidence*. In these areas large settlements can be expected.

In order to minimise the damage which could be caused to buildings due to mining subsidence, one of three different methods may be used:

(1) Allowing the building to act as a single unit so that it may tilt without cracking even though its support by the ground may be reduced to a few localised areas. This demands that the whole of the building is strengthened by reinforcement or other means.

(2) An alternative method of allowing the building to tilt but without cracking, is to specifically design the foundation either as a strong reinforced concrete raft or as a structural system of beams and slabs with three-point support from the ground. Soil movements will then cause tilting of the foundations and hence the building.

(3) Allowing the building to be flexible, so that relative movements in the soil are accommodated in the structure in a predetermined way. In this case details of connexions and claddings become extremely important and have to be carefully worked out, so that there is no damage or cracking to structural elements or finishes. Easy replacement of cladding units is sometimes essential in order to meet cases when the relative movements exceed a specified minimum.

Cracking of a brick wall in a new building the end of which has been built on a wall to an existing building without making allowance for the settlement of the new building

2. Changes in moisture content in clay

(a) Clay and sandy soils

As changes in moisture content play an important part in the movement of cohesive soils and particularly clay, it is necessary to draw a basic distinction between clay and non-cohesive soils. The latter, i.e. sandy and gravel soils, consist of non-absorbent and indestructible particles of rock, chiefly quartz. Thus once these particles have been completely compacted there cannot be any movement due to changes in moisture content which may occur in the voids between the particles.

Clay, on the other hand, consists of very much finer particles of matter. As a result there is much more absorption of water by clay—the material is colloidial in character and much water is adsorbed—which results in a considerable change in size according to the moisture content present. Like other materials there is expansion on absorption and contraction when the water is evaporated.

(b) The problem

Most of the problems of cracking due to moisture content changes in clay soils is found with small-scale buildings, generally with light loads, and particularly housing which falls

Cracking of wall of a house seriously effected by mining subsidence (Courtesy: Building Research Station (Crown Copyright))

Examples of serious structural failures resulting from mining subsidence:- Damage resulting from a combination of bending and shear action after the formation of an artificial fault. The effects of surface tension on the cobblestones can also be noted (Courtesy: Building Research Station (Crown Copyright))

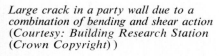

Large crack in a party wall due to a combination of bending and shear action (Courtesy: Building Research Station (Crown Copyright))

Cracks in a garden wall caused by severe surface tension in the ground surface (Courtesy: Building Research Station (Crown Copyright))

into this category. The reason for these failures can very often be associated with the lack of knowledge of the behaviour of clay, which, because of the comparatively light loads to be transmitted, leads to the use of conventional shallow strip foundations. For certain types of clay the latter are unsuitable.

(c) Behaviour

Under average conditions certain clays may shrink to a depth of 2·4m from the surface during a spell of a few weeks of dry weather in the summer. However, the amount of shrinkage and the depth to which it may occur depends on the amount of *shelter* that the ground has from the sun. In addition, the disposition of *vegetation* and particularly *root systems* which remove water from the soil are also important. However, under grasses for example changes in the moisture content of the clay can extend to a depth of about 1·07m and foundations shallower than this will be affected to varying extents. Generally, the greatest amount of shrinkage occurs at the surface, involving a settlement of about 25·4mm. However, settlements of more than 25·4mm (under grasses for example) have been measured at the surface between April and September. The seasonal nature of the moisture content changes of clay soils in Britain are significant.

Where the clay is not sheltered by the building from climatic changes and in the absence of vegetation, a differential movement occurs between those parts exposed to the weather and those parts covered by the building. This has contributed to the failure of shallow strip foundations on certain types of clay soils. The shrinkage of the clay, it should be noted, occurs both vertically and horizontally as shown in diagram D.2.03/32. The diagram also shows typical stepped diagonal cracking of a building as a result of these combined movements. It will be seen from the diagram that the cracking results from the movement of the clay at the periphery of the building.

The situation can be worsened when trees and other vegetation are near the building as the roots of vegetation penetrate the soil to considerable depths and dry the soil when rainfall is low in the summer. Permanent drying to depths of up to 4·6m (3m or so is not too uncommon) with a shrinkage of 75mm or more have been measured in the UK beneath large trees and shrubs. Thus although shrinkage to a depth of about 1·5m in the absence of vegetation may not be significant, the same is not true when tree roots penetrate to greater depths as they can cause particularly severe damage—see diagram D.2.03/33.

The reverse action can occur where established trees are cut down or removed. Clay soils re-absorb the moisture previously removed by the

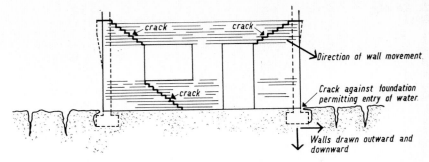

D.2.03/32 *Cracking associated with shallow foundations on shrinkable clay (From BRS Digest 63 (second series)). Below, the diagonal cracking has been caused as a result of the cantilevering of the house at the right-hand end (Crown Copyright)*

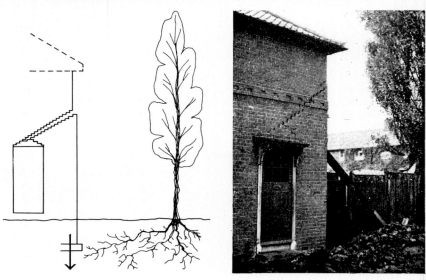

D.2.03/33 *Particularly severe damage to external brick wall in the form of stepped diagonal cracking due to changes in moisture content of clay soil caused by tree roots (Based on BRS Digest 75 (second series)) illustrated in the photograph (Crown Copyright)*

138

roots, and thus swell and lift foundations unevenly as swelling is most marked close to the site of the trees giving rise to a relative movement. The resulting upward movement shown in diagram D.2.03/34 can continue for several years. During a five-year period BRS has shown the upward movement in an office building built on a site cleared of trees to be about 6·4mm per year and estimate that these movements may continue for up to 10 years.

Shrinkage of clay soils beneath ground-floor slabs may occur by artificial drying from boilers and furnaces inadequately insulated from the clay beneath them. As a result of the shrinkage of the clay the concrete ground-floor slab can crack through lack of support.

(d) Precautions

The likelihood of cracking from the movement of foundations can be reduced by using foundations that are so deep that soil movements are unimportant. An alternative, and one which is sometimes found to be more economical, is to support the building on bored pile foundations, with the piles designed with adequate strength and sufficient resistance to settlement so that relative movements of piles are unimportant.

Where it is proposed to erect buildings close to *single trees*, shallow foundations should *not* be used if the buildings are to be nearer than the mature height of the tree. Where there are roots of *groups or rows of trees* competing for water over a limited area, the limiting distance should be one and a half times the mature height of the trees. These distances are only *rough guides* and while existing trees have been specifically mentioned it is important to note that young trees should not be planted closer than the distances suggested.

When trees are felled to clear a site for building, considerable time should be allowed for the clay, previously dried by the tree roots, to regain water.

D.2.03/35 *The results of frost heave of foundations. Chalk used as hardcore under oversite concrete froze while waterlogged and lifted the oversite concrete and brickwork over it. See photograph bottom right (Crown Copyright)*

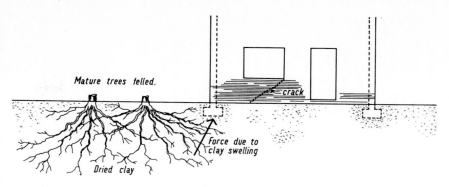

D.2.03/34 *Consequences of tree felling. Clay soil previously dried by the tree roots reabsorbs water. The pressures developed are often greater than those applied by shallow foundations. The resulting upward movement can continue for several years. (Based on BRS Digest 63 (second series))*

An example of a flexible joint in the Clasp system, one way of minimising the effects of mining subsidence

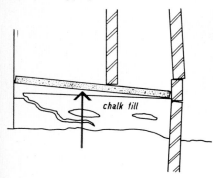

Although the type of clay and the presence of vegetation in close proximity to the building will determine in the first instance whether or not special precautions are necessary, it may be noted that greater shrinkage of clay can be expected on the sunny sides of buildings. Sometimes it is considered sufficient to reflect as much solar radiation as possible falling on the ground in the immediate vicinity of external walls. This is usually done by the use of light coloured pavings. Although such pavings may assist in some cases, it should be noted that the efficiency of any surface in reflecting solar radiation depends largely on its whiteness. At ground level it is often difficult to maintain a clean, let alone white, surface in this country.

Finally, the special case of heating appliances. These should be provided with adequate air ventilation or water channels, that is a cooling system, between the appliance (furnace or boiler) and the base. The cooling system should be installed as part of the foundation.

3. Freezing of the soil

Expansion of soils can take place in any soil that is capable of holding water either within its particles or in voids between the particles. Soils most commonly associated with what is termed 'frost heave' are fine sands, silts and chalks. Generally, it is not normal to anticipate expansion from freezing at a depth below 0·46m, although during severe winters in the UK frost may penetrate to a depth of 0·61m or so.

The comparatively small amount of damage to buildings as a result of 'frost heave' is usually confined to severely exposed parts of buildings founded on predominantly chalky and fine sandy soils. In some of these, there may be a build-up of ice layers that cause the foundations to lift, but then only in exceptionally severe winters. The example in diagram D.2.03/35 illustrates some typical effects, from a house that was newly built on chalky soil with chalk fill under the floor slabs. As it was unoccupied and therefore unheated, the parts most affected were those most exposed. Although heated buildings are unlikely to be affected in this way, it should be noted that garages and other outbuildings which are often built on concrete slabs and footings shallower than those of adjoining houses may be effected. As a precau-

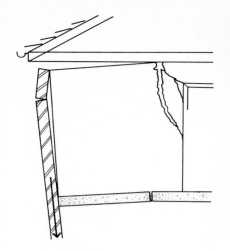

D.2.03/36 *Illustration of the consequences of building on unconsolidated made-up ground. The bungalow from which this example was taken was built partly on made-up ground which was not properly consolidated and probably contained much unsuitable material (*Based on BRS Digest 75 (second series)*) (*Crown Copyright*)

tion fine sands, silts and chalks should not be used as fillings beneath ground floor slabs even in buildings that are eventually to be heated on completion.

There are, of course, special types of buildings, such as cold storage rooms, where problems of water freezing in the soil beneath them, especially in the early life of the building, can be expected. These are exceptional cases and accordingly require specialised treatment. (It has been known for a cold storage room to be completely lifted off the ground due to water freezing in the soil beneath the floor slab. This was due to inadequate insulation.)

4. Vibrations and other causes

(a) *Vibrations and sandy soils*

Sandy soils more than any other may be compacted by vibrations. As already pointed out under 'Cracking due to vibration', the precise effect of vibrations on buildings in general is still not conclusive.

(b) *Loss of ground*

Although dense beds of sand are normally excellent foundation soils, the finer particles may occasionally be washed away by water thus leaving the coarser material in a less stable condition. Under such conditions the soil can lose much of its bearing capacity, particularly if an excavation is made.

(c) *Lateral movement*

Natural or geological phenomena, artificial agencies or a combination of both can cause some foundation movements. Slopes and landslips (clay soils notable) and swallow holes (chalk and limestone areas significant) are the chief natural or geological phenomena. Mining subsidence referred to earlier is a good example of an artificial agency.

(d) *Organic soils and made-up ground*

Organic matter in the form of decaying vegetation cause peats and other soils to vary greatly in their volume as their water content changes, while such soils are very compressible and settle readily even under their own weight. The behaviour of made-up ground is very similar and unless it is good material, carefully placed and compacted in thin layers, settles for many years. The bearing capacities of sites filled by end-tipping are often poor and variable. Consequently these sites require deep foundations passing right through the fill. It should be noted that poorly compacted fill is unsuitable for foundations no matter how long it consolidates under its own weight. An example of cracking in a bungalow built partly on made-up ground which was not properly consolidated and probably contained much unsuitable material is shown in diagram D.2.03/36.

2.04 strength and the use of materials

In many ways the mechanical properties of materials are primarily used in conjunction with structural mechanics in order that the design of the structural elements may be determined. Structural mechanics, in terms of structural design, is essentially based on mathematical formulæ, which, in turn, are based on certain assumptions which generally agree with experimental results. In those cases where structural analysis and design cannot be undertaken on the basis of established formulæ or methods, it is then necessary for model or other tests to be undertaken. On the other hand, experience and tradition have also provided a fund of information upon which some structures may be determined by rule-of-thumb methods. In many instances even the latter are making way for the 'calculated structure'. However, despite these apparent anomalies, it is still true to say that, in general, the use of the strength of materials, insofar as structures are concerned, is a far more exact science than those aspects which are to be considered in this section, which concern some of the main uses to which building materials may be applied from structural elements at the one extreme to fixtures and finishes at the other.

The strength characteristics of materials required for purposes other than those customarily used in the design of structural elements as such, are in many ways of great importance. The aspects of strength which are to be considered here are those *primarily* related to the factors which affect the manner in which materials may be used *either* during the manufacturing processes *or* on the building site and also to those factors which influence the way in which materials will perform once they have commenced their 'working life' in a building. In a great many cases it is usually impracticable to employ calculations with the result that, in the main, it is extremely difficult to formulate any precise quantitative bases for assessment. Resort, therefore, has to be made to the results of experience. Where such experience is lacking, it is then necessary for some form of test to be carried out in order to provide

An example of pressed metal work. A portion of pressed steel louvres and frame. Note that all arrises are rounded (Courtesy: The Morris Singer Co. Ltd.)

some reassuring basis on which to proceed. Despite the fact that it is not always possible to have some quantitative basis upon which to work, it is nevertheless important that some form of *check list* should be developed so that strength, as it affects the use of materials, may be given its due consideration. At a time when there are so many new materials from which to choose, including traditional materials manufactured in new ways, such a consideration would appear to be more significant than it was in the past.

In the absence of any realistic or reliable quantitative methods of assessing the strength of materials in relation to use, this study is being presented in an extremely *liberal,* and in some cases graphic, form. The subject matter has, for convenience, been divided into the following general headings:

(1) Shaping by bending. (2) Cutting. (3) Fixing. (4) Abrasion. (5) Impact. The first three are concerned with use of materials during building construction: the last two primarily with damage which may occur *either* during building construction *or* during the life of a building.

Shaping by bending

All building materials, with the exception of the naturally occurring materials such as timber and stone, may be shaped whilst in a liquid or plastic state by the use of moulds, as in casting or dies as in extrusions. Strength development of materials shaped in this way takes place during the setting or hardening processes after shaping. However, the strength of a material before shaping is of importance when the shaping occurs while the material is in the solid state, even if heat treatment is used to modify its mechanical properties. In addition, the very act of shaping will modify some of the mechanical properties of materials, particularly when the shaping is by means of bending. *Bending* is the only method of shaping to be considered here, as some of the other methods by which materials may be shaped, such as cutting and grinding, are covered separately.

The use of bending as a means of shaping materials, sometimes into highly complex forms, may be required for a number of different reasons and uses. Some of these include: handrails for staircases; pressed metal frames for windows, doors, cladding and other prefabricated systems; water exclusion on roofs and particularly as weatherings in flashings, gutters, etc., or within constructions as damp-proof courses; pipes carrying water, gas or electricity as in sanitation, heating or ventilation systems, etc. The actual process of bending may take place *either* under highly controlled factory conditions *or* on the building site itself. Wherever the process takes place, the materials which are to be bent in the solid state must have certain basic structural characteristics. These are: (1) enough flexibility to allow bending without fracture; and (2) the capacity of remaining in the deformed state after bending.

Some materials under normal room temperature and/or humidity conditions are not flexible enough to allow adequate bending, but may be made more flexible with suitable heat and/or moisture treatment. On the other hand, materials which are inherently or are treated specifically to be, flexible enough for bending, may be too elastic to remain in a deformed state. Thus it is sometimes necessary for the internal structure to be changed, i.e. to 'engineer' a permanent set.

All materials which are shaped by bending have one common characteristic as regards their *arrises*. These can never be absolutely sharp and are consequently always rounded. In general terms, the thicker the material the more rounded the arris. The radius of the arris is primarily governed by the minimum radius through which the material is capable of being bent. In part, the minimum bending radius will be influenced by such mechanical properties as tension, compression and shear. In addition, smaller radii are possible when materials are bent over a former, i.e. support, than when they follow their own bending radii—most bending is, in fact, carried out over a former of one kind or another. In general, however, the thicker a material the larger the minimum bending radius. In the shaping process, as in normal bending encountered in structural mechanics (*Section 2.01*), the outer face of the material will be in tension while the inner face will be in compression. For a given radius, which is here measured from the inner face, the outer face will have to stretch much further as the thickness of material increases. At the same time there will be greater compression of the inner face. Failure of the material may then occur if either the tensile or compressive stresses are excessive; on the other hand, an excessive differential between the tensile and compressive stresses may lead to shear failure. The relative differences, in terms of dimensions of the inner and outer faces, for various radii and thicknesses of material are illustrated in diagram D.2.04/1 and the comparative chart C.2.04/1.

In practice it is uncommon for elaborate calculations to be under-

Bending of solid timber with inner and outer faces supported (Courtesy: Forest Products Research Laboratory (Crown Copyright))

Below, the 'tearing' of a flat steel plate as a result of the thickness/bending radius ratio having been greatly exceeded. (Thickness of metal approximately 13mm)

Below, breakpress used in a factory for bending metal. The operative on the left is holding a portion of a pressed steel door frame (Courtesy: The Morris Singer Co. Ltd.)

Below, part of a laminated Douglas fir right-angle frame after the clamps have been removed and before final planing and trimming (Courtesy: CIBA (A.R.L.))

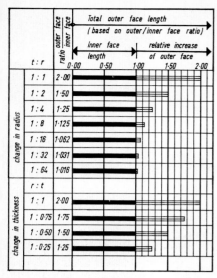

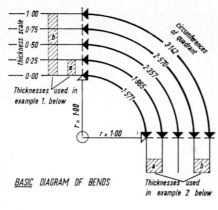

BASIC DIAGRAM OF BENDS

Thicknesses used in example 1. below

Thicknesses used in example 2 below

Examples of relative difference between circumference of outer and inner face (based on outer/inner face ratio)

1. CHANGE IN THICKNESS

(a) $r = 1.00$ $t = 0.25$ $(1:0.25)$

ratio : $\dfrac{\text{outer face}}{\text{inner face}} = \dfrac{1.965}{1.571} = 1.25$

∴ outer face is 0.25 longer than inner face

(b) $r = 1.00$ $t = 1.00$ $(1:1)$

ratio : $\dfrac{\text{outer face}}{\text{inner face}} = \dfrac{3.142}{1.571} = 2.00$

outer face is 1.00 longer than inner face

2. CHANGE IN RADIUS

(a) $t = 0.25$ $r = 1.00$ $(1:4)$

as 1(a) above

outer face is 0.25 longer than inner face

(b) $t = 0.25$ $r = 1.75$ $(1:7)$

ratio : $\dfrac{\text{outer face}}{\text{inner face}} = \dfrac{3.142}{2.750} = 1.14$

outer face is 0.14 longer than inner face

C.2.04/1 *Above, comparative graph showing the relationship of lengths of inner and outer faces for different thickness/radii (t:r) and radii/thickness (r:t) ratios*

Right, a composite diagram illustrating the effect of bending (through 90 degrees) on the dimension of the inner and outer faces of a material with changes in radii and thickness of material, with examples of the relative differences between the two faces

Below, bending of sheet copper roofing at the junction of each sheet to form a watertight joint (All methods of jointing in sheet metal roofs should allow for thermal expansion)

taken to determine the minimum bending radius of a material. Reliance is placed on experience and, where this is absent, on prototypes. The diagram and chart, therefore, are only intended to explain, in principle, the mechanical aspects associated with bending, and also to reinforce the reason for the absence of sharp arrises obtained with *other* shaping processes.

As tensile strength plays such an important part in the bending process, it follows that materials relatively weak in this respect are unsuitable for bending purposes. Thus materials such as brick, concrete and stone, which in addition to being relatively weak in tension are also liable to brittle fracture, are incapable of being bent. Materials which are more commonly shaped by bending are timber, metals and plastics. These are now dealt with separately.

1. Timber

The practice of bending timber* mainly for staircase handrails is fairly traditional. A more recent use of bending has been applied to laminated timber sections, particularly those for structural uses. In principle, the problems associated with bending are basically similar.

In the dry state the maximum stretch possible, i.e. without breaking, of timber is approximately 2 per cent of the original length. On the other hand, in the dry state timber is too elastic to remain in the bent state. Treatment of timber either by steaming, boiling or heating in *wet* sand, alters the characteristics of the material in two important ways, namely, (1) a compression of up to 30 per cent of the original length is possible without breaking, and (2) the fibres of the material are altered in such a way so as to render the timber softer or more plastic, i.e. to allow more bending, and also to allow it to remain in the bent state after drying out.

Where large-radius bends are required it is usually unnecessary for the outer, i.e. stretched, face of the timber to be supported—the inner face is often supported in any case. With small-radius bends support of the outer face by means of steel straps is necessary in order to ensure that it is also in compression. As mentioned earlier, heat and moisture treated timber is capable of withstanding fairly excessive compression.

2. Metals

The bending of metals falls into two categories, namely, (1) that which is done in a factory with elaborate

*A full account of the methods and procedures of wood bending is given in two Forestry Products Research publications, namely:

1. *The Practice of Wood Bending*, Records No. 10, 1936.
2. *A Handbook of Woodcutting*, Bulletin No. 1, 1937.

machines (known as pressing) and whose primary use is the production of actual building components, and (2) that which is done on the building site in connection with flashings, d.p.c., roofing, pipework, etc. Irrespective of where the operation actually takes place, metals do have special bending characteristics which are associated with the changes in the internal structural, i.e. the crystalline, arrangement of the material. Bending in mechanical terms is regarded as work done on the metal and, as explained in *Section 2.02* if the work is undertaken while the metal is in the cold state *work- or strain-hardening* occurs. The effect of work-hardening is to make the metal harder and stronger at the expense of ductility. Thus work-hardening results in making it more and more difficult to continually rebend the metal. (Excessive rebending eventually results in fracture due to the loss of ductility and the corresponding increase in brittleness. Thermal effects may also be involved.) Of the metals which, instead of work-hardening, continue to re-crystallise as a result of bending, *lead* is a notable example. It is for this reason that lead is particularly versatile in the sense that it may be bent and rebent far more frequently than most other metals and, therefore, very often used in those situations where continual bending is necessary, as may occur with flashings for example. Work-hardening may, of course, be reduced by suitable heat treatment, i.e. annealing, when re-crystallisation is made possible and the material made softer and more ductile.

Most of the metals commonly used in buildings, and here lead is again the exception, are far too elastic to remain in the bent state without the use of considerable pressure. The effect of the pressure which must be applied is to harden the material in the zone of the bend and to cause a permanent set. Exceedingly great pressures are used in factory pressing, although regulation of the pressure, among other things, is also used to control the angle of bending. Comparatively thin walled materials, such as pipes, are provided with internal support during the bending process, especially when minimum radii are required. This applies equally as well to lead, although the pressures required for bending are, by comparison with other materials, considerably less. Heat treatment of metals prior to bending also has the effect of reducing the pressures required to 'force' the material to remain bent.

3. Plastics

Shaping of plastics, whether by bending or other means, is an essential part of the basic manufacturing process. Thermosetting plastics are on the whole extremely difficult to shape by bending in the solid state. Special grades of laminated plastics are made

144

The bending required at a welted joint of a zinc roof

Example of the shaping required for sheet metal roofing—the example is lead

Lead weathering to a projection before shaping

A lead flashing to a chimney stack (Courtesy: Lead Development Assn. and Zinc Development Assn.)

Zinc flashing to a sloping roof

Shaped pipework

for what is known as post forming. Such post forming of these still appear to have limitations—radii are comparatively large and there are difficulties in dealing with corners and other junctions.

The thermoplastics, on the other hand, are comparatively simple to bend after moderate heat treatment—in the cold state minimum radii may, subject to the thickness of the material, be relatively large. Bending of these materials, in either the cold or warm state, is as yet not frequently used and appears to be restricted mainly to floor finishes where it may be possible to bend the material at the junction with walls to form a skirting. Bending capacity is, of course, also useful in d.p.c. work. In this respect it is interesting to note that attempts have been made, although not always successfully, to use heat treatment on bituminous d.p.c.'s and roofing felts for negotiating difficult bends. Examples such as these are indicative of the care which should always be exercised when applying heat treatment to materials with relatively low melting points.

Cutting

Cutting is probably one of the oldest methods which have been used for shaping materials of all types in the solid state. Shaping may also be undertaken by planing, chiselling and grinding and, although these are not generally accepted cutting processes, they are included here.

The success with which materials may be shaped by any of these means is not only dependent on primary mechanical properties, but also those strength properties which can only be loosely related to the internal structure of the material, i.e. in terms of grain, porosity or laminar characteristics. The forces associated with these processes are inevitably high and this, in part, accounts for the care which has to be exercised in order to avoid undue damage to the materials. Such damage is often associated with appearance, although it may equally well influence the strength of the material (cutting may cause splitting or other damage) or, more important, the efficiency with which the cut material can be used in conjunction with other materials to form components. As an example of the latter, ragged or otherwise untrue edges or faces present difficulties when sections of material have to be joined together to form an element.

In all these processes the materials have, in general, to be capable of having localised portions of the material ripped or torn away without causing other portions also to come away in the process. In addition, the material may have to withstand considerable compression when pressure is applied on the tools which may be employed. Thus in cutting, for example, soft materials are cut comparatively easily but, because of their

Although this is an example of the mis-handling of lead, it does illustrate the comparative ease with which the material may be shaped (Courtesy: Lead Development Assn)

Below, polishing of stone such as marble or granite is essentially a grinding process using abrasives and water. The photograph shows equipment (known as a 'Graniteer') used in the first stages of polishing granite which gives a coarse grit finish to the slab (Courtesy: The Stone Firms Ltd.)

Above, cutting timber

Below, post forming of a special grade of laminated plastics for the top of a vanitory basin (Courtesy: Formica Ltd.)

M

low resistance to compression, allow the edges of the material to be left ragged. In many cases problems such as this are solved by the careful selection of the tool appropriate for the material.

The use of grinding to shape materials is not common in building practice, although the process is often used to finish materials. Welds on metalwork are frequently ground down, while the whole surface of a material may be ground to provide a particular finish as, for example, with certain metals and stones. (In stonework and other trades the word 'polish' implies a grinding process rather than the application of some liquid or wax substance.) Grinding is generally restricted to the harder and fine grained materials as most of the fibrous materials may have the individual fibres 'pulled up' during the process.

Fixing

1. Aspects considered

The aspects of fixing which are to be considered are those mainly associated with the joining together of two elements with the aid of special fixing devices, such as nails, screws, bolts and nuts, in order to ensure structural stability. Although they are also employed for joining together elements to form the basic structure of a building, *the emphasis* is being placed on structural fixings of those elements which are fixed to the basic structure. These include the fixing of doors, windows, claddings of various types, ironmongery, service apparatus, pipes, balustrades, etc. Irrespective of the precise use of fixing devices, most of which are made of metal of one type or another, strength properties and requirements form rather a complex problem. These concern not only the fixing device but also the materials to be joined together. In making up the main structure of a building other structural mechanical considerations must be taken into account. In order, therefore, to reduce the complexity of an already complex problem, detailed consideration of fixings for the main structure of a building are excluded. Furthermore, only the simplest possible cases will be examined in detail. The principles outlined may in general be applied to the more complicated or unusual cases.

Fixing may also be effected by other methods, namely by the use of adhesives which, for the purposes required here, would include welding and the mechanical interlocking of materials in the solid state. There has been a notable increase in both these methods, particularly the use of adhesives. In addition, both rely on the strength properties of materials particularly for the support of the imposed load. Neither of these methods is covered in any detail. The factors affecting the strength of

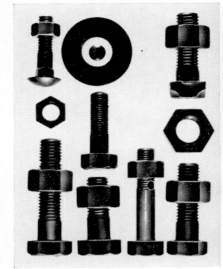

Examples of nut and bolt type fixings (Courtesy: G.K.N. Ltd.)

Right, nut and bolt type fixing for the structure in an industrialized building system

Examples of nails (Courtesy: G.K.N. Ltd.)

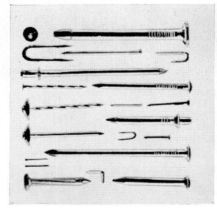

adhesion, although related mainly to the use of traditional adhesives, have generally been covered in *Section 1.11*. Mechanical interlocking, and this assumes the exclusion of such interlocking which takes place when one of the materials is first applied in a plastic state and then allowed to harden (also described in *Section 1.11*), requires the manufacture of specially shaped components. In some systems one of the components is normally made to act with a spring action so as to effect the required frictional grip (frictional grip does also play an important part in the use of special fixing devices, and this is described in detail). In other systems as, for example, those used for fixing stone

claddings a 'loose' form of interlocking is employed.

2. Frictional grip

The precise method by which any one of the various fixing devices may be used may vary considerably. However, in all cases the fixing device is initially 'passed through' the materials of both elements to be joined. (In many cases the device may only pass through one of the elements completely and only partially, i.e. merely housed, in the other. This does not materially affect the principle being outlined.) The success of the fixing, that is in addition to the mechanical

Fixing a timber batten directly to brickwork using a specially tempered steel nail (Courtesy: Douglas Kane (Sealants) Ltd.)

properties and other strength requirements of the materials involved and which are discussed later, will be dependent on the *frictional grip* which can be obtained. Frictional grip is a rather loose but descriptive term used to denote the compressive forces which are permanently created between the surfaces of two elements which will prevent one of them sliding past the other. Frictional grip may be effected at one of two stages, namely: (i) during the passing through process mentioned earlier, or (ii) subsequent to the passing through process.

Nails, screws, rivets and the wide range of expanding bolts (with or without nuts) have the frictional grip created between their surfaces and those of the interior of the materials through which they pass. An additional frictional grip may also be caused between the surfaces of the two elements in contact with one another during the 'tightening up' process. Nuts and bolts and the special range of devices, based essentially on the nut and bolt principle, now available for fixing through thin materials such as the sheet materials which do not have the continuous support of a background, i.e. those which are first fixed to a framed background, primarily rely on the frictional grip caused between the surfaces of the two elements in contact with one another during the 'tightening up' process. (Where these devices are used to support an essentially downward weight along the long axis of the device, frictional grip between the threads is important. This aspect is not included in this general con-

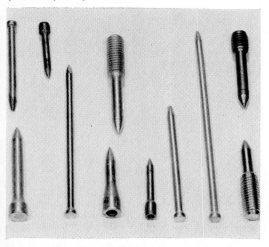

Some of the nails, better known as pins, available for use with cartridge hammers. Below, the use of a cartridge hammer to fire fixings into concrete (Courtesy: Explosive Power Tools Ltd.)

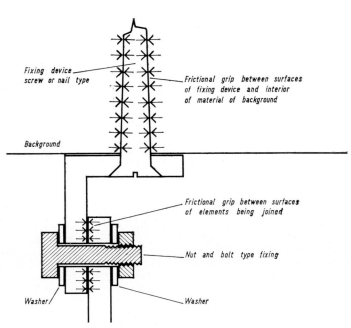

D.2.04/2 Diagrammatic illustration of zones for primary frictional grip for screw or nail and nut and bolt fixing devices

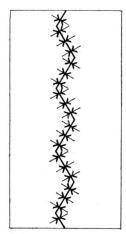

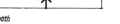

D.2.04/3 Comparison between potential surface frictional grip 'area' of smooth and rough surfaces in contact with one another

147

sideration.) The basic differences between these two methods of creating frictional grip is illustrated diagrammatically in diagram D.2.04/2.

The extent of the frictional grip which can be created between two surfaces is primarily dependent on the permanent compressive forces which occur at the surfaces and this, in turn, is dependent on the compressive strength of the materials concerned. Thus the greater the compressive strength the greater the frictional grip.

In addition to the compressive strength of materials, their surface characteristics are important and this is irrespective of the methods by which frictional grip is created, that is whether between the fixing device and the element or between the two surfaces of the elements in contact with one another. For any given pressure—this may be created during the driving process of a fixing device or alternatively during the tightening up of a fixing device—the frictional grip between two smooth surfaces will be less than either that between two rough surfaces or one rough and one smooth surface, when the materials of both elements have the same compressive strength. The importance of this lies in the fact that rough surfaces, and especially those which may be specially serrated, form an interlocking bond in addition to the fact that the surface area of a rough surface is greater than a smooth one. This is shown diagrammatically in diagram D.2.04/3. In order to take advantage of the additional strength of an interlocking bond, it is preferable that one of the materials has a smaller compressive strength than the other. This then allows, within limits which must not be exceeded, the stronger material 'to bite' into the weaker one. (Although the threads on screws enable the device 'to bore' its way through a material during turning, they also enable greater frictional grip to be created).

3. Fixing processes and procedures

The creation of frictional grip takes place during the fixing process. However, as important, this grip must be maintained after fixing so as to support the imposed loads. For both of these the mechanical properties and the general strength requirements of all the materials involved, i.e. the fixing device and the elements being joined, are important. To deal with these aspects it is more convenient to relate considerations of strength to those required at two distinct stages. These are (a) at the time of fixing, and (b) after fixing.

(a) *Strength required at the time of fixing*

Here the primary relationship of the strengths of the materials relative to the precise method of using a fixing device is important. Those fixing de-

148

Fixings to a reinforced concrete slab for the support of framing for a false ceiling and air conditioning trunking carried out with shot-fired techniques using special threaded ends with nuts

vices which rely primarily on frictional grip between their surfaces and those of the interior surfaces of the materials of the elements through which they pass may be divided into three basic types, each of which may also be related to the method by which the frictional grip is made. These types are:

(i) *Nails* and similar sharp pointed devices with smooth surfaces which are driven through or into materials by impact or a series of impacts. The impact may be by means of a hammer or, as in the more recent developments, by firing. The strength of the fixing device must be related to the compressive strength of the materials through or into which it will be driven and the impact. The fixing device must also be strong enough to resist being bent or otherwise damaged during the whole of the process. In this respect it is interesting to note the development of nails made of specially tempered steel which are capable of being driven into materials of relatively high compressive strength such as concrete, brick and stone. Special nails, sometimes known as 'pins', made for use with firing equipment may also be driven into metals. The term 'nail' or 'pin' for the firing techniques may be a little misleading. Many of these are similar to traditional nails but may have, for example, threaded ends which are left exposed after firing into a background so that other elements may subsequently be fixed by nut and bolt techniques. The comparative brittleness of these newer nails, whether for firing or not, makes it extremely important that the impact is given in the correct way. As an example incorrect manual hammering may result in the exposed portion of the nail fracturing without warning, i.e. in this case without first bending. Fracture results in the exposed portion 'flying off' with the possibility of causing bodily damage to the operative—in this the vulner-

ability of the eyes is an important consideration.

These and other dangers associated with small fragments of the background being projected at great speed in all directions are accentuated with firing techniques. Properly trained operatives are essential to reduce the danger of the firing device.

As far as the elements are concerned, the ease with which they can be pierced will depend primarily on their resistance to crushing. Thus, materials of low crushing resistance are likely to be pierced more easily than materials of high crushing resistance. However, pierced materials of low crushing strength resistance will form a weaker frictional grip per unit length of the fixing device than materials with a high crushing resistance. In addition, the ability of materials to accommodate the expansion which takes place within the material with the introduction of the fixing device will be related to the tensile strength of the material. The total tensile strength which any material is capable of providing will to some extent depend on the volume of material available to resist the stresses created. Thus, materials which might otherwise be able to resist the tensile forces if the fixing device is driven into the centre of the element, might not be capable of resisting the same tensile forces if the fixing device is driven in nearer and parallel to one of the edges. This is shown diagrammatically in diagram D.2.04/4. Failure of materials to resist the tensile forces involved usually results in cracking. In *isotropic materials,* such as brick, stone, concrete, the cracking may occur in any direction. Initial failure of materials such as these is often seen at the surface of the material which receives the first impact. In *anistropic materials* cracking will occur along the plane which is weakest. Thus, in timber the weakest resistance to tension occurs when the fixing device is driven in perpendicular to the grain, which causes the timber to split, as illustrated in diagram D.2.04/5. Once the material has been pierced and been able to resist the tensile forces, it must then be elastic enough to provide the necessary permanent compressive forces at the surface of the fixing device for the required frictional grip.

In all these cases the success of the frictional grip will depend, in addition to those mechanical properties already described, on maximum surface contact in order to obtain the

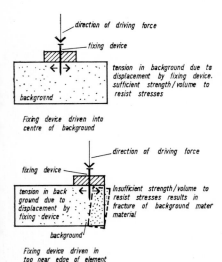

D.2.04/4 *Diagrammatic representation of the relative weakness of the edges of an isotropic material to resist the tensile stresses due to displacement by a nail or screw type fixing device. (Note: The inherent weakness of the edge is greatly increased as the impact driving force is increased. Special care is, therefore, always required when firing techniques are used)*

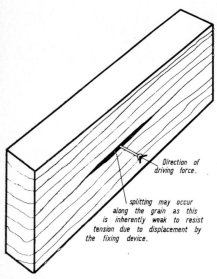

D.2.04/5 *Diagrammatic representation of the inherent weakness along the grain of timber relative to the displacement caused by a nail or screw type fixing device*

maximum surface compressive force possible. Maximum surface contact depends, in turn, on the ability of an operative to ensure that the fixing device is not unnecessarily deflected during the driving process. This means that there must be as little sideways movement as possible. On the other hand, such deflexion may take place when stronger particles may be encountered by the sharp end of the device. (This may, for example, frequently occur in concrete.) Failure in this respect sometimes occurs with firing techniques when the nail may be capable of 'disintegrating' the internal structure of the material and thus reduce considerably frictional grip. For this reason the efficiency of each fixing should be checked and carefully related to the imposed loads that the fixing will be required eventually to carry prior to actual loading taking place.

(ii) *Screws* and similar devices which are capable of 'boring' through materials. All these require that the device is tapered and that most of the shank has a thread. The boring process takes place while the device is continually being turned, usually in a clockwise direction. Resistance to torsion forces is one of the main requirements of the fixing device and this, in turn, will be related to the resistance to turning provided by the materials through or into which it has to pass. In addition, the fixing device must have sufficient compressive strength in order to displace the material through which it is passing, while at the same time it must be capable of indenting the material by means of the threads so as to increase frictional grip. In most cases the strength requirements of the fixing device may be considerably reduced if the material through which it must pass is predrilled with a hole slightly smaller in diameter than that of the fixing device. This also has the effect of reducing the tensile forces which the element will have to provide, as a result of displacement by the fixing device, because the drilling of holes results in a substantial volume of material being removed. There is thus less material to be displaced by the fixing device and thus lower tensile forces created in the element. This, in turn, and subject to the elasticity of the element, will reduce the compressive forces supplied by the element. However, this is partly compensated for by the grip provided by the threaded surface of the fixing device. The strength requirements of the fixing element are, in the main, the same as in the case of nails, already outlined.

(iii) *Nuts and bolts* and all fixing devices which rely on pre-drilled holes through or into which the device is initially made to pass prior for the creation of frictional grip. In these cases frictional grip may be created between the device and the interior surface of the element, as in the two

previous types, or between the two surfaces of the elements in contact with one another. Despite these differences, either of these sub-types require sufficient resistance to torsion as a 'tightening up' process takes place in both. The elements, on the other hand, require sufficient compressive and tensile strength to resist the forces created during drilling. Strength requirements for frictional grip will be the same as those outlined previously under that heading.

As the manner in which the frictional grip may be created varies, the two distinct methods will be dealt with separately:

Frictional grip between the device and the interior of the element. There are a variety of detailed methods available. However, in each case reliance is placed on frictional grip being obtained by expansion of a special device which is inserted into the pre-drilled holes. The hole is normally made fractionally larger than the insert, i.e. only big enough to facilitate insertion. In the simplest case a comparatively thin walled cylinder or plug of fibrous or other material (plastics are also now being used) is inserted into the pre-drilled hole. A screw is then subsequently screwed through the centre of the cylinder, and during the process the cylinder walls are compressed against the walls of the hole. Although some plugs are made with smooth outer surfaces, others are made with suitably patterned surfaces to increase the frictional grip. Slightly more complex devices are available, known generally as *expansion bolts*. These consist basically of an expandable sheath, usually of metal, over a bolt. After insertion of the sheath and the bolt and during the tightening up process the sheath is made to expand and compress against the walls of the hole, by the use of cones or by suitable shaping of the end of the bolt. All these are proprietary fixing devices. It is interesting to note that the increased use of these devices has partly resulted from the inadequacy of other methods of fixing, particularly into concrete, which were previously undertaken by casting in blocks of timber or other material in predetermined positions. These have proved inadequate for a number of reasons, chief of which are: difficulties generally encountered in accurate positioning of the fixing block; comparative short life of the fixing blocks—those of timber are liable to decompose if not properly treated; and the possibility of the fixing blocks working loose. Thus, with developments in drilling techniques, it is now sometimes more advantageous and labour-saving to use one or other of the proprietary fixing devices.

Frictional grip between the surfaces of the elements in contact with one another. The traditional nut and bolt normally has little frictional grip between the surface of the shank of the bolt and interior of the material through which the bolt is passed. This is mainly due to the fact that if the diameter of the pre-drilled hole were not slightly larger than the shank, then it is possible for the threads to be damaged. The frictional grip between the surfaces of the two elements in contact with one another is dependent, in addition to those factors previously outlined, on the area over which pressure can be exerted when compression takes place during the tightening up process. In this the crushing strength of the materials of the two elements will be important. Low crushing strength, among other things, allows little spread of the load. In these cases it is sometimes necessary to increase the spread of pressure by the use of washers. These, in turn, also prevent local crushing of the material at the bolt head and at the nut. One of the disadvantages of the traditional nut and bolt technique is the requirement

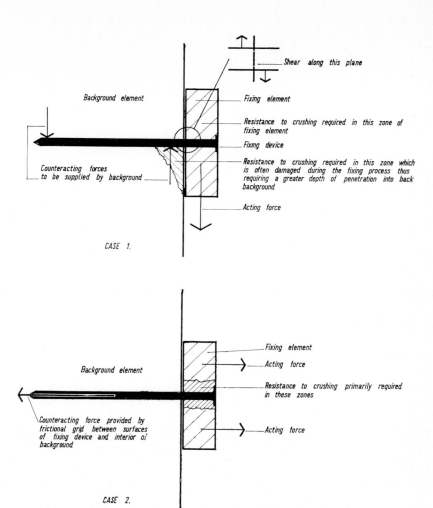

D.2.04/7 *Effects of loading on fixing device and elements to be joined*

Examples of expanding 'Rawlbolts'. Left: loose bolt type; right: bolt projecting type (Courtesy: Rawlplug Co. Ltd.)

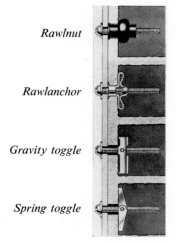

D.2.04/6 *Examples of proprietary cavity fixing devices (Courtesy: Rawlplug Co. Ltd.)*

150

for both bolt head and nut to be firmly gripped during the turning process. In the case of metals, this is sometimes overcome by welding the bolt head or the nut to one of the elements. Techniques such as this must be used when access is difficult. However, thin sheet material fixed to framed backgrounds present problems of fixing as there is no access to the space behind the material. To overcome these difficulties a number of proprietary fixing devices are available, all of which are similar, in principle although not in detail, to traditional nut and bolt techniques. Some of these are shown in diagram D.2.04/6.

(b) *Strength required after fixing*

Once the required fixing has been effected, it is then necessary that the strength of all the materials involved, i.e. both of the fixing device and of the elements joined, should be sufficient to support the total weight or load imposed. The total weight or load may consist of only the dead weight of one of the elements or of the combined dead weight of one of the elements plus a live load. As regards the latter, it has been common practice only to consider seriously the effect of wind on roofs, both pitched and flat. Subject to the design and

shape of the roof and of surrounding obstructions, considerable suctions, i.e. negative or indirect pressures, may be created above the roof. These suctions result in an upwards movement, which is capable, as has been shown in many examples, of lifting either individual elements or the entire roof structure. The problem of suction resulting from wind is now receiving serious consideration, particularly insofar as high buildings are concerned where the problems appear to be acute. The results of investigations to date suggest the necessity of regard being paid to the fixings of more recent cladding materials (essentially lightweight when compared to stone for example), as these may be subjected to considerable suction.* On the other hand, considerable pressures, both direct and indirect, may be exerted on such elements as windows and so, even with these live loads may need special consideration.

*See (1) Newberry, C. W., and Wise, A. F. E., *How wind shapes buildings* in Building Research Current Papers, Design Series 9.
This paper outlines in general terms the implications of wind on all aspects of the shape of buildings, but also gives a clear summary of direct and indirect pressure zones.
(2) BRS Digest (1st Series) No. 98, *Light cladding—Part 1*, pp. 1 and 2, for some practical assessments of wind pressure and remarks on high factor of safety requirements for fixings, especially on high buildings.

In order to determine the particular strength requirements of all the materials it is first necessary to analyse the forces involved. Although the latter may be highly complex, it is more convenient to resolve the forces into essentially simple cases and to relate them primarily to the fixing device. Diagram D.2.04/7 illustrates the two basic cases.

Case 1

In the example the load acts perpendicular to the axis of the fixing device. Such loading is usually associated with, although not entirely confined to, fixings in the vertical plane. Frictional grip is here important in that it must be sufficient to prevent any movement of the fixing, particularly in that element in which it is housed, i.e. the background element, plus any tendency to 'pull out'. In the main, the fixing device is acting in the form of a cantilever. The device must, therefore, resist any tendency to bend. However, the cantilevering effect may be modified due to the contact of the two elements, i.e. background and fixing, with the result that under load the shank of the device must resist shear as shown.

The background element has to resist crushing. At one extreme, i.e. at the external face, an upward counteracting force must be supplied, while at the other extreme, i.e. at the end of the fixing device, a downward counteracting force is required. Materials which are comparatively weak in this respect require for any given load a greater unit length of the fixing device in order that the forces may be distributed over a greater area. On the whole the interior of the material is capable of resisting the forces involved more than the material in the immediate vicinity of the external face, which may in any case be damaged during the fixing process. However, for the interior to act in this way it is nevertheless necessary for sufficient volume of material to surround the fixing device. (The weakness of most thicknesses of plaster requires that all fixings must be securely housed into the background material.)

The fixing element has to resist crushing mainly in the zone of the fixing device and opposite to the direction of the acting force. Materials with comparatively low crushing resistance may require the shank of the fixing device to be larger in diameter than for materials with high resistances to crushing. The increase in diameter assists in reducing the force per unit area. Resistance to crushing is important in order to avoid excessive indentation of the fixing element by the fixing device. In addition to this, the material of the fixing element must resist any possibility of splitting or other damage. The area of material available to resist the forces involved relative to its strength has to be taken into account. However, in general there is

greater risk of splitting occurring when fixing devices are used near the edges of the fixing element than when used in the interior. (It is axiomatic that it is also possible to reduce the forces involved, and hence the resistance required to be supplied by material, by reducing the distances between fixings.)

With those fixings which rely on frictional grip between the surfaces of the two elements in contact with one another, the situation is in some ways similar to that already described. However, in these cases, once the frictional grip has been overcome, the shanks of the fixing device must then resist the acting forces and thus shear and crushing strength are included. As the fixing devices are not normally securely housed in the elements through which they pass, the leverage action is far more accute than in the example given. Thus, the strength requirements of all the materials are required to be greater in some respects.

Case 2

In the example the load acts in the same plane as the axis of the fixing device. Such loading is usually associated with, although not necessarily confined to, fixings in a horizontal plane. In this case frictional grip is primarily responsible for the success of the fixing. On the whole, the frictional grip has to be greater than generally required for Case 1. The shank of the fixing device must be capable of resisting the tensile stresses imposed. In general, resistance to shear is unimportant. Tensile resistance of the background element is important. The fixing element, on the other hand, requires to have sufficient resistance to prevent crushing. The zone most susceptible to this is under the head of the fixing device. (This may be either the nut or the bolt head.) Here again the compressive stresses may be reduced by ensuring greater distribution of the compression. This may be accomplished by increasing the diameter of the head or, as is more common, by using washers under the head. In some cases greater diameter of the head together with the use of washers may be necessary. As in the previous case, account has also to be taken of the proximity of the fixing to the edge of the material. And this, as before, has to be related to the strength of the material.

Abrasion

In simple terms, abrasion is essentially a scraping away process whereby the surfaces of materials are worn away.* It may occur whenever the surfaces of two materials are rubbed against one another. The extent to

*In BS Code of Practice, CP 3, Chapter IX, 1950, 'Durability', abrasion is defined as 'the wear or removal of the surface of a solid material as a result of relative movement of other solid bodies in contact with it'.

The disastrous effects of the lifting of flat roofs to houses at Hatfield New Town, as occurred during a gale with the wind blowing up to 42·5 m/s in November, 1957

which surfaces are worn away is more important than the fact that rubbing will theoretically cause wearing away. The factors which basically influence the extent to which surfaces will be worn away are briefly:

(1) The period of time during which the rubbing takes place.

(2) the surface characteristics of the two surfaces in contact, and

(3) the resistance to rubbing, i.e. friction, provided by the two surfaces.

The latter is directly related to the surface characteristics of the two materials and the pressure exerted during rubbing. These factors are expanded later, as it is first necessary to examine the significance of abrasion insofar as damage to materials is concerned.

151

1. Significance

During some manufacturing processes positive use is made of abrasion either to shape or to provide particular surface finishes to materials. In some cases it may be necessary to roughen an otherwise smooth surface so as to provide a key for subsequent application of an adhesive. The roughness required may be accomplished by chemical or mechanical means. The latter implies abrasive techniques. In all these cases the surfaces of materials are purposely 'damaged'. However, during the construction and life of a building, abrasion may lead to actual damage of a surface of a material. Such damage as may occur is normally confined to comparatively small areas and may, at best, only slightly affect the appearance of a material or, at worst, render the material unsuitable for the use for which it was intended. An important factor which must always be taken into account is the fact that the removal of or damage to the surface of a material may lead to more rapid deterioration of the material as a whole by other agencies, such as water, in addition to the possible increase in the rate of abrasion. For these reasons the problems associated with abrasion, do merit serious consideration.

2. Finishes

The fact that abrasion is essentially concerned with the wearing away of surfaces of materials accounts largely for the association of damage, which may result from abrasion, with finishes. However, even this requires that consideration be given to the nature of the finish and particularly the ease with which it can be replaced if damaged. Finishes may then be divided into the following three categories:

(a) Applied finishes

These are applied as liquid coatings, such as paint, plaster, granolithic concrete flooring, etc. Although not strictly a liquid, polish may, for convenience, be included in this category. One of the more significant factors to be considered is the fact that all these coatings require a *background* upon which they can be applied. Thus, the precautions required for good adhesion are of prime importance. When considering abrasion, this aspect increases in importance as the thickness of the coating is reduced. (As abrasion is not the only criterion upon which good adhesion relies, it is important that the need for proper precautions to be taken is not relaxed as the coatings increase in thickness.) Another factor which is also important is the fact that the surface pattern of a background will not necessarily be obliterated by the comparatively thin coatings such as paint.

The ease with which any of the

Use of special strips to sub-divide a terrazzo floor finish into smaller units. The photograph also shows the use of post-formed laminated plastic for rounding the corner of wall panelling (Courtesy: Formica Ltd.)

coatings may be replaced varies considerably. Generally, the thicker coatings, such as plaster, would be more difficult to replace than the thinner coatings. Ease of replacement may, however, be assisted if the thick coatings are conveniently subdivided into smaller units, with definite joints between the units. This often occurs in granolithic or *in situ* terrazzo floors when the reason may be to reduce cracking due to drying out shrinkage rather than for ease of replacement.

With most of these finishes it is sometimes possible to make good the damage. The success of such making good will partly depend on the age of the surface which has been damaged. Thus, freshly painted finishes are comparatively easy to 'touch up'. On the other hand, finishes applied in a factory under controlled conditions may be virtually impossible to make good on site. Stove enamelled finishes are good examples of this.

(b) Thin solid materials

Normally comparatively *thin* and specifically manufactured so as to possess at least one surface which is suitable as a finish. These materials may have a finish which is inherent in the material or the finish may be applied (again either in a factory or on the site). All these materials have to be fixed to backgrounds, whether solid or framed up, either by means of an adhesive, nails, screws, or other fixing devices. Examples of materials which fall into this category are floor finishes, laminated plastics and many other sheet materials including metals. The condition of the background in terms of surface unevenness may be important when the thinner and more flexible materials are applied. In cases such as these the applied finish may follow the unevenness of the background.

Ease of replacement is dependent

on the manner in which the materials have been fixed and on the size of each unit. In general, the use of adhesives makes replacement more difficult. However, even fixing devices can present difficulties. Where frequent replacement is envisaged it is then necessary to devise special fixing methods.

(c) Thick solid materials

Normally comparatively *thick* and which possess surfaces considered to be sufficient to provide a finish. Although basically similar to the materials outlined in (b), the main difference with this category is that the materials do not require any support. In some senses they may be regarded as structural materials and would therefore include bricks, stone and concrete (both *in situ* and precast).

The materials which fall into this category are usually the most difficult to replace. In most cases it is not normally possible to devise methods of construction which will facilitate replacement.

3. Factors influencing abrasion

It has already been stated that the period of time during which the surfaces of two materials are rubbed against one another will be *one* of the factors which will determine the extent to which the surfaces will be worn away. However, the susceptibility of the surfaces of materials to be worn away is, in the first instance, far more important. In this the surface characteristics and the resistance to rubbing provided by the surfaces have to be considered. These two factors are inevitably closely related.

During abrasion both of the surfaces in contact with one another will be worn away. However, in most cases it is convenient to regard as *the abrasive* the material whose surface is worn away *least*. The abrasive potential of materials was first seriously investigated by mineralogists, who discovered that some minerals were capable of scratching—the simplest form of abrasion—more than others. Their researches showed that the harder the mineral, the greater its potential to scratch. Conversely, the harder the mineral the less likely it was to be scratched. As a result, minerals were classified in terms of their hardness with the diamond—the hardest known mineral—given a value of 10.

In conjunction with the hardness of a material, its surface characteristics are also important. Thus sharply pointed materials are capable of scratching other surfaces comparatively easily. The combined effects of hardness and sharpness tend to increase the basic abrasive potential of a material. Thus, materials which are particularly suitable as abrasives, such as carborundum, are hard and sharp. (The sharpness is not necessarily an inherent characteristic of the material and in most cases is obtained when the material is split into smaller particles.)

For any abrasive material to function efficiently there must be as much friction as possible between the abrasive and the surface to be worn away. Sharpness reduces the contact surface area of an abrasive and so, with any given pressure, there is likely to be less friction. (The frictional resistance may be increased by increased pressure, as explained later.) However, the cumulative effect of the arrangement of a number of sharp particles fixed to a background, such as occurs with glass or emery paper and in another way with a file, is to increase the frictional resistance for any given pressure. It is, therefore, more realistic to consider the frictional aspect of sharpness which results from the cumulative effect of a number of sharp particles rather than from a single particle. This does not in any way mitigate the fact that scratching may occur with sharp pointed objects. Such scratching is often associated with what may best be termed a grazing action and is important particularly when accidental damage is being considered.

Despite the increase in frictional resistance which the cumulative effect of a number of sharp pointed particles are potentially capable of providing, and assuming a given pressure, the net frictional resistance will then be governed by the surface characteristics of the material to be worn away relative to the abrasive. In general, smooth, hard and shiny surfaces will reduce frictional resistance, as the abrasive will only tend to 'glide' over the surface. This then reduces the amount of scratching that can take place. If, however, a surface is inherently capable of increasing frictional resistance, this resistance may be reduced by ensuring that a lubricant is interposed between the abrasive and the surface.*

Thus, to produce a given amount of abrasion, an efficient abrasive requires to be applied with considerably greater pressure when the basic frictional resistances of the abrasive and surface is low than when it is high. In the same way, less efficient abrasives must be applied with greater pressure than more efficient abrasives to effect the same amount of wearing away.

Another factor which is equally as important is the evenness with which any wearing away may occur. As efficient abrasives are a collection of sharp pointed hard particles, it follows

that each particle actually scratches the surface of another material during rubbing. The eventual wearing away process is, therefore, the net effect of innumerable scratches. The overall evenness is dependent on the evenness of distribution of the scratches which, in turn, is dependent on the distribution of the particles in relation to the rubbing action and the area covered. Thus, localised rubbing will cause localised abrasion. However, evenness is also dependent, in the practical terms being considered, on the relative flatness of the two surfaces in contact and particularly the background, i.e. the surface being scratched or worn away. As far as the latter is concerned, there is likely to be more wearing away of 'high spots'. These high spots may not necessarily affect the eventual evenness of wearing away, i.e. over a period of time. However, what is important is that these high spots are worn away *first*. To summarise, uneven wearing may be caused *either* by localised rubbing or unevenness in the background ('high spots').

4. Assessment considerations

In terms of the damage which may be occasioned by abrasion in buildings, difficulties have been encountered in making any positive quantitative assessments of the susceptibility of materials to abrasion. These difficulties arise mainly because of the complexities associated with the extent of abrasion which may occur and which have been outlined in the considerations above. Thus, the whole question of abrasion has to be treated primarily on the basis of experience.* Some conditions within buildings are known to be more conducive to damage by abrasion than others, while at the same time some materials are known to be more resistant to damage than others. Thus, once the severity of the conditions has been assessed, it is then possible to deal with the situation in one of three ways: (1) to protect the surface of materials with some form of applied, usually thin and often temporary, finish and to ensure renewal of the applied finish as necessary; or (2) to select finishes which although they may be liable to damage in the severest conditions anticipated—not all areas are necessarily liable to the same amount of abrasion—are used in such a way that affected areas may be easily replaced. Generally small unit materials, i.e. with many joints, are easier to replace in small areas than, at the other extreme, jointless finishes; or (3) to select materials which are known to resist the anticipated abrasion, including the severest conditions.

5. Agencies causing abrasion in buildings

In order to determine the severity of conditions likely to lead to damage by abrasion it is necessary to consider the agencies which cause the abrasion to take place. The abrasive potential of, say, glass paper can most probably be readily appreciated as the abrasive materials are more or less fixed to a background of stiff paper. Thus, the scraping of a surface can be comparatively easily accomplished. However, the abrasive particles are still capable of scraping the surface even when they have come away from the background. As loose particles they are not, under any given pressure, as efficient as when they are fixed.

In most practical building examples it is uncommon for abrasives to cause damage by being purposely fixed to surfaces of materials. Damage is, therefore, more often accomplished when abrasive material is interspersed between two surfaces which are being rubbed against one another. As in the case of the glass paper, the abrasive action of the particles is made more efficient if one of the surfaces is capable of 'housing' the particles. Thus, if both of the surfaces are of equal hardness and unable to house the particles, there is likely to be equal wearing away of each of the surfaces. If, in addition to being hard, the surfaces are also smooth and shiny, then the overall abrasion will be slight and possibly insignificant, although localized scratches may be noticeable. On the other hand, if one of the surfaces is hard and the other soft and resilient, then the softer material is capable of 'housing' the abrasive

Floors are not normally subjected to abrasion caused by footwear shown below. However, it is not uncommon for building site operatives to wear boots of this type and so, in some cases serious consideration should be given to the temporary protection of floorcoverings before a building is handed over (Courtesy: J. K. Sankey Ltd.)

---

*Reduced frictional resistance allows gliding or slipping to take place comparatively easily, and so in another context, i.e. with floor finishes, may be undesirable. In cases such as these, and within limits, it may be necessary to employ the principles of abrasion positively for the safety of the users of buildings. Nosings to treads in staircases are often covered with special non-slip materials. Finishes which are cement based may have two or three rows of carborundum cubes inserted. Hard finishes such as clay tiling, may have each joint filled with a mortar containing carborundum dust. Many applied finishes, such as polishes, may include a proportion of abrasive material or otherwise made to ensure an abrasive finish.

*The Building Research Station has been carrying out work to determine the wearing qualities of floor finishes by employing machines which simulate foot traffic. The results obtained from the machine tests have, as yet, not been correlated with actual conditions, nor have any positive methods of assessment been published.

Paint used in a position liable to excessive abrasion is easily worn away.
For protection and appearance frequent re-painting would be necessary

particles and thus causing the hard surface to be worn away. In the process the soft material will be indented and in this sense may be damaged.

Dust, dirt and grit generally account for the most common abrasives encountered in buildings. These are easily and sometimes readily available on horizontal surfaces such as floors where, as an example, the abrasive particles may be interspersed between the soles of shoes and the floor finish. The action of walking does in some degree constitute a rubbing action and so, under conditions such as these, abrasion results. Wheeled traffic may be regarded in a similar way. The severity of conditions, insofar as the floor is concerned, will be dependent on: (1) the amount and efficiency of abrasive material available: (2) the relative properties of the two surfaces rubbing against one another and (3) the amount of traffic, whether foot or wheeled.

6. Floors and abrasion

As it is the abrasive material which accounts for the damage, it follows that regular cleaning of floors is likely to reduce the amount of wearing away. There are certain building types and notably industrial buildings where not only is the amount of traffic normally excessive, i.e. by comparison with other building types, but also the amount of dust, dirt and grit. However, even in buildings in which there is excessive traffic or large amounts of abrasives, it is not uncommon for special areas such as entrances from the outside to be particularly susceptible to damage by abrasion, due mainly to the ease with which abrasives may be introduced, i.e. by soles of shoes, etc. and wind. The traditional doormat does in some ways provide a means for reducing the ingress of grit. Thus, in office, public and other buildings it may

nevertheless be necessary to ensure that the floor finish is specifically selected for its resistance to abrasion, albeit in local or special areas.

When dealing with abrasion damage to floors it is probably of prime importance to try to reduce as much as possible the likelihood of it occurring. If this cannot be done, then temporary protection or replacement as mentioned earlier may be practical. Furthermore, such abrasion as may occur should take place as evenly as possible. Among other things this will be dependent on the intensity of traffic in various areas, although the juxtaposition of materials with different resistances to wearing may be a contributory cause. In addition to these, it is important to note that a greater degree of uneven wearing will take place if there are any 'high spots' in the finish. As an extreme example consider linoleum laid directly on warped floor boards. The linoleum soon reproduces the unevenness of the timber sub-floor and thus presents high spots. Invariably these are worn away first, thus reducing the life of the finish. Thus, for maximum resistance to abrasion, comparatively thin and flexible floor finishes should be laid on completely even backgrounds.

A rather specialised aspect of abrasion sometimes occurs with cement based finishes such as granolithic. These finishes, however well made, are liable to what is known as 'dusting', i.e. the surface of the material gradually comes away as a fine dust as a result of traffic over it. When this happens the dust acts as an abrasive, thus accelerating the whole abrasive process. The liability of dusting can be reduced in the first place by correct selection of materials, mixing, placing and curing. If further resistance to dusting is required than can be obtained by proper control, then it is possible to obtain this by special surface treatments. None of these surface

treatments, it should be noted, is suitable for application on surfaces which are weak, friable or otherwise of poor quality.*

7. Maintenance, cleaning and abrasion

Damage by abrasion may also occur as a result of the maintenance and cleaning of various surfaces in buildings. For the sake of cleanliness and appearance, such maintenance and cleaning may occur regularly and is, in any case, to be commended. However, this does not in any way mitigate the care which many finishes require during these processes. At a time when there are so many different types of finishes available, it is of the utmost importance that commercial abrasives are not used indiscriminately. The appearance and surfaces of many materials may be prematurely ruined when the incorrect cleansing agent is used. In this context it should be noted that the lubricating effect of water when used with certain abrasives is often insufficient to prevent damage as a result of abrasion. Without in any way reducing the usefulness of commercial abrasives in many situations, it is nevertheless salutary to note that a great number of finishes may be quite easily cleaned with soap (including detergents) and water. In cases such as these the use of water may very often provide sufficient lubrication to reduce the abrasive effect of any dust, dirt or grit which may be present on the surface to be cleaned.

The degree of cleaning and maintenance required will largely depend on circumstances. Where extremely frequent cleaning or maintenance is required it may be practicable to give special consideration to the effects of

Granolithic concrete, concrete tiles and terrazzo flooring, BRS Digest (2nd Series) No. 47, page 2, outlines three surface treatments, viz: (i) Sodium Silicate, (ii) Magnesium or Zinc Silicofluoride, and (iii) Sealers.

abrasion, in terms of either protection or selection of materials.

8. Working surfaces and abrasion

Working and other similar horizontal surfaces may also be subjected to damage by abrasion, the cause of which is in some ways the same as traffic on floors. Many objects, some of which may be potentially abrasive in character, are liable to be pushed or otherwise scraped along surfaces. Such surfaces may, of course, also have abrasive material on them. The severity of conditions will again depend on circumstances.

Regular cleaning and maintenance of surfaces of building materials does help to preserve appearance and to increase durability, provided the correct cleansing agent and method are used. In the photograph a floor is being scrubbed by a machine capable of a variety of cleaning and maintenance operations (Courtesy: Columbus Dixon Ltd.)

Worktops and other horizontal surfaces may be subjected to abrasion damage and, subject to conditions, require careful selection of surfacing materials

9. Handling of materials and abrasion

It is only in special circumstances during the life of a building that occasional scratching by hard sharp pointed objects may be reasonably anticipated. However, during the construction of a building the liability of such damage to the surfaces of materials is far greater.

Damage generally occurs during the handling of materials, but may also be

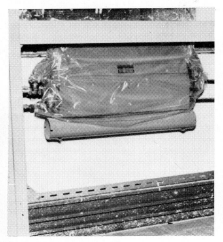

The use of transparent plastics sheeting to protect an undercill air-conditioning unit during building operations and until the permanent protection, i.e. in the form of a casing, has been completed. Although primarily intended to prevent dust and dirt from entering the unit, the sheeting also affords protection from abrasive damage

caused by plant and equipment. Surface finishes which are easily prone to scratching under construction conditions or which are not easily touched up on site (this would include many of the self-finished materials) require that some consideration be given to protection of the surfaces. The use of temporary transparent plastics protective coatings (these are usually 'peeled off' once the liability to damage has been removed), as now often used on aluminium or stainless steel components, is generally more effective than many traditional opaque materials. This can be partly accounted for by the fact that the transparent coatings do, in addition to providing protection, also enable the material to be seen, thus making it easier for those handling the material to be forewarned.

Impact

1. Context

Under *Mechanical Properties (Section 2.02)* it was stated that impact is not generally considered to be of importance in buildings, particularly as the cases where it may have to be considered are for the time being comparatively rare. This generalisation

is meant to apply to the loadbearing or structural elements of buildings only, and especially insofar as impact may affect the design of these elements. The aspect which is to be considered here is related to what may be loosely termed 'local damage' which may result from impact. Accordingly, it is necessary to use the term 'impact' in a more liberal sense and in effect to use its literal rather than its strictly structural mechanical meaning.

By definition, impact is concerned with the sudden application of a load on a material. If, therefore, this definition is broadened enough and, in fact, taken out of its conventional structural mechanical context, it is then apparent that there are innumerable instances, both in building practice and during the life of buildings, when materials may be subjected to sudden applications of loads. Whenever this occurs the impact results in stresses that are momentarily higher than those due to the same static load.

In order that the damage caused through impact may be applied to all elements of a building, i.e. whether they are primary structure or not, it is necessary to consider both of the factors which must be involved for an impact to actually occur. For the purposes required here, impact, in simple terms, results when *two* objects, one of which is in motion, collide with one another.* As a result of the collision with the static object, the object in motion may (1) be brought to rest, or (2) have its direction of movement changed, or (3) have its speed slowed down. Depending on the *relative* strengths of the materials of which the objects are composed and the intensity of the forces produced as a result of the impact, there may be structural failure, i.e. weakening or damage, of *either* the object in motion, *or* the static object *or,* in some cases, both. Strength and intensity of force are obviously closely related, but it is convenient to consider these separately.

2. Strength characteristics

The strength characteristics which determine the liability of a material to suffer damage whether this is, at best, deformation or, at worst, fracture, as a result of impact are rather complex. This complexity is partly governed by the fact that damage results when a material is unable to absorb completely the kinetic energy involved during impact. In metals ductility is *a guide* to the amount of energy that can be absorbed by the material and, generally, the more ductile a material is the more energy it is capable of absorbing, and thus resisting failure. Accordingly, the brittle metals are more easily susceptible to damage and this usually results in fracture.

The difficulty of clearly defining

*It is, of course, possible that both objects may be in motion prior to the collision with one another. Considerations such as this are normally outside the scope of most practical building examples.

other building materials in the same way has led to the use of pairs of comparative terms such as 'hard' and 'soft' or 'resilient' and 'plastic'. Many materials, as, for example, bricks, clay products, stones, concrete and glass, would be regarded as being *hard* when compared to, say, many of the fibre building boards, which would be regarded as *soft*. These hard materials may also loosely be described as brittle. This partly accounts for the fact that when these materials are damaged by impact, the damage will be in the form of fracture. The softer materials, on the other hand, are likely to be more easily damaged than the hard materials. The damage, however, of the former is more commonly in the form of severe indentation or gouging. In extreme conditions fracture may occur, but even this is not of the same kind, as with the hard materials. *Resilient* materials are broadly those which, although they may be deformed as a result of impact, are capable of 'springing back' once the impact force has been removed. Timber is often regarded as a resilient material. *Plastic* materials, on the other hand, are incapable of springing back upon removal of the impact force and are, more often than not, likely to remain permanently deformed. It is, of course, possible that there may be some recovery once the impact force has been removed, but such recovery is usually insignificant.

It is possible to summarise in general the potential of these two broad categories of materials to resist impact as follows :

(a) *Hard materials* are more likely to resist impact damage than soft materials. Damage to hard materials is normally in the form of fracture, while soft materials are damaged in the form of indentation or gouging.

(b) *Resilient materials* are likely, within limits, to recover the temporary deformation caused by impact, whereas *plastic materials* are likely to be permanently deformed.

In conjunction with the basic strength characteristics of materials relative to their resistance to suffer damage as a result of impact, account must also be taken of the manner in which a particular material is actually used. In this, the material as an element and particularly the size, shape and 'fixing' of the element, becomes important. Many metals and sheet materials may be fixed in panels. Unless adhesives are used to fix these panels to a continuous background, i.e. not framed, it is normal for the fixing to be such that the panel may be regarded as being capable of a certain amount of 'drumming' when struck. The effect of this is to give the element, so to speak, a spring action. This then lessens the intensity of the impact.

Another aspect which is quite different from the last is concerned with the amount of support an element may receive from a background. Hard

plaster will serve as an example. Proper adhesion between the plaster and the background implies that there are no gaps between the plaster and the background. Any impact, therefore, will be resisted by the plaster and the background together. If, on the other hand, there has been poor adhesion which results in gaps being formed between the plaster and the background, i.e. planes of weakness, and impact occurs in the zone of the poor adhesion, then the plaster must resist the impact alone. Unlike the panels mentioned earlier, the plaster is unlikely to possess any springing action and, therefore, is more likely to suffer fracture. Hard tiles, particularly those used as wall or floor finishes, may suffer in the same way if they are not bedded properly. Failures are more likely to occur when specially made adhesives are used for the adhesion of the tiles to the background. The reason for this is not due to the fact that the adhesives cannot form the necessary bond, but rather because the adhesives, generally speaking, cannot 'fill in' except to a moderate degree unevenness in the background.* Thus, in cases such as this, it is important that the background is level.

Finally there is the comparative weakness which is inherent at the corners of hard materials, and these frequently require some form of reinforcement. For different reasons, soft materials may also require protection.

3. Intensity of forces

Although it is possible to make quantitative measurements of the forces which may be involved during impact, it is not usually easy or practicable to rationalise these measurements in order to assist in the problems associated with local damage. Some of the difficulties may be apparent when it is realised that the intensity of forces involved during an impact are dependent on a number of factors. Firstly, there is the weight/speed relationship of the moving object and, secondly, the area of the object which comes into physical contact with the static obstruction. Finally, there are the various ways in which movement of an object may be initiated. Chief among these are :

(1) By simply dropping. (2) By a throwing or projectile action. (3) By a ramming action.

On the whole, the manner in which movement of an object is initiated is relatively unimportant insofar as the extent of damage is concerned. Collectively, however, they are important because they do illustrate that impact may result in a variety of different ways. In view of the difficulties of making rational quantitative assessments, it is then necessary to rely

*The traditional material, i.e. rendering, used as an adhesive is better able to fill in unevenness in the background than some of the newer adhesives. The latter, of course, are potentially able to effect better adhesion.

heavily on the results of experience when dealing with specific materials and conditions. However, it is possible to draw some basic conclusions, albeit extremely elementary ones, concerning both the moving and static objects. These are essentially related to the contact surface areas of either of the objects at the time of impact. (The comparative examples which are given assume that the weight and speed of movement is the same.) A sharply pointed moving object, at one extreme, is likely to cause greater damage than, at the other extreme, a flat moving object. On the other hand, if the moving object is weaker than the static object, then the sharply pointed one is likely to be more easily damaged than the flat one. The principle involved here can equally as well be applied to corners of either moving or static objects. Thus the external corners of either moving or static objects are far more vulnerable to damage than the general body or flat and level surfaces of the object.

4. Significance of damage

The nature of damage which may result from impact is extremely variable. In some circumstances it may result in corners of elements being chipped; in others the element may be deformed leaving dents or impressions, while in the worst case the element may be severely cracked leaving it structurally weakened if not unusable. It is thus possible that such damage as may occur may not necessarily adversely affect those properties for which a material has been primarily selected. This would include strength, i.e. mechanical properties. Despite this, there are good reasons why other factors, such as appearance but perhaps more important the susceptibility of the damaged material to further deterioration, need to be taken into account. In this connection it is as well to remember that damage of any kind, and however slight, may, subject to exposure and other conditions, encourage deterioration from sources against which the material in its 'whole' state may be quite capable of withstanding. As an example, cracks always provide potential paths for the ingress of water, which, in turn, may have deleterious results.

All the difficulties associated with accurate assessments of the likelihood of damage being caused by impact, plus the fact that in a great many cases it could be argued that the damage only affects appearance, and even then only slightly, have in many ways led to the treatment of the problems with a certain degree of scepticism. One extremely common attitude adopted accepts that most damage can most easily be remedied by making good and/or 'patching up'. Although as a theory this is viable, it is not always practicable or, for that matter, always successful. So far as finished surfaces are concerned, it is often extremely

Cracking of a Georgian wired glass panel at ground-floor level due to impact. (This is one of many similar failures found on a housing estate and appears to be indicative of unforeseen vandalism in the particular area)

Fracture of a vitrolite sill insufficiently supported to withstand the impact causing the damage. (Sill is near pavement level)

An example of the obstructions created by dismantled formwork. Obstructions make the careful handling of materials difficult

difficult to match new material satisfactorily with the existing surrounding areas which have not been damaged. However, this does not mean to say that such procedures may not in certain circumstances have to be adopted.

It has obviously to be accepted that it would be unreasonable to guard against impact damage due to unforeseen circumstances, particularly accidents. At the same time there are nevertheless a number of known situations where the possibility of impact actually occurring can be forecast. In situations such as this there are, basically, three alternatives. These are either (1) to use materials which are unlikely to suffer from damage due to impact—this would include using special materials in localised areas, or (2) to use materials which, although they may suffer damage as a result of impact, may be easily or conveniently replaced—this may include the making good concept previously mentioned, or (3) to provide some form of guard which prevents a moving object from impacting with a static object. Although it is not possible to lay down any hard and fast rules as to which of these three may be used, the final choice will, to a large extent, dictate the manner in which a particular material is to be used.

Having broadened the scope of impact and having explained the principles generally involved, it is now convenient to consider damage which may be caused during building practice, on the one hand, and during the life of the building on the other.

5. Building practice

In this context building practice includes the whole of the time during which a building is under construction and until it is occupied. During this time damage may result *either* in the moving *or* the static objects.

Damage to moving objects is mainly associated with the handling of materials. Nowadays it is significant that many of the mechanical aids used on building sites, such as cranes, trucks, etc., are potentially capable of causing much more serious damage than is the case with purely manual handling of materials. However, this is not to say that the problems of impact damage resulting from mishandling of materials will be caused only by mechanical aids. The latter require special techniques and care. Thus the problem has to be seen in its entire perspective.

In the main there would be no problem if materials were always handled with care. However true this might be, it does have wide implications. Among other things, care requires a tidy site so as to reduce the necessity of overcoming obstructions, which make handling difficult. In conjunction with this, there are limits of the care with which materials may physically be handled on building sites. For this reason it may be necessary to provide adequate protection which would

157

relate the strength of a material to resist impact damage and the care in handling which may be reasonably expected on a building site. Other factors which may determine the degree of protection to be provided are the ease or economic viability of replacing or otherwise making good to damaged materials. At one time it may have been considered expedient to regard small unit materials, such as bricks, as not requiring any protection at all, especially as partially damaged bricks may still be conveniently used in wall constructions and badly damaged bricks as hardcore, etc. However, the cost of handling units of this kind singly, together with the cost of breakages which result from the frequent handling necessary in the brick's journey from works, to supplier, to site, have led, in recent years, to developments in packaging bricks so that a given number may be handled 'singly' at the same time. The use of mechanised equipment for lifting these heavy 'parcels' has naturally made this now practicable. Even in cases such as this it has to be remembered that special care is required in handling.

Many building techniques now incorporate the use of fairly large panels of materials. Some of these are hard and may suffer comparatively easily from impact damage, particularly at corners. In addition, the largeness of size, coupled sometimes with considerable weight, makes the liability to

Fork lift trucks are a common form of mechanised aid used in the handling of materials. Loaded or unloaded the truck, if not properly controlled, can cause impact damage to the fabric of a building. The photograph also gives some indication of the care that is required to prevent impact damage to the materials being handled (Courtesy: Levertons (Industrial) Ltd.)

One method of packaging bricks. The delivery vehicle is equipped with a gantry and delivers bricks in packs of 500, fully protected from damage and soiling. By remote control, one man can off-load 5,000 bricks in less than 20 min (Courtesy: National Federation of Clay Industries)

Large panels require special handling techniques and care to avoid the possibility of impact and other damage (Courtesy: Quikbuild Homes Ltd.)

damage so much easier. There is also the unwieldiness of large panels, irrespective of their hardness, heaviness or lightness. Many of these panels, but also others smaller in scale must be included, may come self-finished, i.e. the finish has been applied in a factory under controlled conditions. This means that the likelihood of satisfactorily making good such a material which has been damaged all the more difficult, if not impossible. These and other factors point to the necessity of ensuring that, wherever practicable, the materials are suitably protected. Such protection may only be necessary to corners or other inherently weak areas. All of these

problems require real consideration in terms of both packaging and handling. Suitable solutions may often only be found after some experimentation.

Fixed elements may suffer damage not only during the handling of materials but also during the handling of plant and equipment. Here it may be necessary to protect either the fixed element or to provide some form of guard or cushion to the moving objects likely to cause impact. Sharp pointed items such as ends of pipes, etc. can be lethal and in many cases it would be a simple expedient to ensure that the exposed ends are covered with a resilient material. Protection of a fixed element may involve the use of a temporary guard. A typical example occurs with many heating elements, such as radiators, convectors, etc., which, although they may eventually have some form of permanent protection, may require temporary protection. In some cases problems of protection could be mitigated by careful programming of work.

6. Building life

The susceptibility of materials to suffer from impact damage during the life of a building are, when compared to building practice, somewhat less. There are basically two reasons for this : (1) the obstacles inherent in building practice, i.e. those which make handling difficult, are for the most part removed, although some of a different kind may be introduced; (2) during the life of a building, materials are damaged by moving objects.

Thus, during the life of a building, the severity of conditions, i.e. the likelihood of impact damage occurring, is governed, not so much by building type, but rather by the frequency of the use of moving objects in and about the building. In this the exact nature of such objects will be important while, as before, mechanised objects are likely to be far more lethal and therefore require, in addition to greater care in use, special consideration of vulnerable areas. In many cases these may only be corners.

In many ways there would seem little reason to doubt that, on the whole, industrial buildings present by far the severest problem. This partly derives from the fact that this building type, when compared to others, obviously has by far the largest amount of movement of objects of all kinds. In many cases these objects are not only wheeled, but also mechanised. However, it is still more realistic generally to include all building types insofar as the likelihood of damage by impact is concerned. This is important because in all buildings there is a continual movement of objects. On the other hand, there may be localised areas where the movement is intense enough to warrant special consideration. For example, service areas to all buildings need special attention. In these areas, even if motorised wheeled traffic such as cars or commercial vehicles are not anticipated, there is always the potential hazard of the dustmen, milkmen and other deliverymen. Maintenance of many buildings now requires the use of special travelling cradle equipment and this needs not only special design, but also appropriate care in use. Many of the problems associated with servicing, maintenance, etc., may be solved insofar as impact damage is concerned, not only by ensuring protection to the building fabric, but also by the use of resilient materials for containers, etc., i.e. those elements which may be regarded as the moving objects. For example, the increasing use of disposable paper or permanent

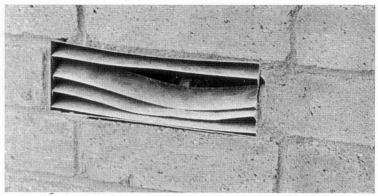

Impact damage to a metal ventilator positioned adjacent to the ground level entrance to a building, i.e. a vulnerable position. (Similar ventilators positioned at higher levels have not been damaged)

Damage due to impact of a concrete plinth coping in a service area, and adjacent to a store for wheeled rectangular metal refuse containers

Fracture of the corner of a reinforced concrete structural column, probably due to 'accidental' impact damage. (The column is in a pedestrian zone)

Bollard used to protect the corner of stone cladding in a service area— entrance to a loading bay

159

Concrete curb at service entrance aimed to guard against impact damage

The vulnerability of corners to chipping (far left) due to impact damage can usually be avoided by rounding the exposed edges (left). Both examples occur in service areas

Damage of reinforced concrete bollards caused by impact from motor vehicles

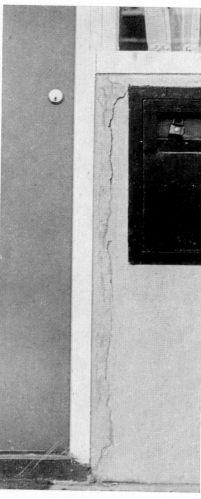

Left, cracking of rendering due to impact caused by banging of entrance door to a flat. (Unforeseen user habits may lead to damage of this kind—other entrances in the block had not failed at the time of taking the photograph)

Below, the use of metal angles to protect the vulnerable height of the corners to a column in the public 'service area' to a railway station

Above, failure of concrete bollard to protect the upper part of the corner of a brick pier to a service entrance used mainly by lorries. (The rear part of a lorry often oversails the wheels. The height of the protection, therefore, needs to be increased)

Below, 'Expamet' angle bead used for the protection of the corners of plasterwork. Photograph shows the angle bead nailed to a breeze block wall, which has been rendered to receive plastering—unrendered area to receive tiles. The photograph bottom right shows details of 'Expamet' angle bead (Courtesy: The Expanded Metal Co. Ltd.)

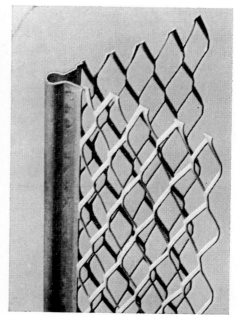

N

plastics dustbins immediately reduces, even if it does not completely eliminate, the likelihood of impact damage.

As in all cases of assessing the severity of conditions, all likely factors must be taken into account. Another point which is particularly relevant in this context is that, in a great many cases, the likelihood of impact damage may be confined to localized areas or zones. Corners are an obvious example. In cases such as these it is often possible, as in the case of plasterwork, to reinforce the corners comparatively simply with specially made corner metal plastering beads. Concrete columns or walls with sharp corners may be protected from damage by motor vehicles by the insertion of special steel corner pieces. On the other hand, the use of such protection may very often be dispensed with if the corners are rounded.

The stiletto heel, and especially that made of steel and with steel tips, was a good example of an extremely sharp-pointed moving object. Even floor finishes, such as timber, traditionally well-known for their resilience, were quite unable to withstand the impact*. In some instances it was even found that extremely hard finishes such as terrazzo were not necessarily immune to damage—in these cases damage was usually confined to small areas around joints between slabs. One of the more interesting results of the stiletto onslaught was the concerted effort on the part of manufacturers to produce floor finishes, such as plastics and linoleum, so that these possess surfaces strong enough to resist damage but with interiors still comparatively resilient, i.e. within the limits of the thickness of the material.

Traditionally there is nothing new in the concept of bonding together various materials each with different properties to form one unit or element and thus taking advantage of the combined effect of the properties. By so doing, it is possible to select materials for specific purposes in the knowledge that any deficiencies in one material can be made up by others. At the present

*Although the stiletto heel was a fashion of the immediate past, the extensive damage it caused to floors should not be overlooked. The lessons to be learnt from it in terms of impact are still relevant. On the other hand, fashion being what it is nowadays the stiletto may return.

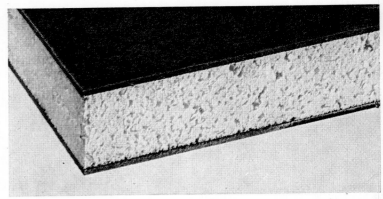

A 'sandwiched' board. The core consists of expanded polystyrene between two sheets of hardboard, all of which are bonded together (Courtesy: Venesta Manufacturing Ltd.)

The stiletto—a passing fashion but one that caused untold damage to many floors (Courtesy: Nairn-Williamson Ltd.)

time there is a marked increase in the production of what may best be termed 'sandwiched' materials, especially in sheet or board form. An example which is particularly relevant when considering impact is a board which has a core of expanded polystyrene in between two sheets of hardboard, and intended as a walling material. Among other things, expanded polystyrene is, within practical limitations, too weak to form a walling element, while it would suffer too easily from impact damage. The hardboard, when properly bonded to the expanded polystyrene, provides the additional strength required and also reduces the susceptibility of the core to impact damage. The resilience provided by the expanded polystyrene further assists in reducing the liability of the element to impact damage.

GLOSSARY OF TERMS

Abrasion The wear or removal of the surface of a solid material as a result of relative movement of other solid bodies in contact with it

Absorption The more or less uniform penetration of one substance into the body of another. Cf. *Adsorption*

Acids Compounds of acidic radical with hydrogen which can be replaced by a metal (usually sodium) either wholly or in part. Acids turn blue litmus red. Cf. *Alkalis*

Adhesion The property of matter by which close contact is established between two or more surfaces when they are brought intimately together. Force is required to separate the surfaces. Cf. *Cohesion*

Adsorption A special type of absorption in which only the surface functions as the absorbing medium. Cf. *Absorption*

Alkalis Soluble bases or hydroxides. A base is a compound which reacts with an acid to yield a salt and water only. Alkalis turn red litmus blue. Cf. *Acids*

Anisotropic Different physical properties in different directions. Cf. *Isotropic*

Atom The smallest uncharged particle of an element which can enter into, or be expelled from, chemical combination. The particle is said to be uncharged in order to distinguish it from an ion. An atom consists of one or several of each of three sub-atomic units, the electron, the proton and the neutron. Cf. *Ion* and *Molecule*

Atomic Weight The atomic weight of an element is the weight of the atom of the element as a multiple of the weight of an atom of hydrogen. Cf. *Molecular Weight and Equivalents*

Capillarity The capacity of a liquid to move upwards against the force of gravity

Capillary Circular tube of narrow bore. Term also applicable to narrow spaces or pores in materials

Carbonation The process of saturation of a liquid with carbon dioxide or converting a compound to carbonate by means of carbon dioxide

Chemical Change A change that is (in building terms particularly) permanent and that results in completely new substances being formed that are completely different from the original substances and with entirely new chemical properties. Cf. *Physical Change*

Cohesion Forces between the particles of any given mass by virtue of which it resists physical disintegration. Cf. *Adhesion* which is associated with forces at interfacial surfaces

Cold Working The operation of shaping metals at or near atmospheric temperature by rolling, pressing, drawing, stamping or spinning. Cf. *Work Hardening*

Colloid A substance consisting of a continuous medium and particles dispersed therein. More generally known as a *disperse system*

Compound Has a fixed composition and formed as a result of chemical forces uniting two or more elements. The properties of a compound are different from the properties of the combining elements. Cf. *Mixture*

Covalent Bond	The sharing of two electrons by two atoms
Creep	The time-dependent part of strain resulting from stress—the additional deformation that takes place in materials subjected to a constant load over a period of time
Crystal	A body, generally solid, where atoms are arranged in a definite pattern, the crystal faces being an outward expression of the regular arrangement of the atoms. Cf. *Space-lattice*
Deformation	The changed shape of a material due to the application on or inducement of a force in a material
Ductility	The capacity of a material, usually a metal, to be drawn out plastically before breaking. Cf. *Malleability*
Durability	The quality of maintaining a satisfactory appearance and satisfactory performance of required functions. Cf. *Maintenance*
Efflorescence	Deposits of soluble salts at or near the surface of a porous material as the result of evaporation of the water in which the salts are dissolved
Elasticity	That property of a material which enables it to return to its original shape and form once the stress causing the deformation has been removed
Electrolyte	A substance (other than a metal) which when fused or dissolved in water conducts an electric current
Electron	One of the three sub-atomic units. It is the constituent of negative electricity. Cf. *Proton* and *Neutron*
Elements	The basic 'building units' from which all matter is made. They are substances which cannot be broken down or decomposed by chemical means
Equivalents	*Element*: The equivalent of an element is the number of parts by weight of the element which combine with or displace, directly or indirectly, one part by weight of hydrogen. Cf. *Atomic Weight* and *Molecular Weight* *Compound*: The equivalent of a compound is the number of parts by weight of the compound which react or yield, directly or indirectly, one part by weight of hydrogen. Cf. *Atomic Weight* and *Molecular Weight*
Evaporation	A process whereby the quantity of a liquid exposed to air is progressively reduced until it eventually disappears
Fatigue	A phenomenon whereby materials fracture when subjected to a fluctuating or repeated load which is within the stress limit for static loading. Cf. *Impact*
Force	(1) The physical agent which causes a change in momentum. (2) The physical agent which produces an elastic strain in a body. Cf. *Weight* and *Mass*
Gas	One of the states of matter. A gas has no definite volume or shape, but fills any vessel into which it is put, irrespective of shape or size. Cf. *Liquid* and *Solid*
Gel	The apparently solid, often jelly-like, material formed from a colloidal solution on standing. Properties, even when containing appreciable quantities of water, are more like those of solids than liquids
Hardness	The resistance of a material to permanent deformation of its surface
Impact	The sudden application of a load on a material that results in stresses that are momentarily higher than those due to the same static load. Cf. *Fatigue*
Impervious	Said of materials that have the property of satisfactorily resisting the passage of water
Ion	A charged atom, molecule or radical whose migration effects the transport of electricity through an electrolyte, or, to a certain extent, through a gas
Ionic Bond	Formed by the complete transference of an electron from one atom to another
Isotropic	The same physical properties in different directions. Cf. *Anisotropic*
Liquid	One of the states of matter. A liquid has a definite volume, but no definite shape, taking on the shape of its containing vessel. Cf. *Solid* and *Gas*
Load	Imposition of some weight or force on a structural member or element

Maintenance	Work undertaken in order to keep or restore every facility, that is every part of a site, building and contents, to an acceptable standard. Cf. *Durability*
Malleability	The ability of a material, usually a metal, to be beaten into sheets without rupturing. Cf. *Ductility*
Mass	The quantity of matter in a body. Cf. *Weight* and *Force*
Meniscus	The curved, upper surface of a liquid in a tube or other container due to surface tension effects
Mixture	Consists of two or more substances whose individual properties remain unaltered. A mixture has properties which vary from point to point and is said to be heterogeneous. Cf. *Compound*
Modulus of Elasticity	(Young's modulus). The ratio of the direct stress to the strain produced by that stress
Molecular Weight	The molecular weight of an element or compound is the weight of a molecule of the substance as a multiple of the weight of an atom of hydrogen. Cf. *Atomic Weight* and *Equivalents*
Molecule	The smallest particle of a substance capable of independent physical existence and built up of groups of atoms of the elements.
Neutron	One of the three sub-atomic units, a component of the nucleus and with no electrical charge. Cf. *Electron* and *Proton*
Oxidation	The reactions in which oxygen (or an element chemically similar to oxygen, such as sulphur or chlorine) is added to an element or compound, or in which hydrogen is removed from a compound. Cf. *Reduction*
Physical Change	A change that lasts as long as the cause of the change persists. In general a physical change is limited to a change in shape or appearance of the material concerned. Cf. *Chemical Change*
pH Value	The logarithm to base 10 of the hydrogen ion concentration with the negative sign omitted. Denotes the degree of acidity of a solution. Pure water has a pH value of 7·0, acids have a value *below* 7·0 and alkalis a value *above* 7·0
Plastic	Adjective used in connection with wet mixes of mortar, plaster, renders and concrete and implies easy to trowel or spread
Plasticity	The property in a mortar, plaster, render or concrete implying ease of trowelling or spreading
Plasticiser	(1) An admixture in mortar or concrete which can increase the workability or plasticity of a mix with a low water content in the mix. (2) A non-volatile substance mixed with the medium of paint, varnish or lacquer to improve flexibility of the hardened film
Plastics	Artificial materials which are generally of synthetic organic origin and which are plastic at some stage of their manufacture, during which heat and/or pressure are used
Pores	The spaces between the particles of which a material is composed
Porosity	The ratio of the volume of voids in a material to that of the overall volume of the material and expressed as a percentage
Proton	One of the three sub-atomic units, a component of the nucleus and carries a positive electric charge. Cf. *Electron* and *Neutron*
Reduction	The reactions in which oxygen (or an element similar to oxygen, such as sulphur or chlorine) is removed from an element or compound, or in which hydrogen is added to a compound. Cf. *Oxidation*
Resilience	(1) Technically the amount of energy stored in a material. (2) Non-technically the power of a strained body to 'spring-back' on removal of the acting force causing the straining
Salts	Formed as a result of a chemical reaction either between an acid and an alkali or an acid and a metal
Solid	One of the states of matter. A solid has a definite volume and shape. Solids may be either crystalline or amorphous (non-crystalline). Cf. *Gas* and *Liquid*
Solubility	(of a solid in water): The number of grams of a solid which dissolves, at a given temperature, in 100 grams of water to give a saturated solution at that temperature
Solute	The dissolved solid in a solution. Cf. *Solvent*
Solution	(1) A *saturated* solution is a solution which, at a given temperature, is in equilibrium with undissolved solid. (2) A *colloidal* solution, or sol, is heterogeneous and is a system in which one of the components is dispersed throughout the other as small particles or droplets.

Solution—*cont.*	(3) A *super-saturated* solution is a solution which contains more solute in a given weight of solvent than is required to form a saturated solution at the same temperature. Usually an unstable solution. (4) A *true* solution is a molecularly homogeneous mixture of two or more substances
Solvent	The liquid which holds the solid in solution
Space-lattice	The regular geometrical pattern in which the structural units of a *crystal* are arranged
Strain	A measure of the deformation produced in a member by an acting force and relates change in form (length, width, depth or volume) with the original form of the member, that is prior to loading. Defined as a *ratio*
Strain Hardening	Increase in the resistance to deformation (that is hardness) produced by earlier deformation. Cf. *Work Hardening*
Strength	The ability of a material to sustain loads without undue distortion or failure
Stress **(Intensity of Stress)**	The intensity of internal forces called into play by the external forces. The intensity is expressed as units of force per unit area
Surface Tension	Property of liquid surfaces to assume minimum area and in so doing liquid surfaces exhibit certain features resembling the properties of a stretched elastic membrane
Thermoplastic Plastics	Class of plastics which can be softened and re-softened indefinitely by the application of controlled heat and pressure
Thermosetting Plastics	Class of plastics which undergoes a chemical reaction during the hardening process and cannot subsequently be reshaped by the application of heat and pressure
Thixotropy	The property shown by certain gels of liquefying on being shaken and of re-forming on standing
Valency	The property of an atom which enables it to enter into chemical combination with other atoms
Viscosity	A property of liquids which appears as a dissipative resistance to flow
Weight	The effect of gravitational force acting on a body. Cf. *Mass* and *Force*
Work Hardening	The increase in strength and hardness (that is the resistance to deformation) produced by working metals. It is most pronounced in cold working. Cf. *Strain Hardening*

IMPERIAL/METRIC (S.I.) CONVERSION SCALES FOR MECHANICS

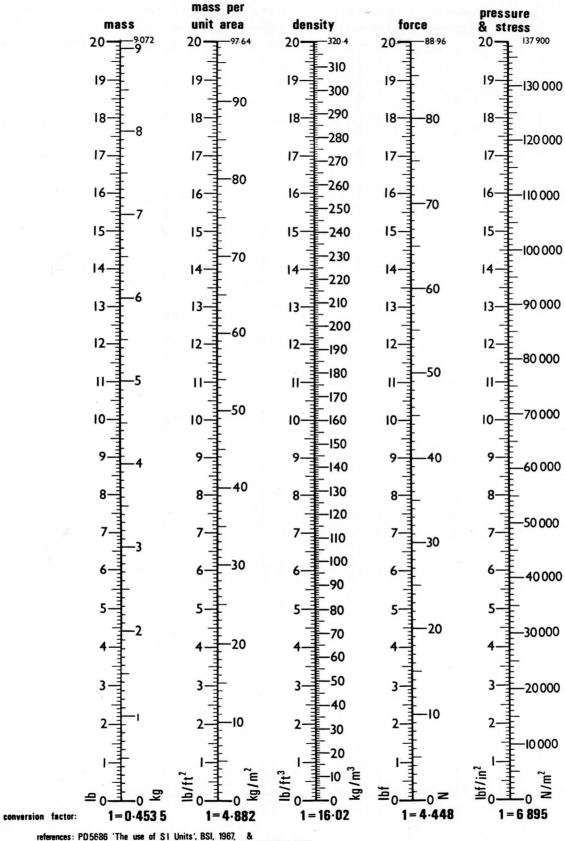

mass

20	9.072 / 9
19	
18	8
17	
16	7
15	
14	
13	6
12	
11	5
10	
9	4
8	
7	3
6	
5	2
4	
3	
2	1
1	
lb 0	0 kg

conversion factor: **1 = 0.453 5**

mass per unit area

20	97.64
19	90
18	
17	80
16	
15	70
14	
13	60
12	
11	
10	50
9	
8	40
7	
6	30
5	
4	20
3	
2	10
1	
lb/ft² 0	0 kg/m²

conversion factor: **1 = 4.882**

density

20	320.4
	310
19	300
18	290 / 280
17	270
16	260 / 250
15	240
14	230 / 220
13	210
12	200 / 190
11	180 / 170
10	160
9	150 / 140
8	130 / 120
7	110
6	100 / 90
5	80 / 70
4	60
3	50 / 40
2	30 / 20
1	10
lb/ft³ 0	0 kg/m³

conversion factor: **1 = 16.02**

force

20	88.96
19	
18	80
17	
16	70
15	
14	60
13	
12	
11	50
10	
9	40
8	
7	30
6	
5	20
4	
3	10
2	
1	
lbf 0	0 N

conversion factor: **1 = 4.448**

pressure & stress

20	137 900
19	130 000
18	120 000
17	
16	110 000
15	100 000
14	
13	90 000
12	80 000
11	
10	70 000
9	60 000
8	50 000
7	
6	40 000
5	30 000
4	
3	20 000
2	10 000
1	
lbf/in² 0	0 N/m²

conversion factor: **1 = 6 895**

references: PD 5686 'The use of S I Units', BSI, 1967, & NPL Changing to the Metric System' 2ᴺᴰ edition (HMSO) 1967.

IMPERIAL/METRIC (S.I.) CONVERSION SCALES FOR HEAT

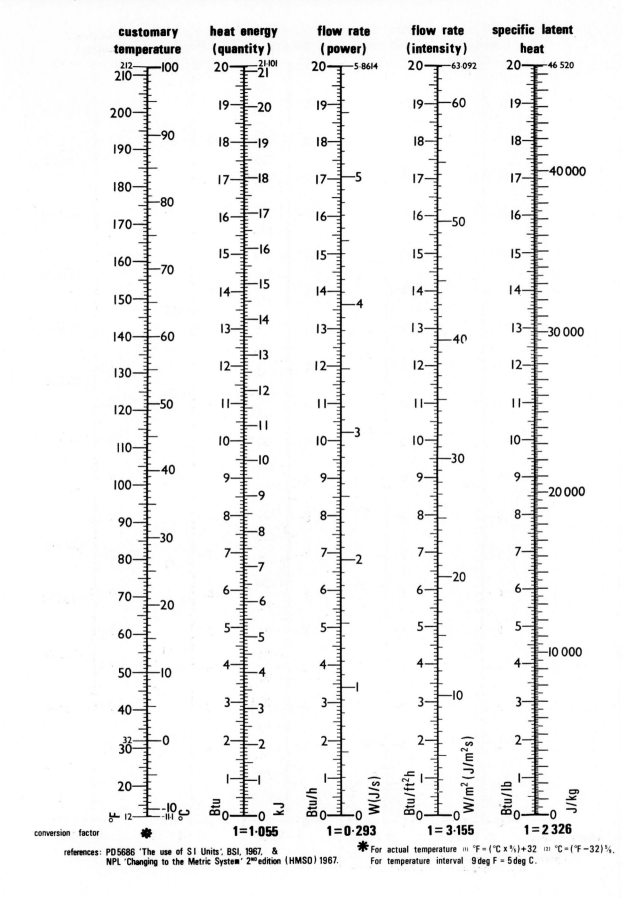

customary temperature	heat energy (quantity)	flow rate (power)	flow rate (intensity)	specific latent heat

conversion factor

✱	1=1·055	1=0·293	1=3·155	1=2326

references: PD 5686 'The use of S I Units', BSI, 1967, & NPL 'Changing to the Metric System' 2ND edition (HMSO) 1967.

✱ For actual temperature (1) °F = (°C x 9/5)+32 (2) °C = (°F −32) 5/9.
For temperature interval 9 deg F = 5 deg C.

IMPERIAL/METRIC (S.I.) CONVERSION SCALES FOR HEAT (continued)

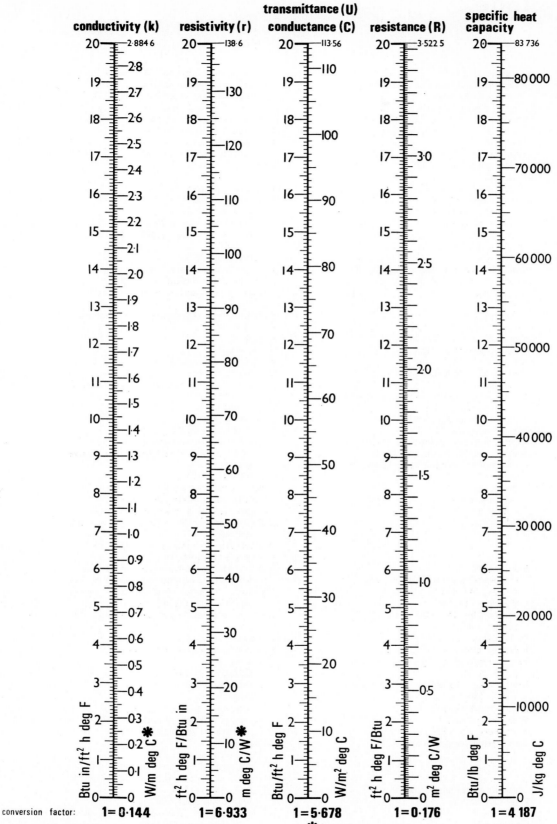

conductivity (k)	resistivity (r)	transmittance (U) conductance (C)	resistance (R)	specific heat capacity
Btu in/ft² h deg F → W/m deg C	ft² h deg F/Btu in → m deg C/W	Btu/ft² h deg F → W/m² deg C	ft² h deg F/Btu → m² deg C/W	Btu/lb deg F → J/kg deg C

conversion factor: 1 = 0·144   1 = 6·933   1 = 5·678   1 = 0·176   1 = 4 187

references: PD 5686 'The use of S I Units', BSI, 1967, & NPL 'Changing to the Metric System' 2ᴺᴰ edition (HMSO) 1967.

✳ These units look unfamiliar due to cancelling the metre thickness
i.e. (k) Wm/m² deg C = W/m deg C & (r) m² deg C/Wm = m deg C/W.

Index

Index

Index

Index

Index